About the Author

DOROTHY MCRAE-MCMAHON was born in Tasmania, but has lived in Sydney for the last half of her life. She has been a pre-school teacher, a development educator and was ordained as a minister in the Uniting Church in Australia in 1982. She was a minister with the Pitt Street Uniting Church in Sydney for 10 years and then spent 5 years on the national staff of the Uniting Church. Her key interests in life are reflected in her community awards, which include a Jubilee Medal from the Queen for work with women in NSW (1977), an Australian Government Peace Award (1986), the Australian Human Rights Medal (1988) and an Hon Doctorate of Letters from Macquarie University for work with minorities and contribution to the spiritual life of the community (1992).

She now spends her time mostly writing, speaking, reflecting, working for a just Republic of Australia, looking after her granddaughter and reading her favourite detective stories.

Previous Publications

Being Clergy, Staying Human (Alban Institute, Washington 1992)
Echoes of Our Journey — Liturgies of the People (JBCE 1993)
The Glory of Blood, Sweat and Tears — Liturgies for Living and Dying (JBCE 1996)

Everyday Passions

A Conversation on Living

Dorothy McRae-McMahon

ABC BOOKS

Dorothy McRae-McMahon is a reformer. It is by reform that the Church of Jesus has renewed itself over two millennia. The path of the reformer is a difficult one — but as Dorothy's life teaches us, dishonesty, complacency and hypocrisy are the complete antithesis of the message Jesus brought.

The Hon Justice Michael Kirby

Here is a book which makes contact with us where we are. It tells a story about life from within life, about community from within community, about love from within love and about faith from within faith. Dorothy McRae-McMahon writes about what she has experienced and, in doing so, invites us to connect with our own experiences. As we read stories from her life, and her reflections on them, we are introduced to new visions about life and what it means to us, especially in our relationships with others. There is a warmth about this book which conveys a strong sense of the worth of life and the value of living it to the full.

Reverend Dr Charles Biggs

Tolerance and personal integrity are at the core of this book. Spirituality at its best.

Jenny Brockie

This timely book will sustain us in our continuing quest to build a just, humane and honourable society. One of Australia's truest and most controversial Christian leaders tells her story with enriching honesty and insight. It is a wise and friendly book. It will reassure readers, whatever their frailty or struggle in life may be, that they are not alone, and that there is always hope.

Caroline Jones

Acknowledgments

My thanks go to:

My children Christopher, Robert, Lindy and Melissa and my son-in-law, Scott McDonald for their kindness to their rather odd mother; Barrie McMahon who was a companion over many years of learning and his generous wife Sara; Jenny Chambers for the fun; my loved sister Carmyl and brothers John and David, whose loyalty never wavered; Colin and Beth McRae, my parents; the people of the Pitt Street Uniting Church in Sydney for sharing 10 very significant years with me and teaching me much; the staff of the Assembly of the Uniting Church, especially Margaret Tasker, Gregor Henderson and Gwenda Davies, for the love and support they gave me, even when they knew who I was; Vladimir Korotkov and John Rickard, dear friends in many brave conversations; Gwenda Davies, Carmyl Winkler, Florence Spurling and Felicity Reynolds, whom I could trust to give me honest feedback on my manuscript; those whose stories mingle with mine in this book; Jill Hickson who believed this book was possible; ABC Books for taking the risk of publishing my efforts and Brook, my little grand daughter, whose two years of life have already been lived with passion and for whom I will keep struggling to live out a larger dream for the world.

To Ali

Published by ABC Books for the
AUSTRALIAN BROADCASTING CORPORATION
GPO Box 9994 Sydney NSW 2001

Copyright © Dorothy McRae McMahon 1998

First published 1998

All rights reserved. No part of this publication
may be reproduced, stored in a retrieval system
or transmitted in any form or by any means,
electronic, mechanical, photocopying, recording
or otherwise, without the prior written permission
of the Australian Broadcasting Corporation.

National Library of Australia
Cataloguing-in-Publication entry

McRae-McMahon, Dorothy, 1934- .
Everyday passions: a conversation on living.

   ISBN 0 7333 0667 5.

   1. Uniting Church in Australia – Clergy. 2. Women in
   the Uniting Church in Australia. 3. Christian life.
   4. Self-actualization (Psychology). I. Title.

287.93082

Designed and typeset by Brash Design Pty Ltd
in 10.5/16.5 Slimbach
Printed by Griffin Press

5 4 3 2 1

Contents

	Introduction	1
1	Living Life in the Face of Death	13
2	Living Within Set Boundaries	35
3	Living with Miracles	47
4	Living as a Non-victim	59
5	Living Life under Attack	73
6	Living with Your Own Truth	84
7	Living with Failure and Forgiveness	115
8	Living with a Bigger Dream	131
9	Living in Community	149
10	Moral and Ethical Living	178
11	Living with Power	193
12	Living in Our Landscape	198
13	Living with Humanness and Fun	212
14	Hard Questions for God and Some Equally Tough Possible Answers	218
15	Some General Thoughts about Surviving Well Enough	239
16	In the End, the Passion	249
17	Rituals and Liturgies for the Journey	255
	For those who feel wounded or betrayed	255
	A ritual of support	258
	Grieving the child	260
	Ritual for those who are betrayed by the church	264
	Hold your heads high, our liberation is at hand	269
	In the end, the passion	272

Introduction

'I think I'll write a book about the meaning of life,' I said to my friends.
  'Oh, just about the meaning of life?' they said.
  And we all laughed.
  Understandably.

※

WHEN I began to think about it, I realised that we all search for a viable life, and some of us search for a viable God within that life. Conversations about the meaning of life don't belong just to experts. They belong to ordinary people. Most of us learn our survivals and our meaning from each other. I am not a therapist, psychologist, nurse, doctor, counsellor or social worker. Many people need these specialist people to help them make life viable. This book does not attempt to enter such fields of advice and health care. It is, rather, about the accompanying we offer to each other for lives that have an average level of trouble, dysfunction and joy.

It seems to me that to live life to the full is not just about meaning, but about life which is sometimes lived with a passion in the face of the tough questions, the hard times, the setbacks and our ordinary human frailty. It is about heading into it all as though vivid and many-coloured life is possible, if we all hold on to each other. Some of us also take our God with us.

I will begin with a conversation through stories and some possible learnings of life, from my life and the lives of others. I will ask some tough questions of God and give some equally tough possible answers about the nature of life in general. Then I will give some ideas for developing one's spirituality, and rituals and liturgies to mark the journey through life.

The sixty-three years of my own life have included a brain-damaged son, a loved sister and her husband killed in a car accident at twenty-two years of age, two years of spasmodic attack by a neo-Nazi group while living mostly alone, a father who died from violence, an ending of a marriage after a thirty-year struggle to decide on my sexual orientation, plus all the other 'normal' hassles about being human. I am joining my journey with the journeys and stories of hundreds of others whose lives have interconnected with mine.

My life was born, as a child, into a Christian religious environment but has spread itself into relationships with people of other faiths, non-religious faith and no faith. My world view has been formed from all those relationships as well as from the above experiences. The longer I live, the more I see that none of us has the whole truth. Each of us chooses a framework for the way we will live, often because of our cultural environment or the chances of our birth. If there is one thing which I do know it is that, somehow at the very heart of things, no matter what our choice of framework, there are some close relationships.

Truth is truth no matter where it comes from, and I don't find that a cause for fear, even if it challenges my own framework of the Christian faith. The invitation to people who search for meaning is to try to hold open to the laying down of our perceptions alongside those of others and to walk an exciting journey of discovery together. This does not mean that we must be lukewarm people for whom anything goes. On the contrary, in my experience, the genuine truth searchers are those of strong but not dogmatic belief. They live from what they believe as part of the testing of truth, and that cannot be done from wishy-washy approaches to anything.

THERE were three very focused moments in my journey towards the interpretations of life and God, and they are reflected in this book. The first was long ago, when I was about fourteen years old. I had a Sunday School teacher whose name was Miss Stubbs. I think she was probably in her sixties, as it is my memory that she was a retired schoolteacher. Interestingly, I can't remember a single thing she said in her classes with us. I remember two things about her that have stayed with me for the whole of my life.

The first was a profound sense that I was in a very privileged relationship with a woman of integrity and courage. She was a single woman, which in those days was usually regarded as something to be pitied. But I knew that there was nothing to be pitied about Miss Stubbs. She had a quiet dignity of person and communicated a sort of firm goodness without giving us anything that I registered as rules or dogma.

She was absolutely unflurried by the disrespectful antics of some of the Sunday School class and handled us with calmness and love. I knew that she was a person of courage, without understanding why I recognised that. Maybe her face told me of a life which had been deeply lived and of a costly peace within her. All I knew was that I wanted to grow up to be a woman like her.

The second gift she gave me happened when she invited her class to her house for afternoon tea. We all sat uneasily in her neat little lounge room and nervously held her obviously delicate china. We had not thought of ourselves as 'afternoon tea' people — that was for our mothers. The boys, in particular, gave each other digs in the ribs and yet I remember we all behaved ourselves as though we needed to rise to the auspicious occasion.

After we had eaten her cakes and sandwiches, Miss Stubbs said, 'Now, young people, I am going to play you some beautiful music on my gramophone. I want you to sit still and just listen to it.' She then proceeded to play a whole record of music from Johann Sebastian Bach. We all sat there, mostly trying not to fidget. I listened and tried not to show that, for me, it was the music of my soul and I had never heard it before. As we left, the others talked about how boring it had been, but I knew that it had been a special gift for my journey.

It took me some thirty more years before I really connected with that music again. My family never had any records or anything to play them on and we rarely listened to the radio, other than the news and the ABC's Children's Session. We were literary people, people of the word (many, many words!) and we sang our songs around the piano rather than listening to music. We had no money for concerts, so the whole world of classical music only returned to me much later in life when a dear friend, called Murray, shared his love of music with me.

❦

T H E second focused moment came about sixteen years ago when I studied the Book of Habakkuk in the Hebrew Scriptures, the Old Testament. My teacher was Rev. Dr Keith Carley, who has since returned to his home country of New Zealand. Keith was a gifted teacher, who was prepared to hand over the tools which he held for learning and then trusted that adults he taught could go on their own search for truth. He believed the journey could begin with one's own life experience rather than the well-formed and abstracted ideas of others, even though these, in the end, might become part of the testing of truth.

At the end of the course, I painted a picture as part of my assignment because words could not express the significance of what I had discovered about my own faith, alongside that of Habakkuk, who had written all those centuries before. To his credit, Keith did not think it strange to receive a painting as part of an academic essay. Even as I write this paragraph, I am playing some music because, as the sound rises and falls in adventurous harmonies, in its exquisite longings and triumphs, it honours the same longings and triumphs of human life, far beyond my halting words that is the power of art in all its forms.

The Book of Habakkuk is only three chapters long. It begins as a writer, from long ago, cries out to his God about the injustices which he sees happening to his people. Why do the wicked win and why are the good people defeated? Where is God in all of this? What is God doing? Seemingly in response to his cry, the people of Israel are attacked and defeated again.

Habakkuk is devastated, but he hears the voice of God say:

Write the vision; make it plain... so that a runner may read it.
For there is still a vision for the appointed time;
It speaks of the end, and does not lie.
If it seems to tarry, wait for it;
it will surely come, it will not delay...
The righteous shall live by faith.

(2:2–4)

Habakkuk is captured by this challenge to live as though justice will prevail, in the face of no signs and few reassurances. He goes into an Israelite funeral song, announcing the death of the oppressors of the people, in the face of their destructive life. Then he ends with a song which (somewhat paraphrased) goes like this: 'The fig tree will not blossom, the vines will not bear fruit./But I will exult in the name of my God who carries my feet into the high places' (3:17,19).

Somehow I knew that, if Habakkuk's faith could not be mine, then I could have no faith at all. It may sound strange, but the very struggle for faith in the ultimate triumph of good over evil, seemed to me to be what a glorious life would be like. Like the music and the paintings, like the beauty of the mountains and the skies, life at its best was something which lay beyond ordinary 'happiness'. It was about the indescribable dignity and courage and determination in Habakkuk's song. That was the sort of life and faith which I wanted, even if I only lived it out in small glimpses, just enough to remind me of my destiny as a proud and hopeful human being.

※

THE third focused moment came in 1997, when I did the very last subject to attain my first academic degree. That, in itself, was a special moment. My family was quite poor and I was the eldest of five children. I knew it would help my family if I did not stay at school to matriculate, but accepted a scholarship to train as a preschool teacher after five years at high school. My sisters and brothers were exceedingly bright and I was given subtle messages that probably I would find university difficult, compared to them. Added to that, my ambition to go to university and train as an art teacher was downgraded as a less than worthy ambition — what did art offer to the well-being of the world? In retrospect, I imagine that I might have been oversensitive to suggestion, but I was always trying to be extra 'good' and suggestions were powerful. My sisters and brothers knew nothing of all of this until many years later and all well and truly earned their educations with scholarships.

Anyway, I dutifully trained as a preschool teacher. When I studied for the ordained ministry as my second profession, much later in life, the theological college where I trained did not have degree status until the year after I left!

So I spent eleven years of some full-time and some part-time study and, at sixty-three years of age, finally graduated Bachelor of Theology. As I went up to receive my degree, I had the widest smile of anyone and the little thought in my head, 'So there, dear mother, I can do it!' If I give this story as a little detour in among the grander thoughts it is because grander thoughts are not really that, they are all part of the determined little journeys we make.

My very last subject for my degree was, ironically for a number of reasons, a study of the Book of Job. Again, I am indebted to the Hebrew Scriptures, the accounts of life and faith in the Jewish tradition, for another life-shaking understanding. Job has probably gone into the English language, and others, as the representative person for the hard questions of life and faith.

It is quite a long book and is written in a tantalising and somewhat puzzling form. At the beginning and end of it there is a story. This story gives a setting for the life of Job (almost certainly a mythical character) in which Satan has a wager with God that there is no such thing as a person who will do good for its own sake. Satan's view is that, if there are people who appear to be very virtuous and believing in God, they are only that way because life is rewarding to them and that, if life was tough, they would lose their faith.

In the story, God takes on the wager and agrees that Satan can put Job, an apparently good and godly man, through endless and severe suffering to see if he will fall from his faith in God. So Job enters a time of suffering. His family also suffers, but that is not the focus for the story (or maybe it is not considered as important!). After a terrible time, at the end of the book, the story tells us that God rewards Job and he lives happily ever after. This happy ending lacks credibility for people like me, so we focus on what lies in between, which is far more ambiguous.

What does lie in between the beginning and the ending of the story is a long series of dialogues between Job and his wife, his friends and, finally, between Job and God. These dialogues, if you take the surrounding story away, are more like the encounters which happen to people as they experience a real and suffering life. Job and family are going along well and in great prosperity and suddenly they experience not just one tragedy, but repeated tragedy, both personal and corporate. The responses to these tragedies by Job and his family and by people around them are reflected in the dialogues, and they remind us of the same in our own real life situations.

Job is significant because he refuses to believe that he has deserved what is happening to him. In the face of friends who urge him to see that he has offended God, either by doing something wrong in the first place, or by his loud and angry protests to God because of what is happening to him, he sits there and refuses to be 'repentant' or to remain silent. He is not due for this suffering and he will not politely accept his lot. He will tell God what he thinks and, if his friends don't like his honesty, well, tough! He will do as much cursing and shouting as he likes and, if God can't see the truth in his situation and defend him, then he will have to find another advocate for himself.

Again, I had a very special teacher, one who did not invite us to take the easy path as we looked at this ancient writing, which echoes the questions of all ages. His name was Rev. Dr Roland Boer and his ability to live with unanswered questions and possibly unpalatable answers, gave us the chance to choose to live with maturity and courage. I do not believe that the church always offers this opportunity to people. It often chooses to take people on a lesser journey which sometimes requires them to deny reality and to live with 'easier' and simplistic faith answers.

Roland invited us to live with honesty and perhaps a tougher God than some of us would like to live with. Whether he intended it or not, he offered me a grander and greater possibility of interpreting life than I had ever had before. I say, 'whether he intended it or not' because I still don't really know what he believes himself — quite a change in a teacher. This does not mean that he did not teach. On the contrary, he paid us the respect of giving us all that he had in information and then allowing us to work with that. Many teachers say that they are doing that, but few really mean it.

In God's response to Job, I suddenly saw myself in two ways. I imagined myself as 'heard' and 'known' in my life journey. This was not a new belief, indeed it had always been my perception, rightly or wrongly. What changed was that I, this heard and known speck in the universe, became part of a much grander cosmic endeavour and life system. Maybe I did not need to think that my experiences or efforts were part of a plan or pattern which was confined to the human race or even to this planet.

I heard a God speaking to Job and saying, 'I see you Job, sitting there protesting and suffering. I give you the ultimate dignity of responding to you. Come on, Job! Look around you at the brave river running alongside you and all the creatures living and dying in passionate life. See, I have given you a lotus flower to lie under. Go and lie under it, refresh yourself, then get up and go on. You can do it! Don't just sit there. Your life is part of a cosmic struggle for existence and survival, a part of creation beyond your imagining. Don't look for simple justices, but be part of greater ones.'

In some ways it was simply an extension of my experience with the perceptions in Habakkuk, but it gave me a whole new perspective on life, a canvas for living which stretched far beyond my sight. It took me beyond the mountain tops and skies into the endless galaxies of corporate existence. Oddly enough, this did not move me into a lostness in space but rather gave to me an increased dignity as a respected part of the mystery of life. It called me like a song from the stars and the singing which lives beyond the stars into an even more passionate commitment to my little part of life which could be much larger than I had thought.

My company was the wind, the brave river and the lotus flower, the tiny ant and the leaping dolphin, alongside all who tread as human life in all its choices and ambiguities.

I BEGAN, early in life, believing that I can change, others can change and the world can change. I think my whole environment taught me that and I still believe it. Maybe this conviction comes from a deep and unquenchable optimism about reality which lies within some people, including me, and which is nurtured by kindness around us, even though life is not easy. While I don't think I had a perfect family life, I did have loving parents and great brothers and sisters who are still among my best friends. All of us believe that change can happen and we were brought up to believe that we could be part of the changes and sometimes initiate change.

Because of this, my life views have also been formed by being part of some of the great twentieth century movements for change in this country, and, to some extent, internationally. I feel that I have even been part of history as we moved to try to bring an end to many forms of racism — in the White Australia Policy, in apartheid, in various struggles for the rights of Aboriginal people and in relation to the evolving of a multicultural and multi-racial society in our country.

I was part of the movement to end the Vietnam War and other efforts for peace. For nearly thirty years I have been part of the Women's Movement and now I struggle for the liberation of homosexual people. All these movements have been part of the forming of my understanding of life and its viability. They have both empowered me for life and challenged me in my powerlessness.

IN all these life experiences, I have always had a fascination with raising questions for God and faith while trying to form patterns of meaning. I began with a childlike trust in what life would bring me and have now gone through more than six decades of living which, on one level, have taught me that life is not to be trusted. In response to that, and my journey with others and with God, I can see that the 'rational' option is to be cynical. However, I have come full circle and now choose to live still with something of a childlike trust, because that is the reinstating of hope and courage and the way through to the possibility of the victory of love.

This is a costly way to live because trust, love and hope lead us into inevitable vulnerability. However, the greater cost is really to lay down hope, love and trust because we live defended against the possibility that they will, in fact, be there for us in among the wounding and the betrayals. I began by believing that life is about choices between good and bad but I believe now that the choices are rather between life and death. When you live from those choices and take on the risks of vulnerability, life takes on a passion, a vivid colour and songs of both grieving and celebration.

HAVING imaged my sense of call to an exciting cosmic existence, in the following chapters of this book I will think aloud about the human journey by taking moments, events and issues in the facing of real life. Not that real life removes from us this cosmic call, in fact in many ways it reinforces that call, but not as something experienced in a journey of contented peacefulness, but in the rigour of challenge, pain and celebration. Many of the stories and reflections overlap with each other because I am coming at them all from the same conviction that our calling is to be part of our personal liberation and the liberation of the world. It is really all about refusing to be determined by the events of life, to see bigger possibilities and the creative power in life which is lived together rather than alone. When I have finished the stories, I will gather up what I have learnt in my life and reflect on the way I now put it all together for myself. I do this even as I recognise that tomorrow I may see it all differently.

Living Life in the Face of Death

MOST of us fear death. We fear the possible pain involved in it. We fear the endings of relationship associated with it and we may fear what lies beyond it. Some of us limit how much we live because we fear death. Almost all of us respect death. As a present generation, we are spending a lot of our resources trying to avoid death as we swap more and more organs and even try to clone life or deep-freeze ourselves as we die. And yet, as soon as we are born, we receive the gift of death, the inevitability of our mortality.

So, what is death?

That may seem a strange question and I am not answering it in a theological or philosophical way. The way in which I have understood something about death is by looking at people who have died to see if I can see what is there and what is not there. I have only been able to do this in the later decades of my life. Our culture in the middle decades of this century, at least, has not encouraged us to look death in the face.

This stands in contrast to some other cultures that have never lost that connection with reality and mortality. I recall having the honour of sharing a time of mourning with a Vietnamese family whose father and grandfather had died back in Vietnam. The family members remaining in Vietnam had sent photos of the grieving process and of the funeral for the one who had died. This included many photos of every family member, down to the smallest child, beside the body of the dead man as he lay in his bed for a week before the funeral. At the end of the week, the whole family tenderly placed his body in the coffin they had prepared and carried him in procession into the church where his funeral would take place.

As I have looked at people who have died, I have always been struck by the absolute emptiness of their bodies. Even though our bodies are critical to our life, there is obviously some essence of our being which departs from us when the body stops functioning. The person we knew is not lying there dead, the person has somehow gone. I always find that in some sense comforting, alongside the loss of their going. Even though I will grieve the going, the person is not lying there experiencing death or the grave or the fire: they are either ended, or elsewhere.

Living with death

I have never yet faced my own physical death, but I have had the indescribable honour of accompanying many people towards that moment. As I write this book, I am making arrangements to go back to doing that, or at least to the conducting of funerals. If I do that, it is because I have experienced around death some of the most truth-filled and life-filled moments.

Of course, people approach their death in many different ways for many different reasons. I believe that this is their right and should always be respected, no matter how inappropriate and unhelpful it might seem to be to the observer. This doesn't mean that we can't be useful to each other as wise and loving company on the journey towards death. Rather, it means that the choices at that time belong to the traveller, as far as is possible. I have seen people die in deep and serene peacefulness. I have also seen them die protesting, denying reality, partying, in anger, in laughter at life, in terrible endurance, in loneliness and in fear. The lonely and fearful exit is the most terrible and I always hope that people might find some company in death to reduce that terror of dying.

The best dying, in my view, is related to people who decide to live until the moment of death rather than to start dying in preparation for death. This involves a commitment to the risk of loving on in the face of parting from people — a risk for the lover and the loved. It involves stretching the boundaries, rather than pulling them in. As I have watched someone making this choice, I am always struck by the reality that life is less about length than about fullness and wholeness. I have seen people live a more passionate life as they approach death than many people will experience if they live to be a hundred. It is as though people who do this demonstrate the difference between significant and insignificant life. Facing death, if one has warning, does tend to make some of these issues starkly clear. And it does this for dying people as well as for those around them.

I remember Nerida, who talked and laughed as she remembered her years as an outstanding teacher and the loved children she had taught. I remember her deep concern for her elderly mother who would find it hard to face the fact that her daughter had died before her. We talked about whether it was the right moment to make explicit with her mother that she had been in a long-term relationship with another woman — something she longed to do. She decided to respect her mother's obvious preference that this not be named. She died, a vivid, strong, clear and loving woman, still fully alive to the needs of those around her.

If many of my stories of dying are connected with gay men, it is because so many of them die in the prime of their life and know they are going to die. I remember Bill, a party person, a direct and lovable man. As he lay dying, there he was still organising people, honestly telling all and sundry exactly how he was experiencing his journey towards death, sending out for lavish titbits from the local deli, rejoicing in the art around him — an ongoing party person, a direct and lovable man.

Then there was Don, a deeply thoughtful man, one who refused to settle for other people's philosophies and religions; a gentle soul, a caring man. He died being even more than he had been. He discussed his understandings of life and death with his friends. He refused to be defeated by his failing body and would plan his trip to meet you for coffee and get there even if it took him a painful hour to do so. His gentle earnest face would light up as he talked about important things, not just about his world but much wider. He would puzzle over the future of us all and wrestle with the realities of his past and future life. We would talk about his exact desires for his funeral and plan it as though it was a sort of wedding — his last commitment in love to all who had loved him.

In his last days, Don carefully made cards with a photo of himself, at his strongest and most beautiful, and arranged for them to be sent out after his death. They contained words of thanks and ongoing life. I remember looking at the face of a Don full of health, one I had never seen in life. I was confronted by the cost of that last life-filled journey which was evident on the face I had known but all I could see, even in his earlier photo, was the beauty of soul of the dying Don looking out at me.

Then there was Bruce. Bruce was something else! He was very young and very gay. He was also in the first stages of dementia, but somehow I had the feeling that Bruce had always been reasonably wild. Bruce had possibly never been very introspective. Life had not been easy for him and he had dealt with that by sort of rocketing along. To stop and struggle with what it all meant was too hard.

I asked him if he wanted to think about what it all meant as he lay dying, because I sensed that sometimes he was deeply troubled. He at first said he did and would I help him with that please? I put down on paper some possible ways into his questions. In the end, he said he was just too tired and weak to try and did I think it would be alright just to die as he was?

He held my hand as tightly as his weakness would allow, and I remember still my strong sense of love and grief as I thought of the way life had been for him, for reasons often outside his control. I knew that the God in whom I believed would also look upon him with love, would receive him as he was. That God would see the integrity of his struggle. At the end, he rallied a little and quietly and very graciously lived the last days of his life, just being himself, organising odd and unexpected things. I will tell the story of his remarkable funeral later in this chapter.

Then there are those who live with death for a long time. I think of my friends Pam and Judy. Several years ago, Pam was diagnosed with lymphoma. This was a total shock to us all, as Pam seemed to be one of those strong people who would live to be a hundred. The doctors decided to give her the 'big bang' in chemotherapy, as that can sometimes successfully defeat lymphoma. The risk was that you can only do that once. Because Pam, and Judy her partner, were prepared to go through the entire trauma openly and honestly, we were able to share in it with them, as far as people can. We talked about it all together, watched Pam's hair fall out and rejoiced when it grew back.

We faced, with them, the fact that the 'big bang' had not worked — the cancer was still alive in Pam's body. Judy and Pam, who have one of those rare relationships which allow for not only living but working together, then had to decide how they would live with death. They did some wise things in changing lifestyles for Pam so that life became as restful and healthy as possible, while maintaining all that was important to them in work, social life and the things they enjoyed, whether very healthy or not.

Following their lead, while we did not refrain from mentioning Pam's illness, neither did we dwell on it. It became a natural part of the conversation. Most times, when the next blood test was due, they alerted some of their friends so that someone would be thinking of them as they went through the stress of waiting for the good or bad news of the progress of the cancer.

We watched as Pam set about restoring the ceiling of her lounge room, a rather intricate old pressed metal one. Being Pam, we knew that this would be a long and perfectionist process. Judy would have to put up with ladders and planks over a long period of time as each patch of ceiling was laboriously rubbed back to its origins and finally painted. In fact, it took years. In the end, we watched with a degree of anxiety. We thought to ourselves that maybe this was a sort of symbol of Pam's life — that as soon as she finished this major project she would die. We contemplated the thought that she was actually stringing it out because she thought that too. As we saw the final painting approaching our anxiety rose. Eventually, however, Pam finished her perfect ceiling and put her ladders and planks away. Now she threatens to start another ceiling and we all laugh at our little theories about symbols of living and dying.

Meanwhile, through it all, Pam and Judy get on with their life together, doing the things that are important to them. They look after their young nephew for regular weekends, letterbox-drop for political campaigns which involve justice in their terms, and spend a lot of time planning which sample bags they will buy at the Royal Easter Show (much to the mystification of some of their friends).

If I notice anything about them which has changed, it is perhaps a stronger commitment to friends who they feel can comfortably accompany them on their journey with death. I watch Judy at odd moments preparing her life for a different future and collecting around her, at regular intervals, all that has been life-supporting in her tough life journey in the past. I also watch them both develop a greater and greater love for the somewhat tacky and absurd (hence the showbags). Pam loves watching mice go round and round on a turntable while Christmas carols churn out, and key rings that open when pressed to reveal little cows moving around inside — she informs me that this is a cultural advance!

Pam is uncompromisingly herself as, even in the face of death, she rejects a religious interpretation of life. One of my most precious moments was when I decided that she would receive me, an equally uncompromising religious person, as a respected friend. Her integrity goes beyond religious formulations for me and her life makes its own statement of truth. Judy, who has always lived alongside Pam with her own view of life and faith, has gathered together the understandings of the spirit which are true for her, with perhaps a little more seriousness than before.

I hope that my journey towards death can be as loving, honest, free, true and significant as that of Pam and Judy's.

Fearing the pain of death

This is obviously a normal human fear — if we did not fear pain all our lives, we would be constantly at risk. The fear of pain is one of our survival mechanisms, a warning system to protect us from danger. The fear associated with the pain of death is something else, because we imagine ourselves in terminal pain which really does lead to the destruction of our life. No one can actually remove that fear from us, even as medical science finds more and more ways to alleviate or remove pain from our existence. Most of us know that this capacity does not cover every path to death. We also add to our fear of literal physical pain the fear of the pain of possible indignities, dependencies and meaningless life, which seem worse than death.

We live in a time when medical science pushes further and further in the effort to sustain life, regardless of its consequences for the individual concerned. Some of this is genuinely part of an effort to advance our living and, I suspect, some of it seems like human curiosity which pays scant attention to the well-being of the whole person. Because of this, I believe that we are well overdue for serious reflection, between all the stakeholders in the debate, about how decisions are made around the ending of a person's life.

At present, most of the determining discussion involves a relatively small group. There is the medical profession, which has a rightful responsibility to heal and protect life. There are some parts of the religious community, who have a rightful responsibility to contribute to our thinking because they have a strong interest and tradition in relation to values, ethics and life and death issues. Then there are the politicians who have a responsibility to legislate in response to community concerns. While there may be some disinterested citizens influencing the debate, it is not really evident, in my view, that a widespread discussion is actually taking place.

Perhaps this is because few of us like to discuss death in all its aspects. Perhaps it is also because the stakeholders are powerful and are not often interested in moving beyond their own agendas. It is interesting that politicians regard the issue as beyond party politics and therefore allow a 'conscience vote'. They assume that the community has a less valuable conscience than themselves and presume to decide this life and death issue on our behalf, sometimes against the evidence of public opinion.

The whole area of the prolonging of life in the face of unrelieved pain, indignity and other suffering is ambiguous and risky in its complexity. We cannot really release the medical profession from its commitment to the sustaining of life. This should mean, however, that we should not give it overpowering control in the decision-making process.

If religions are to participate, they need to state clearly the grounds on which they make their judgments. It is not enough nowadays to say with simplicity that the time of death is in the hands of God when we are making significant interventions around life and death from birth onwards, and even more so around the prolonging of life, often at any cost. We are long past a 'natural' journey through life.

It is also not convincing to say that, if we have knowledge, it follows that it should be used. We have many forms of knowledge that relate to life and death. Some are good and some are not. Many are, at the very least, ambiguous. For example, if we feel we are at enough risk, we judge it appropriate to kill each other in self-defence, or even in anticipation of the need for corporate defence. In other words, we use our knowledge of armaments to end life. We also use it because we believe that it will save other life.

We do not often now sustain life when a person is judged to be 'brain dead'. Why not? Strictly speaking, the person is still alive and we can keep that person functioning on some level. We know how to do that. We choose not to do it because we have decided that the level of life being lived is not worth sustaining. We are choosing not to use our knowledge to save that life.

If I refer to these issues, it is to emphasise that all along we are intervening, making choices for people, making choices about the sustaining of life. Every decade we have more knowledge with which to work. It is not so long since renal failure meant certain death — God's time to die? We intervened with dialysis and kidney transplants. God's mind changed? Or have we always had freedoms and responsibilities in this very difficult area? If we have, then it is time we all entered a tough and honest discussion on the matter so that we can create some agreed guidelines for ourselves and probably save some of us from life which is not worth living.

In the meantime, most of us will fear the pain of death and we will do that together. And as we encounter that pain in those we love, as they die, we may well become participants in the discussion about what it means to prolong life.

The fear of ending relationships

This fear usually lies in the living and the dying. If we dare to love another, we risk the pain and loneliness of parting. If we decide to protect ourselves from this pain by not loving too much, then we diminish our living and we suffer from loneliness in that living.

I have known many people who, when faced with the terminal illness of someone they love, or their own illness, decide that they can prepare themselves for the ending of a relationship, for the death or a loss. I suppose that, given notice of death, there are some things that can be done in preparation — practical things or making sure some things are said one to the other. However, most of us find that there is really no preparation for the moment of ending.

I always think there are safe and dangerous forms of pain. Guilt would be an example of a dangerous form of pain. Grief, hard though it is, does not usually destroy us — it wounds like a bruising of the heart, it bleeds like a raw tearing of our flesh, but it is a clean, non-festering wounding and therefore can be healed in the passing of time. As with all woundings, sometimes we can do a good deal of the healing ourselves, but the cherishing of us by others and being open to the cherishing love of God (if that is meaningful to us) is critically important.

A good funeral helps us

I will never forget Bruce's funeral. More than two hundred people poured into the church to celebrate the life and grieve the dying of this very young man — all sorts of people — plus his huge dog, Zorro. Zorro sat beside the casket and stood and sat with the rest of us as though he understood exactly what was happening. People read poems they had written about Bruce and one talented young woman gave a 'rap' for him. His mother remembered all his life for us. I am sure that everyone who was there pondered the fact that this young man had created so much love around him, however he saw himself.

Most people dread funerals — they try to have them as soon as possible after the death so that they can move past the ordeal. However, a good funeral is something which people often find enormously helpful. It is probably useful to ask yourself what would make a good funeral for you, although those who know about taking funerals may have some ideas you haven't thought of and may wonder about.

For me, a good funeral has the following characteristics:

- It is respectful of the authentic journey and spirituality of the person who has died.
- It takes into account the people who will be there to grieve.
- It is not 'used' to achieve anything other than the honouring of the journey travelled in life in respectful honesty for the caring of those who are left. For me, this rules out heavy religious funerals for those who had no connection with organised religion. I believe that this is a violation of the life decisions of the person concerned, a mockery to the mourners and a lack of self-respect by the church. Having said that, I do not believe that it is appropriate to assume that, because a person had nothing to do with the church, that the person had no spirituality or sense of God.

How does a minister of religion then act with integrity in the centre of varieties of funerals? I believe that it is ethical and appropriate to say in a funeral, 'It is clear that I am a minister of the Christian church. I am honoured to be asked to lead this service of a person who was not connected with the church and to help create a special occasion for the grieving and celebrating of this human being who is to be respected in her/his choices.

We will not pretend things here in the face of death. I, as the church, will simply share in this significant and honest occasion. Sometimes within that, I will share some of the things that I believe. I will also honour and respect a person who believed differently. That is my gift to you and the sharing in this moment is your gift to me.

There is something about a well-done tribute to the person who has died which can give huge satisfaction to those who loved that person. If the person is described with satisfying reality, people feel as though there is a true recognition, a naming of the life that has gone, a marking and honouring of the journey of that person. The tribute 'holds' it for people, like a recording of something in perpetuity — a sort of reference point. As the person conducting the funeral, it is possible to do this for people, whether you ever met the dead person or not. It is a matter of listening carefully to the words and phrases which people use to remember their friend or family member, the stories they tell in laughter and tears.

The strength of a funeral is in its ritual power to mark an ending. We should never underestimate the power of corporate rituals. As we gather for a funeral, we make a caring place for all who suffer the loss to face that it is indeed an ending. We make an opportunity for others to close around those concerned and offer them healing and company into the future.

Funerals are usually more than the particular event around one person. Most of us bring to a funeral all the funerals and deaths we have experienced. It was deeply moving and interesting to watch the mourning processes around the death of Princess Diana of Wales. In a quite extraordinary manner, it was as though the people of Britain created for themselves a massive funeral. They chose the place for their grieving, outside Kensington Palace. They placed their flowers and their own written tributes to Diana.

They made small and large shrines all around the site and then they kept gathering in that place as they waited for her casket to arrive. The place became a sacred 'cathedral' for their funeral rites. So devoted were the people that their very grieving presence created an environment which people wanted to visit. They stayed there for long periods and spoke of experiencing a connection with other loved ones who had died. They noticed that others around them were hushed and 'engaging with their own inner worlds' in meditative reflection.

Millions of people around the world watched what the mourners were doing and felt deeply moved. I doubt that we were all focused on Princess Diana, even though we were sad that an almost fairy-tale princess and her chaotic and sometimes kindly life had gone. Speaking for myself, I found myself connecting with a corporate grieving for things and people lost, for love and a lightness of life which we long for and which keeps going from us as a world. I found myself connected with the goodness of tears and feeling from the heart.

In modern Anglo-Celtic culture we have a tendency to try to protect ourselves from the reality of death, especially at a funeral. We sit well back from the casket. We often arrange for people's eyes to be closed in prayer or cover the casket with curtains as it leaves the crematorium chapel. We make the service as brief as possible. We often deny ourselves the opportunity of the goodness of real tears and real feelings of loss and the direct facing of our mortality. Many other ancient cultures do much better.

The longing to weep

Stoic cultures often long to weep for their life in general. They lack grieving rituals and this fact often means that their celebratory life is weak as well. It is hard to celebrate (except by drinking yourself stupid!) if your griefs have rarely been named or recognised. It makes a celebration seem a sort of mockery.

I believe we who live in Australia bear layers and layers of unrecognised grief. We carry the grief of Aboriginal people who have never recovered from the wounding of their life since the invasion of their land. We have the pain of those of us who were sent here against their will to an alien and hostile land and often to a life of slavery and oppression, together with those who were sent to guard them far away from family and homeland. We have wave after wave of refugees and immigrants, many of whom would not have chosen to come, or if they did choose, still suffered the loss of their homeland and cultural base. And we have all the grievings of our life together with its injustices, misunderstandings, struggles and vulnerabilities. When have we ever shared our stories of weeping? When have we ever honoured the pain of our history?

If you read a few lines of 'An Absolutely Ordinary Rainbow' by the Australian poet Les Murray to a group of people, you almost always see eyes filling with tears. Part of the poem reads:

There's a fellow crying in Martin Place. They can't stop him...

The crowds are edgy with talk
and more crowds come hurrying...

The man we surround, the man no one approaches
simply weeps, and does not cover it, weeps
not like a child, not like the wind, like a man
and does not declaim it, nor beat his breast, nor even
sob very loudly — yet the dignity of his weeping
holds us back from his space, the hollow he makes about him
in the midday light, in the pentagram of sorrow,
and uniforms back in the crowd who tried to seize him
stare out at him, and feel, with amazement, their minds
longing for tears as children long for a rainbow...

(from *Anthology of Australian Religious Poetry*, Collins Dove, 1986)

There is also an Australian Christmas carol by Norman Habel of Adelaide which has verses beginning with such things as:

*Lay this child to the ground,
one with us, one with earth...*

*Send this child down the road,
let him ride hard the track...*

*Lift this child to the night,
to the silence of God;
Let this child cry for us,
and the silence be heard.*

(From *Outback Christmas*, Rigby, 1981)

This was the one non-Aboriginal Australian song chosen by the World Council of Churches for its Assembly in Canberra in 1991. The international committee that made the selection from hundreds of hymns and songs felt it connected best with the ethos of this country which they experienced as outsiders. When it is introduced to Australian groups, many of us recognise in ourselves and our hearts that we long for grieving but are too self-conscious, perhaps too vulnerable to do other than laugh when we could cry.

Processes of grieving

There are many books written about the process of grieving which give much fuller ideas about what happens to most people and what they can do. In my experience, after the initial numbness, anger and shock most grieving is about talking, telling stories and remembering.

It is as though we hope that in this way we can hold the loved one to us, or maybe we fear that, if we don't keep putting our memories into words, the loved one will go from us. We can't, of course, hold the loved one any closer than our memories and these change over time as though we select the most valued ones.

Talking and talking for a while is a comfort — some people need more time than others. Remaining silent doesn't usually stop the talking in our head anyway and the tears that accompany the talking in caring company are healing and respectful of our feelings. To have someone who does no more than empathically and comfortably be with us is a great help. Those who try to 'cheer us up' in various ways are rarely the best company.

It is our right in grief to choose our own company.

Beyond death

None of us knows what lies beyond death. We can only listen to each other's stories from around death or near death and reflect on possibilities that arise from our understanding of life.

If I were reflecting from my understanding of life, I would say that death takes many forms. I like to think of human existence as an eternal travelling between life and death, and beyond death. I see it as eternal because I think that, from the moment we are born, we begin choosing between life and death. As we value life-filled things in ourselves and others, so we absorb into ourselves things that we carry beyond the boundary which we know as physical death.

The things of life have an eternal quality about them. They are somehow linked with the more lasting factors in life. Of course we can never tell in a precise way which things, moments, qualities and actions have a lasting value, but I think most of us have some sense of that. If we look at which people are recognised in history as special people, those whose lives we celebrate on down through the centuries, we have clues about life-giving and life-lasting factors in human existence.

We remember the Hitlers of this world but we do not celebrate them. It is the Martin Luther Kings, the Ghandis and the Mandelas who we hold as our historical treasures because, while not being perfect, they remind us of costly choices for life, choices that are about love, sacrifice for others, justice and courage. History, because of its bias, has not delivered to us many stories of well-rounded women treasures. However, most of us can add our own: women close to us whose lives told us what lasting life was about — our mothers and grandmothers and friends.

I will always remember a young woman from the Philippines who sat next to me at the Assembly of the Christian Conference of Asia in Penang in 1977. Her name was Jessica Sales and she was doing supportive work with the families of political prisoners during the Marcos regime. When she had finished conducting a group in which she described her work, she sat down beside me and said, 'Dorothy, I think those words may cost me my life.' I did not know what to say as it sounded so melodramatic. She went on, 'But I can only live as Christ calls me to live. I can only live, or I will die anyway.' There were indeed Marcos spies, even in that Christian gathering. As soon as she returned to her home country, she disappeared. After some months, she was found in a mass grave, her body shockingly abused by torture. She lived the way she did rather than die an inner death, even if that almost inevitably led to her physical death. Even now, my eyes fill with tears as I think of her young courage and vibrant life.

In all this, I am suggesting the possibility that, as we choose between life and death values on our journey, so we determine whether we are part of life which links with the ongoing cosmos. We also determine whether our own person is filled with life or death. This is, of course, affected by the degree of life-threatening or life-giving things around us, although our responses to that are still important.

I am not suggesting here that this is about reward and punishment but about what survives death in this life as well as the next. I believe that there is one. I am saying that what we call death is only one sort of death, but of course a very significant one.

After the death of this life

As one who tries to travel in the company of God, as best as I can, I am not prepared to believe that there is a God of judgment, heaven and hell, awaiting us at the moment of death. To believe that would be to deny the God I experience now as one of infinite loving kindness, grace and endless understanding of my journeyings and wanderings. It is also to deny the God who Jesus represented as loving parent.

My father once said to me, 'If you ever find you are more loving than God, Dorothy, you are on the wrong track.' Even as a fair to average parent, I can say that there would never be a moment when I would draw some sort of line for my children beyond which hope ends and my judgment descends upon them for eternity, even if that decision was mine to make.

To those who tell me that it is precisely because God is infinitely good that God has no option but to pass final judgment on humankind, I would say that their God is not in fact infinitely good at all. An integral part of holiness and perfection is always profound love, forgiveness and healing in relationships.

There is no such thing as total goodness without love and there is no such thing as final judgment — the ending of possible reconciliation — that can be likened with love. Can any of us think of a truly good person who would be like this judgmental God?

That is not to say that there is not a moment of truth at the time of death. Many people who have had near death experiences tell stories of a new 'knowing' or 'seeing' — a heightened awareness of reality about themselves and others which has accompanied that experience. Sometimes they tell of a grieving about some of that but this is rarely (if ever) described as being in the presence of any sort of punishing judgmental presence. Of course, this is not conclusive as they did not die, however, it may be a clue to the truth.

Stories around death

As I began writing this chapter, I met with a man called Dudley who was telling me about his children. He told me the story of a little daughter who at a very young age became ill with leukemia. The doctors had advised him and his wife that there was nothing more that they could do for their child and they decided to take her home to die. They put their daughter in a cot beside their bed so they could watch over her, expecting that she would have a week or a month to live. That night they woke and Dudley said he could hear music. He asked his wife whether she could hear anything and she said she could hear a choir singing.

As they listened, the little girl woke and asked to be taken into their bed. They placed her between them and she gave each of them a hug. When they woke again she had died. For some time they could still hear the singing and they experienced that as a welcome to their daughter, wherever she was going. The man mused that people said they heard a choir when a child arrived in Bethlehem.

I had a special sister-in-law who was dying of cancer. She suffered much in the last weeks of the illness. I sat with her not long before she died and we talked together about her experience of having already left us. She described her peace and her sense of separation as she related to her family and watched over them with a different sort of detached but deep caring. It was, indeed, as though she was already dead and in some safe and caring space. I have seen this happen to others as they neared death. It was as though the line they crossed in death was a very thin line of separation — quite near to being in what we understand as life.

I once had an old friend who was not very easy to live with. She had few friends. Her dearest love was her cat, Deci. She asked me to be the executor of her will and to come and get Deci when she died. One night, in the early hours of the morning, I woke very suddenly and could hear her voice calling me to come and get

Deci. I thought I was dreaming but rang her the next day only to find that she had died in the night. Maybe she called me just before she died and I heard her telepathically, or maybe she called to me from beyond death. I will never know.

The other story is clearer. I had a dearly loved sister who, together with her young husband, was killed in a car accident. Three days after she died I was walking home from the local shops with our two little boys. At this stage in our life we had been on an endless round of doctors and specialists trying to find out why our eldest son, Christopher, had gone into a total autistic withdrawal at the age of two years. By then he was five years old and having psychotherapy in an effort to bring him out of the withdrawal, which had been diagnosed as behavioural. As we walked home, Christopher threw himself down on the footpath and screamed and banged his head, as he commonly did.

I stopped and said to myself, 'O God, what will I do?'

I heard my sister's voice say, 'Derth [my family nickname], take Christopher to Laura Nesbitt in Collins Street.' Collins Street was the street in Melbourne where many medical specialists have their rooms. I went home and looked up the name, which I had never heard before, in the phone book.

Sure enough, there was a Laura Nesbitt listed in Collins Street. I rang and Laura Nesbitt answered the phone herself. I said, 'Look, I feel a bit silly asking this, but what sort of specialist are you?' She said, 'I am an allergist. Are you by any chance Thais Worner's sister?' I said, 'Yes, I am.' She said, 'The presence of your sister came to me this morning and said you would ring.'

We took Christopher to her and she diagnosed brain damage due to an allergic response to the Salk polio vaccine and asked his psychiatrist to arrange for an electroencephalogram. The psychiatrist agreed and the neurologists independently confirmed brain damage which was, in their view, a typical allergic response to the Salk vaccine.

I found out later that my sister had consulted Laura Nesbitt when she, as a young adult teacher, had been vaccinated and hospitalised after a severely allergic response to the Salk vaccine. All of this was new to me and obviously not something my sister connected with Christopher's situation until after she died. All I know is that she knew more after death than she had known in life and that her love for us continued and reached beyond death. While it was hard indeed to know our son was brain-damaged, it was less hard than going on trying to find out what was wrong. It almost certainly saved his sister, who had the same allergies, from brain damage as she would have been vaccinated as well.

As we participated in the double funeral for my sister and her husband, John, I looked at the two caskets and knew their life did not lie within the caskets. I experienced them hovering above us in comforting love and care, even as we grieved. All of that experience removed from me the fear of death and the experiences around it, even if I still don't know what death ultimately contains for us. Even as I personally believe in some sort of ongoing, I obviously don't know if that is true. It is a matter of belief.

Maybe my sister, after her sudden death, stayed close to us for a while and then there was nothing more for her. Maybe death really is an end to all consciousness and being. Maybe we go on in some sort of individual journey in another place. Maybe we are reincarnated for another turn at our sort of life or another. Maybe we are absorbed into all life in a cosmic community of life which swirls around the universe in many forms and emerges again in the ongoing of earth, sea, wind, water and all forms of other life. Maybe we emerge on another planet. Who knows?

But, if there is nothing beyond what we see, then this existence becomes more important, not less, unless all life is meaningless. It gives us a greater emphasis on what it is that contributes to the life that we leave behind us, which is incorporated into the lives of those who knew us or were impacted by our existence. That, in itself, becomes our future, our eternity.

Death will always fascinate us

Perhaps this is because it is one thing which we cannot avoid, all of us, no matter how rich or poor, good or bad, well or ill, religious or not. It is all the more reason for talking about it together.

Living Within Set Boundaries

SOMETIMES we have little option but to live within limits set on our choices and freedoms, by factors outside our own control. My most significant experience of this limiting was that which related to the brain damage of my son Christopher. We started out together in the normal way. He was our first child, a bright little boy, going through all his stages ahead of time and, at a little over two years old, speaking in sentences.

Then, quite suddenly, in the month in which his brother was born, he went into a total autistic withdrawal and never spoke to us again. His intellectual development regressed to something like a chaotic sort of babyhood and he stopped relating to us in other than the most minor ways.

We began a round of visiting doctors and paediatricians, none of whom could tell us what was wrong. Much later, in a remarkable way, as I have mentioned, an allergist, a psychiatrist and two neurologists told us that it was likely that he had been allergic to his Salk polio vaccination and was permanently brain-damaged. Then I remembered how very distressed he had been at the time of his booster dose of the vaccine.

I need to say at this point that, in spite of Christopher's brain damage, I do believe in vaccinations. I remember well the terrible disease of poliomyelitis, which afflicted some children in every school class in my childhood, and we do appear to have wiped out some serious diseases through vaccination programs. Two of our children were vaccinated and the other two were not, depending on signs of allergies.

It is hard to tell what the truth really is about vaccinations but, given the family history, we were advised by the several doctors we consulted to be cautious. Maybe, one day, we will have some simple tests that can check the safety of vaccines before they are administered. I hope so, because what happened to our son should not happen to any child.

For the next fourteen years, during which we had two more children, making four, it felt as though the boundaries of my life were set by the boundaries on Christopher's life. In the early days, right at the time when my head and heart were full of questions and needings to share things, a great silence descended around us. We were living in a new housing estate where we had all compared notes daily on the progress of our children and life in general. All of a sudden, the discourse stopped.

No one wanted to ask me how Christopher was getting on, probably because they feared I would become emotional and because they don't know what to say anyway. There was nothing me of their own healthy children who had been Christopher's playmates. I was about twenty-five years old. Had I been older, wiser and more confident, I could have said to them, 'Please talk to me. Don't worry if I cry — it's good for me to do that. There is nothing that I need you to say. Most people say stupid and unhelpful things when they speak. I just want you to be there for me please.'

The ones who did speak often said things like, 'What could you have done that this has happened to your child?' or 'God must have a reason for doing this to Christopher' or, one even said, 'Don't worry, Christopher will be an angel in heaven because he will be sinless'! Interestingly, not all of these comments came from people who would see themselves as religious. I thought to myself, often with tears of rage, 'Well I don't believe in a God like that' or

'How dare you blame me for what has happened to my son!' and 'What a load of rubbish!'

At the same time, my own response to God was one of pleading. 'Please make our son well again. I know you can work miracles. I was only trying to care for him, surely you can stop his suffering.' Much later in my life, I felt free to be really angry with God who created a universe where such things could happen. Even had I then the view of life and God which I have now, I would still see a response of anger and protest at this tragedy as entirely appropriate.

I will reflect on miracles later, but whether you believe in them or not, why should a mother not cry out into the universe her pain and pleading in response to the suffering of her child and herself? Why should we not have the confident relationship with God which allows us to be angry, to challenge what has happened? Surely we do this in self-respect, in authenticity and in response to our own valid sense of justice?

Even as I write this account, I realise that, while I understood what I wanted from my friends — just kindly and consistent company, rather than solutions — I thought then that God ought to be able to do better than that. To a God who, in my inner insights offered me never-failing company and seemed to me to be saying 'And that will be enough', I said, 'No. I want answers and solutions. Your company is not enough.'

I guess that was understandable. After all, we do expect God to be able to do better than ourselves in these times. In the end, I realised that the offer was 'I am with you always'. I could decide to live from that, or live in protest against its inadequacy. I believe that is an actual decision we make, even if we fall from our decision here and there. Whatever we decide about that determines our life from then on. I never felt I was other than self-respecting in deciding that I would accept the company of God as the totality of the answer and to live as fully as possible from that.

The question of faith also lay before the rest of the family and they made their own personal responses to the question. I recall our daughter, Lindy, coming home from Sunday School and saying with great heat, 'I am never going to sing that song again!' When asked what song, she said, 'That one called "Nothing is Impossible to God". It is just not true. I asked God to make Christopher better and he didn't, so I don't believe that song.' She worked out her own faith in her authentic way as life went on.

What we all found, as do others living with any disability, either as the person concerned or as carers, the boundaries were in place. I wish to make it clear at this point that we all live with some form of disability of body, mind, heart or soul. We are all differently abled. Some of these disabilities make it more difficult than do others to live in fullness and freedom in our society. There are also some people who live joyfully and creatively within their own boundaries. Many are especially gifted in loving relationship. Christopher is not one of those people. In his years at home with us, when he was unmedicated, he was often a distressed and confused person and severely isolated from relationships. The type of brain damage he sustained breaks up his thought patterns every few seconds so that he is unable to think in any useful way, or to speak. All this was our ongoing grief, rather than the disability in itself.

Our whole family was affected by Christoher's boundaries, of course. We could rarely go out together as the stress of handling the entirely unpredictable Christopher made it so much trouble that it often wasn't worth it. We only went on holidays to family, as anywhere else was unlikely to be manageable. Even staying with family had its stresses, because their houses were not set up for Christopher. It was only really viable because both his father and myself could take turns in watching him. And in it all, I had to decide whether I would settle down and live carefully and quietly within those boundaries or move towards them and try to push them out a bit further for more life.

It was very tiring being carer for a brain-damaged toddler as well as a baby and, later, when he became a fully grown brain-damaged adolescent and we had three younger children. From seven to sixteen years of age, Christopher attended a great Rudolf Steiner School for Children in Need of Special Care for several hours in the middle of the day. We had to raise a lot of money to keep the school going. I remember, as I sewed literally hundreds of items of clothing for the school fete, being outraged about the absence of free state facilities for our child.

I used to think to myself that, if we had twenty healthy children, the state would have provided relatively free schooling for them, but not for this one needy child, and myself as a needy parent. In New South Wales, at that time, there was literally no government-provided day care for a child like Christopher.

At sixteen Christopher was still not toilet-trained, in spite of my efforts and the efforts of the school. He used to run away, just take off into the distance — our house became like Fort Knox in an effort to keep him safe. Fortunately he liked eating and liked shoes, so I could sometimes track him through milk bars where the astonished owners had watched as an apparent teenager raced into their shop and grabbed a handful of sweets. He was then likely to take off to the shoe shop where he sat and stroked the shoes on display. At home his activities were infantile, like taking a jar of honey and gloriously mixing it with a container of flour in the bottom of my wardrobe or dropping things into the backyard incinerator to watch them burn.

He loved eating almost anything, including paper, children's homework, library books, anything. Sometimes you had to laugh rather than cry. On one occasion, his three-year-old sister, Melissa, called out, 'Mum, come quickly! Chrissie has eaten the angel and the wise men and he is just about to eat Mary and the baby Jesus!' Her cardboard nativity scene was fast disappearing! We had to hastily drive to Parramatta before the shops closed to buy a plastic one.

Always there was the strenuous effort to try to rescue the other children from the hardships of having this brother who did not understand what he was doing, to calmly say 'Never mind, we'll fix it or get another one.' I said that so often that I would hear the words come back to me from the other children as they spoke to each other — sometimes quite inappropriately. I began to fear that they would value nothing because it could always be replaced or fixed, and as though we had endless money to do so, and as though it didn't matter.

In actuality, we had to devalue things that other people valued, because we stood to lose them. In some ways that was a way of choosing to live beyond the boundaries we were set. We could choose to grieve every time we lost something, or we could put less value on material things and decide that the things we retained were more important than anything we had lost. Some of this was, I am sure, quite unhealthy. It could have been good to give each other permission to rage around the place and weep and wail, rather than becoming excessively generous about our losses. On the other hand, I think we did genuinely learn to be less reliant on things that are not very critical in the long and wide view of life.

If a person is responsible for what they do then you can challenge him or her, but with Christopher we all knew that he was only minimally responsible. Even as very young children his sisters and brother knew that before it could be explained to them. They also realised that, in spite of his activities, Christopher was very defenceless — at fifteen years old, he would cower as three-year-old Melissa said, 'No, Chrissie!'

Life was tiring and there was little respite available from anywhere. The question was, 'Do I try to get more rest and cope with this life as it is?' In the end, I realised that the boundaries could only be pushed out by choosing to add to my life, rather than trying to reduce it. When my sons were young I did two matriculation subjects by correspondence and passed them with honours.

Later, I decided that, if I was largely restricted to the house and child care by day, I would volunteer to go on the Life Line phones in the middle of the night when my husband was home to care for the children. Later still, when Christopher was away in the middle of the day, a friend and I organised a monthly lunch for elderly women who were referred to us by the local Community Aid Centre as people with few friends and chances of getting out. We would pick them all up from their homes and take them to our houses for lunch, then drive them back. Then I would race home in time to collect Christopher.

I became part of the Vietnam War peace movement and edited a bimonthly newsletter, mostly for women who were at home, called 'Mothers and Others for Peace'. The whole idea was to offer people at home enough information to be active in letter-writing, phone-lobbying and talking with neighbours about the war in an effort to influence its ending.

These activities were a big effort, but they saved my life. In saying that, I am meaning that if you allow your life to be severely narrowed down in order to deal with it, you are likely to lose most of your life. The boundaries were stretched. My life was not determined by the situation. Tiredness was healthy instead of due to depression and a sort of boredom. There could have been many other ways of claiming my life. These days, I suspect I would have arranged more fun for myself rather than all serious and serving things. However, the company of God and that of my friends, who learnt what being company meant, was indeed enough to live on with a level of freedom and a lot of hard-won moments of joy in life itself.

When Christopher was sixteen, harder to handle, bigger than I was, severely epileptic and getting to be a worry for the friends of his siblings, we placed him in a state hospital for children with intellectual disabilities. Some of my Christian friends said, 'Oh, we thought that since God had given you this burden, God would give you the strength to cope.' I thought to myself and sometimes told them, 'That is an oppressive heresy. God gives the strength to cope to the whole community, not to individuals. Everyone has to decide which community has for them the resources they need to cope. This community of the church is not that for us and it never has been. The staff of the state hospital, who are giving us a marvellous gift of their commitment and skill to care for a child like ours, are now our community of care.' And so they were, and have been ever since.

The life of our other children, Christopher's father and myself has been infinitely enriched by their gift to us of their vocation in development disability nursing. I still weep when I think of my gratitude to them.

Having said that, the decision to send Christopher into permanent residential care, while it clearly opened out the boundaries for me, and I should think for his father, was far more ambiguous for his siblings. We, their parents, could see the advantage to them, both at the time and into the future. We believed that we were not only making many more things possible in their present life and lifting much tension, but we were avoiding the possibility that, if anything happened to us, they would be left with the responsibility for his care. Later in life, however, his sisters in particular were faced with the impact that decision had had on their young lives. We thought we had explained in great clarity why their brother was sent away forever, but a seven year old and a four year old create their own interpretations for such a traumatic event. In some respects, their lives were given new boundaries as they tried to respond in their childish ways to what happened, and they still work with that as adults.

For most of the years, I held to myself a dream that one day, somewhere, there would be ultimate justice for Christopher. Somewhere he would live life to the full. Somewhere would be the compensation for what seemed to be the gift of his life so that other children would be free from polio — as a person who paid part of the price for progress. I have never felt bitter about him being such a person. However, I become really angry when I hear doctors say blithely that there is no risk in immunisation, that those of us who say there is are ignorant and irresponsible. I see their dilemma. If they frighten people, no one will risk their children and the great advances from immunisation will be lost. However, I suspect that we parents can be trusted with more honest information and that the medical profession could offer a few more options for checking who is at risk and who is not.

I guess I feel that one small justice for Christopher, and others like him, would be if their costly journey for other children was honoured as real and significant.

If I thought of another more ultimate justice, it was comforting to imagine Christopher born again into another life or leaping around some heaven, shouting and singing with his bright mind released to its fullness again, loving and living. Maybe that is the true possibility for all who live this life with less than their share of health, who live with limits which are beyond their control. None of us can really know.

Just recently, however, I decided to set his life free into the cosmic collection of all life, whatever that may be like. Somehow that was a good and releasing thing to do. When he dies, I will simply imagine that his boundaried spirit is now free to fly and link up with other life. That too will be enough. This decision came from my significant experiences in reflecting on the questions of Job. As I took my place in a more cosmic view of life, so I could take Christopher with me, whether we have a conscious meeting there, or not, and whether justice resides there, or not.

It took me thirty-eight years to arrive at the time when I could write a liturgy of grieving and welcoming for our son. I'm not sure whether, if I was beginning the journey again with Christopher, I could actually participate in such a liturgy. I am told that it has been helpful for some others, however, so I have included it at the end of this book in case it is useful to you. It comes from an earlier book of mine and I did hear that a whole group of people who had children with disabilities had used it together.

Ours is only one story of boundaried lives. It is also only my version of the story. The other members of our family would tell it very differently, I know. Robert, who was much closer in age to Christopher than his sisters, really lost his whole infancy because of our intense trauma in facing Christopher's brain damage and still grieves with tears the brother he never had.

He lived with the boundaries for fourteen years of his life, the whole of his childhood. There are, of course, many other stories within our life and also people who live with far tighter and narrower boundaries than we ever did.

❈

W H E N I think of those who stretch out boundaries to live, I always remember a young friend of mine. She had juvenile diabetes and was gradually going blind. Her family life and church life had been very traumatic and betraying, to say the least, but she had battled her way, on her own, through to a university degree and a graduate diploma in rehabilitation work. I was present when she received her graduate diploma and that was a moment which I won't forget, because I had some understanding of what it had taken to achieve it.

Soon after this my friend established herself in a professional career and later began to buy a house, but she lives with chronic pain and a future that will obviously narrow her life. She was not to be defeated, however. She would come to her friends and say, in her colourful and honest way, 'Life is a shit! Now look what's happening! What's it all about? Why should I have to put up with this?' She would rage and cry. We would not try to answer her valid questions but try to be her friends, and she would pick herself up from the ground again and go on. I remember particular moments of the determined expanding of her life.

She had been very fond of sport at school, but could no longer participate because she couldn't see the balls fast enough. So, after grieving that, she thought a lot and decided to become a great kite flier because the kites were big and colourful enough to see. She believed that she could run with them and fly them by herself. And so she did and her life stretched out again. After a while, the strength in her hands began to deteriorate, so that it was difficult to hold the kites. Not to be defeated, she discovered a leather wristband and attached the kites to her wrist.

Her life was often very stressful. It was also intensely painful, spiritually, psychologically and physically — and this last could only sometimes be relieved with the use of very strong and frequent painkillers. Not all diabetics suffer such sustained and severe pain, but for some inexplicable reason my friend was one who was almost never without terrible pain behind her eyes.

A few years ago, she discovered the form of martial arts called Aikido. She found that this offered a whole new way of living. On the other hand, the doctors advised her that the activity might well have a negative impact on her condition. She decided that her life was still fuller if she went on with the Aikido. Even if it sometimes affected her physical condition, it restored her in other ways and gave her a sense of inner peace. She also loved the physical challenge to go beyond her limitations in strength, courage and discipline.

Recently she rang me to tell me that, after five years of doing Aikido, she had won her Black Belt. In doing this she had defended herself against many opponents who had no idea that she was visually impaired and that ordinary movements and impacts caused her great pain. An Aikido classmate told me that they all watched in hope and wonder as their friend won a major and moving battle against all her disabilities. In winning her Black Belt she defended herself against the boundaries in life which would have always had the capacity to teach her defencelessness. There were tears in my eyes as she showed me her Black Belt with pride. Achieving that Black Belt was the highest point in her life. She will always be for me a sort of 'icon' of courage and intense determination to live.

I AM very conscious that my own life could stretch itself out much more because I had a husband who cared for me and all our children, and some others who encouraged and supported us. I will always remember a quite old woman, Sadie Martin, who was the one baby-sitter who would baby sit Christopher apart from, for a brief time, a very young woman called Ann-Marie. They gave us the only respite we had. Not everyone is as fortunate as I was.

However, I guess I am exploring a principle which may give a clue about how to live with boundaries — that to add something to a tough life, rather than to take something away, is to claim life back in some small way. I am also suggesting that fullness of life is not necessarily what we think it is. It is more about taking charge of whatever there is available to us and living it with determination and a sort of vivid passion.

Living with Miracles

WHAT is a miracle? This is a more important question than it appears to be. Most of us tend to define miracles as having to do with physical events which seem to have no rational explanation. We often attach to them the possibility of some sort of supernatural activity. In doing this, we assume we can distinguish between natural and supernatural. Actually, as soon as you relate across cultural boundaries, this assumption is likely to be challenged, quite apart from the diversity of experience and belief among people in general.

Particularly in the ancient cultures which have not been so overwhelmed by what we call rational thought, the lines are more blurred. Some of us assume that this is a 'backwardness' which will be eliminated with 'progress'. But maybe we are the ones who are 'backward' because we have, in our materialistic view of life, lost some old truths about the natural world. In putting this view, I am not claiming as true or natural every belief which lies in the ancient cultures, just inviting an openness of mind.

On quite another track about the definition of miracles, I would suggest that many of us tend to limit the concept of miracles to the physical and material. I recall, when I was a parish minister, receiving a letter from a group that was interested in faith healing. They asked me to record and send to them descriptions and numbers of any miracles that took place within our parish life. I rang the author of the letter and asked what he meant by a miracle. He obviously thought my question strange — surely a miracle was a faith healing of a physical nature. I asked him which he thought was the greater miracle, a person who was physically healed, or a person who was not healed but retained her or his faith?

I would say that miracles are events and situations that we find hard to explain. They are changes in people and situations which we did not expect, given what we know about the diagnoses, the resources, the courage, the strength that we thought were true and present in the situation or person. Some good thing has happened and we find it hard to imagine where that good event came from. So we say, 'It's a miracle!'

Of course there are 'magic' type 'miracles' — where people deliberately walk across hot coals without getting burnt or acts like that which have a sense of phenomenon about them. I don't pretend to know anything about those events, except to suggest that the power of the mind over matter is something about which we know very little. However, my discussion here is focused on the more random surprises in everyday life which most of us experience at some stage, or observe in the life of others.

BECAUSE prayer is so often regarded as related to miracles in religious circles, I will reflect a little on my understanding of prayer. One of the formative experiences that has contributed to my reflection on the nature of prayer relates to my having the parents I had. My father's family came from what some historians claim was an indigenous clan of Scotland. This clan took part in the defence of the Catholic faith in the highlands of Scotland and in many other battles there. My father was probably influenced by his genes and his heritage.

His family were poor but cultured farmers, in that they enjoyed literature and reading and respected education. My father began training as an engineer and then changed courses and went into the ordained ministry. He was a fine biblical scholar and theologian. He achieved a Masters degree in Philosophy (although that was never conferred because he could not find enough spare money to pay for its conferral). His spirituality, even as a Protestant minister was, in some ways, very 'Catholic'.

He led his congregations into an appreciation of finely crafted prayers, peaceful reflection in the silences, deep thought and a brave and critical analysis of the Bible and the nature of God. His view of God was essentially focused on grandeur, mystery and quiet presence. I never knew him to be connected with any obvious 'miracle' and yet many things changed in people with whom he was associated.

My mother, on the other hand, was a Cornish-Australian hardware merchant's daughter. She was quite intelligent but had to leave school at thirteen years of age to help support the family after both her parents had died. Her spirituality was simple (but not simplistic). She believed that God was involved in every decision she ever made, in the most intimate way. She prayed for guidance before she bought the curtain material and waited for God's quite direct answer about which shop to go to and what colour for the material. She prayed for healing and clearly had gifts in being part of the healing of many people. I saw, as a child and as an adult, people literally rise from their beds of paralysis and walk.

I particularly recall a baby being born with an inoperable cleft palate. The doctors said the child would never speak nor be able to eat normally. My mother and her friends prayed and, to the astonishment of the doctors, the cleft palate grew across and the child was able to speak and eat. The doctors had no explanation for this and said that they had never seen such a thing happen before. I also remember a child with a brain tumour having the tumour disappear after the prayers of my mother and her friends.

I recall, at a period when we were quite poor, the family gathered around our table for a meal and my mother telling us that we needed to pray for food, as we had none. The food arrived at the door, via a generous neighbour. Even then, I had some questions about why we were given provisions when I knew that others, far more hungry, were not. However, we were all grateful for the food!

I also remember a period in my mother's life when she connected with a worldwide movement which believed that the important thing was to wait in silence for messages from God, rather than having a one-way conversation — telling God what you wanted. She used to sit us children down on some days with a notepad in front of us and asked us to 'listen to God' and write down what we had heard. I never heard anything and felt very uncomfortable — but I made up something each day. My very bright and bouncy sister always heard masses of amazing things and I used to feel quite envious of her.

Then two things happened to my mother. She invited a friend, Elsie, who was also part of this movement to live with us for a while. Each day, they sat together for their 'quiet time', when they listened to God. One day Elsie told my mother that God had spoken to her and asked her to tell my mother that she was to be given my mother's finest china teacup and saucer for her personal use each day and that she was to have fruit salad every night for dessert. My mother was speechless with annoyance. It rocked her view of this approach to prayer quite significantly.

Then, later, she actually connected with a whole group of members of the movement for the first time. With great anticipation she went to her first meetings, only to find the messages that most of the group received from God consisted almost entirely of critical and judgmental instructions for other members of the group. As one who had received insights only about her own life and hopeful healing possibilities for others, she found this very nasty and suspicious. She never went back to the group and her interest in the movement faded considerably.

In being part of praying groups, I believe that my mother transmitted to other people a careful and mature understanding of the nature of prayer, and the possible activity of God in response to prayer, especially in her later years. She always worked corporately and no one that I ever saw left the situation damaged by the experience, or in any doubt that God had been with them, whatever the ultimate result. My mother prayed from the heart and the worship she led was informal, intimate and 'homely'. God was essentially her personal friend, her ever-present companion.

My father and mother loved and respected each other's spirituality and way of praying. When they died, hundreds of people came from all over Australia to their funerals, in thanksgiving for the fruits of the particular spirituality which they had experienced in one or the other. In fact, when my mother died very suddenly, the local provincial city paper carried a large headline which read 'Beth McRae Everybody's Friend Dies'.

In sharing these two stories, I am not implying that styles of spirituality are connected with levels of education. One of my brothers and myself are both ordained ministers in the same church. My brother has a degree in Applied Science and another in Theology. He is far more like my mother in spirituality. I, on the other hand, have only last year achieved my first degree (in Theology) and am, I think, more like my father in spirituality, but not in intellect. Having said that, neither of us is a replica of either parent. We are uniquely ourselves, as is our sister and other brother.

So which of my parents contributed most to the possibility of miracles? At different points in my life, I have had a different answer to that question. In my earlier days, it depended on which person was more like myself! Then I realised that spirituality is about the connection with one's own inner life and its relationship with the 'otherness' in human existence — the awareness of that relationship and its true expression. Therefore, in the end, spiritual development must be profoundly connected with the development of authenticity.

I believe that those who live with authentic spirituality add their own authentic dimension to the miraculous nature of life.

I believe that prayer in the church has largely become captive to past bad experience and present poor theology. Most of us in the church who are older, carry with us a heavy burden of memory of dreadful boring prayer meetings where the powerful and/or neurotic held forth week after week at great length and with infinite repetition. Most of us remember switching off from 'around the world trips' in prayer from the pulpit, or prayers of admonition directed towards the captive congregation.

Most of us also have in our hearts what we perceived as 'failures' in prayer at important moments in our life which were never resolved or even helpfully explored and which took away our confidence in praying. We were often taught as children, if we went to Sunday School that, of course, as good Protestant Christian children we must pray and read our Bible every day, preferably at a fixed time. It was a relief to discover when I was much older that, of course, most of us did not do that. For a while there I thought that I was the only one. For some people spiritual activities fit well into a fixed pattern, but for many others the development of spirituality takes an entirely different form.

Are some people especially capable of producing miracles? I don't really know. There do seem to be some people around whom miracles appear to collect. That tends to be related to the more obvious definition of a miracle as physical healing, however. There are other people whose lives relate in a far less obvious fashion to transformations that are not often recognised as miracles. By this, I mean people who seem to have a radical impact on the lives of others with whom they relate. You see an unusual number of people given a whole new courage or strength or hope, or a gift of being able to forgive, after they have associated with the person concerned. Maybe far more of us perform miracles than we have noticed.

However, I have no problem with the thought that some particular people offer special talents in this area. Maybe they have a clear connection with dimensions of life that other people don't even believe in. Maybe that is simply their skill, like any other skill. Maybe it doesn't matter why they are as they are.

How can we understand prayer and its connection, or not, with miracles? In one sense, I don't see prayer as related to the supernatural. I see it as a 'natural' connecting with the resources of the universe, including God. I believe that energy, courage, strength, faith, endurance and healing are as transferable between people as love is transferable. I can do that myself and have received it from others. I have held someone's hand and said, 'I will give to you some of my energy and peace,' and have felt, particularly the energy, leave my body at that moment. I have certainly received a sense of calmness or courage from someone who intentionally offers it to me. I have also received many resources from what seems to me to be a source outside myself, and beyond other people.

When I participate in a group of people who pray, or indeed are together sharing care and hope with each other about somebody or some situation, I imagine us as pooling all our resources. If we do this consciously, I believe that the gathering together of everything we have within us and around us is effective in enlarging the creation of good. As a Christian, I believe that as we also include the idea of God in this pooling of creative good, we are able to tap into resources for good that are beyond ourselves. When we do that, I put no limits on the possibilities for change that are before us.

I am comfortable with people asking for anything, or with people who simply engage in a communal and silent hoping for an expanding of the good around them. Our way of connecting with the 'otherness' in the adding to life must be authentically our choice. I do not mean that I believe that we can direct God, or that God is responding to specific requests. If we could direct God, we would be God and I don't believe in that sort of intervening God. Rather, I believe that the eternal pouring towards all people of the love, energy for good and healing power of God is something which we can tap into to support and enrich our living. I believe that this enlarging and gathering together of good energies can produce amazing miracles of change in individuals and situations.

There is a passage in the Book of Luke 11:9–12, in the Bible, which has Jesus saying:

So I say to you, ask and it will be given you; search and you will find; knock and it will be opened to you. For anyone that asks receives, and everyone who searches finds, and for everyone who knocks, the door will be opened...If you then, who are evil, know how to give good gifts to your children, how much more will the heavenly Father give the Holy Spirit to those who ask him!

If we are looking for a biblical model of what prayer is about, I would choose this as mine. The trouble is that many people end their reading of the passage before the thoughts of Jesus are complete — we stop at the promise of the door being opened. If you go to the end, you discover that the offer is not that everything which we ask for will be given to us, but that we will receive the gift of the Holy Spirit. The Holy Spirit is the Spirit of God which Christians believe has the capacity to comfort, heal, bring truth, faith, courage, hope and insight — indeed, the resources for the journey of life. So the gift of the Holy Spirit, in response to prayer, means that we wait with expectation for the adding of many different sorts of good gifts to our life. The effects of this adding of good may be many and varied.

As I said, I don't understand any of this to be supernatural or magic. If you think about the extraordinary interconnection between our state of being and our health, then you would have to challenge a very obvious and 'concrete' view of reality. I recall a stage hypnotist inducing a blister to appear on the arm of a subject by suggesting that the person was suffering a burn. My hair goes flat when I am depressed. I recently had all the symptoms of a heart attack when I was severely stressed. We all have our own stories of the interconnections between our own body, mind and spirit. We can also tell stories about huge increases in health and well-being because somebody really loved us. These are not illusions, nor are they supernatural.

I believe that the resources for good in ourselves, between us, and in the universe through God, or some other positive force, are an ever-present dimension of ordinary reality with which we can choose to connect, or not. I don't even believe that this resource is denied to us if we choose not to invite it. I simply believe that when people share all that they are and have, and choose to connect with all that God is, then a remarkable energy for good is set free. Some of this energy for good will so transform our life that we will see it as miraculous.

This view of prayer (or whatever you choose to call it) removes us from the dangerous and punishing possibilities that lie within some views of prayer. I recall going as a guest preacher to a congregation in Sydney. Before I took my place in the pulpit, a parish leader rose to speak. He said, 'You will all know that we have been praying for some time for the healing of one of our members who had cancer. Well, it is my sorry task to tell you that the young man died this week. It is quite clear that our faith was not sufficient, or that some grave sin lies in our midst which prevented the healing.' I watched the whole congregation almost tremble in distress and anxiety as he resumed his seat. Needless to say, I had to 'rewrite' my sermon on the spot. I do not believe that the gifts which we perceive as miracles have anything to do with reward and punishment, or even lack of faith, and that if we teach people that they do, we are likely to be quite damaging to them.

This destruction to people happens in environments where a viable theology of prayer has not been developed. To imply, or say, that our failings are the cause of the death of others in this way is to place on people a terrifying and, in my view, erroneous burden. I have even seen people who, having prayed for a specific form of healing for some person, when it failed to happen, blamed that person for their own lack of healing. They say to the person that maybe they have a hidden sin or a lack of faith which is preventing the success of prayer. This activity can be unbelievably destructive and, quite apart from the damage it does to the person concerned, can certainly discourage people from the risk of praying.

My partner, Ali, tells a story from her childhood. She suffered significant damage to her body as a result of having tuberculosis of the hip as a young child. When she came home from years in hospital, on crutches, her local Catholic Church was visited by a priest, who claimed to heal people with the assistance of a 'holy relic'. Her father told her of this and took her to the priest for healing. She was not healed. She cannot remember how the priest concerned responded to this lack of healing. She only remembers the nuns at her school telling her that people who had enough faith would be healed. One wonders what this did to a vulnerable child, especially as the disability was sustained for the rest of her life.

IS THERE anything we should not pray for? Some people believe that we should not pray for things like rain, because that is not theologically sound — God sends rain on the 'just and unjust', and who are we to decide that our little bit of turf is due for rain when it might bring floods to someone else, or be more needed elsewhere? Or, rain is due to a whole complexity of scientific conditions which have nothing to do with our personal or corporate needs or desires, so prayer is inappropriate.

Probably all of the above is true but, if encouraging people to pray for rain teaches them that rain, or no rain, is a reward or punishment from God, then I would be most uneasy. We are somewhat prone to interpreting such events in our own interests and being quite inconsistent in looking at the facts. If we were honest, we could not but admit that God does not deliver justice in this form.

I recall, with affection, an enthusiastic praying person who was a member of our parish in Sydney. He was also a very keen member of the Labor Party. Although our worship was rather formal, there was usually a point in the service when people were invited to 'lift up their own prayers for the church and the world'. Around election time, the congregation waited with a variety of emotions for our enthusiastic prayer to lift up his prayers for the success of the party in the coming election and sometimes the destruction of its enemies. We occasionally discussed whether his prayers were appropriate. Mostly we felt that in inviting people to pray, we set that moment free for the hearts and longings of people, and that the rest of us were quite capable of choosing whether or not we joined them in their prayer.

There is also something real, refreshing and human in the allowing of ourselves to simply cry out into the universe our response to life. Why should we not say into the cosmos 'Send us rain!' or 'Please, someone, God, give power to the forces of good and stop the power of those who seem to bring oppression to the world'. The biblical Psalms are a great example of the honest crying out of the Hebrew people, and some of them are a little more vicious that most of us would find comfortable. Having said that, there have been occasions when that level of 'Bring down my enemies' is the only level of crying out which helps truly afflicted and suffering people.

The safeguard is if we talk together honestly about what we believe we are doing as we pray. Another safeguard is the setting free of individuals to pray in ways that we all understand is not a prayer which arises from our corporate life, but which is simply gathered up as a prayer from the heart of one person.

I HAVE not discussed in depth the way I understand the activity of God in relation to answers or perceived non-answers to prayer, nor my general theology and philosophy about the activity of God in relation to our lives. I have left that for another part of this book. Here, I am primarily focusing on the possibility of living life with an expectation that it can be more miraculous than we had anticipated.

To live with miracles is to live with expectation. If I like to live as one who believes in miracles, or surprising transformations, it is because I choose to live as though life has resources and dimensions to it that are beyond my knowing. I will never know what is possible, given the power of love which swirls around the universe. I will never know the full dimensions of the transforming power of love which resides in those who love me and within me in my love for them, or simply as a gift from God.

Because of this, I am committed to living with a great expectation of surprises. I am prepared to invite them in myself, in others and in God. I believe that the dimensions of reality with which most of us live, including myself, are very partial indeed and that, just as science keeps expanding our view of reality so our possible life in relationship with love is barely known.

Living as a Non-victim

THE most focused experience I have had in relation to being a victim occurred in the early days of the Women's Movement. During that period we spent much time in groups, sharing ideas about our lives and the possibility of making moves to change them. We recognised that this discussion was, in itself, a process. The name we had for that was 'consciousness-raising' and it came from the liberation movements in Latin America and the great Brazilian educator Paulo Friere. He called it 'conscientisation'.

Consciousness-raising begins with the realisation that you are indeed a victim. Of course that is sometimes very obvious, but not always. To see that you are a victim — that is, that something is happening to you, or has happened to you that is unjust, wrong and to be challenged, is the beginning of the liberation journey. If someone steals from you, or bashes you in the street, or kills someone you love, it is easy to name yourself as a victim. However, if your victimisation is related to prevailing oppressive attitudes in a society, or to the activities within systems, it is not always so clear.

I am not suggesting that in those days, we were radiantly happy women looking for our victimisation and encouraging others to do so. Sometimes people accused us of that. We were women who, at some level were disappointed, disturbed or distressed about our lives. Some of us had not been able to connect with the source of this dissonance in our lives and others had been able to do so. As we reflected together and encouraged each other to articulate things we had not dared to articulate before, the patterns of our corporate truth began to appear.

The superficial, happy appearance of people should not deceive us. I recall at one point in the 1970s a major Christian church making a decision that related to the continuing exclusion of its women from a church position. The members of the body that made this decision, said with confidence that their women did not want to hold this office and that they rejoiced in their role. I was then on the staff of the state Ecumenical Council. Quite suddenly, conservative women's groups from this church invited me to come to speak to them on the Bible and the role of women, knowing full well that I was a feminist. I went to a couple of the groups and simply shared the way the Bible had informed my journey. This released a torrent of anger and accusations of betrayal directed at their church authorities because of that decision of exclusion.

Some of the women were not, in fact, sitting there happily with their role, they were just polite, nice Christian women who could not face what would follow if they were honest. Our group had decided to be honest, for the sake of our life and the lives of other women.

To 'see', is to bring into your consciousness that you are being victimised in some form. Most of us can only sustain that 'seeing' if someone else or a group of people also 'see' it and affirm the validity of our perceptions. A good support group will then free us to be grieved and/or angry about our situation and to name out loud the source of our suffering. At this stage, we are still in victim mode, but the stages are important if we are to decide against living as victims.

This period of recognition of oneself as a victim is important because it restores the self-respect, which comes when you believe your own experience. It is hard to imagine that people don't believe their own experience but it is true. How often have each of us been hurt by something, felt deeply wounded by it and then had someone else tell us that we should not be feeling hurt for some reason which they give us. They say things like the person who hurt us didn't understand, we are strong enough to not notice this experience of being hurt, it is a bit neurotic to be hurt by this, it was really meant as a joke, it is unreasonable to be hurt, our problems are not as bad as others, and so on. We also sometimes add our own reasons for denying pain, which come from our life history. Maybe our mother said 'We women can put up with a lot' and 'The men mean well'.

It is surprising and disturbing to discover how many people simply think, deep down, that their own lives don't matter — that everybody has problems and theirs are no worse than anyone else's, so why should they consider their hurts important? Often, if you challenge this and ask whether they would not be concerned if the same thing happened to someone else, the person will say, 'Oh yes, but that's different'. We often believe that the journey of others is significant, but ours is ordinary.

The ultimate victimisation involves being convinced by your oppressor that you brought your suffering on yourself. This can be done in situations of violence based on domination. It can also be related to a subtlety of attitudes which teach you that only the way of life, of doing things, of seeing things which is that of the dominant culture or class is 'correct'. 'Real women are not like these feminists,' they say, which tells you very clearly that if you are like a feminist, you won't be loved and respected as a woman. I recall on one occasion being in a church gathering with my then husband and having someone come up and ask, 'Which is Mr McMahon?' Very funny? No, it was not. It was a cruel warning to someone who dared to challenge the status quo and claim a stronger life for herself and other women. It was also humiliating for my husband and a warning that he was being less than 'masculine'.

Another common pattern in persuading you that you are the

cause of your own victimisation is to convey in subtle and unsubtle ways that 'You have a problem'. In other words, if you are protesting about things, it is because you are rather neurotic. No one else is complaining, so what's wrong with you? I am truly amazed at how long it takes to move away from this tactic and see it as such. Decades after I have seen through it, over and over again, I still succumb to its power.

I suppose it is partly because sometimes it really is my problem — I am sometimes quite neurotic! I have at least learned to check with others my perceptions about that, however. It is good to go to a group and say 'Who is neurotic — them or me?' Women always need to beware, nevertheless, because down the ages the lives of women have often been diminished by naming them as a 'problem' when they are simply different.

To break through all this and honestly own our woundedness and the injustices we experience is, oddly enough, the first stage of moving from being a victim. I think this might be because, whether we own it or not, when we are wounded in life, our inner being records the woundings and builds its own register of victimisation. To bring this to the surface and look at it is the start of our healing and power.

The next stage is the honest response to this, our life. I was taught, as a child, that anger is rarely an appropriate response to things relating to myself, although it was all right to become angry in a controlled fashion about the pain of others. This, I suspect, is not uncommon in Christian circles, especially Anglo-Celtic Australian circles. Strangely, I don't personally remember being discouraged from being angry with God about life in general or my own life specifically. However, most Christians do feel anxious about being angry with God.

Jewish people are very refreshing in this respect. Their culture, as evidenced in the Jewish Scriptures, the Old Testament, felt quite free to challenge God in no uncertain terms. They obviously had a view of their relationship with God which invited honest and self-respecting relationship.

Whether we believe that God is involved, or not, to be fully human in our response to our realities is part of both maturity and of moving towards not being a victim. To be angry is to lift up an energy and self-respect which is often the beginning of rebuilding our lives.

Sometimes people feel more authentic about beginning with grieving. I have found this helpful myself. Often when we do so, we can see reasons for the way others have acted towards us which make us want to mediate our anger into grief. Having said that, I am well aware that I am still not very good at anger and am writing out of my own lack of freedom in that respect. I am also aware that, to recognise why someone behaved as they did towards you does not in any respect diminish the damage they did to you, and that it is helpful not to be confused about that. For example, the fact that your father was abused himself does not really take away the destructive impact of his abuse of you.

This response stage, or 'rage stage' as women used to call it, can sometimes go on for quite a while. It is often hard to bear in other people (as against ourselves!) and we sometimes wish that they wouldn't 'go on and on about it'. If we ourselves are reasonably happy, we think that after listening once or twice, our empathic and sympathetic reply should be enough to enable the person concerned to leave the pain behind and get on with life. Grieving and anger at injustice take time, however, especially if they are in response to serious abuse.

If another's grief and anger takes more time and empathy than we have to offer, then we can sometimes arrange for a sharing around of the availability of the listening ear and caring shoulder. I have also found that being up front with those who ask for our care is important. Occasionally, when the phone has rung and my heart has sunk at the thought of sharing someone's pain again,

I have said to the person, 'Would you mind caring for me today? I am very tired and I need some space to myself. Would you be gracious enough to allow me to ring you next week?' Often the person feels respected in this request. You have not pushed them away by sounding weary and less interested on the end of the line. You have asked for their support. Sometimes victims don't imagine that they can give support to others.

Having acknowledged that going through anger and grieving and pain takes time, nevertheless I believe that there is a time for moving on. Those who stay beyond a certain point in the rage stage, at the very least become paralysed in their life and, at worst, begin to destroy themselves from within and also destroy their relationships. Friends can't cope with the continuing sharing of pain and begin to reject them, in direct and indirect ways. This adds to the feelings of victimisation. The anger and grief begins to circle within their being, consuming their energy and diverting them from other agendas and interests. They become, at best, boring to themselves and others and at worst, head into breakdown.

It is also helpful to realise that some people's needs may never be met. I mention this thought to people whose friends commit suicide. Sometimes the pain of life is simply too great for fragile personalities and nothing we can do will save them from giving up on life. Sometimes the abuse they have received is so damaging that they can never seem to recover from it and we should not take upon ourselves a burden for them that we are unable to reasonably carry. Sometimes our own needs are also great and we cannot carry those belonging to someone else.

Of course there are always situations where we find the meeting of two pathologies in a relationship. There are people and groups that have an insatiable need to be needed and they attract to themselves those who are insatiably needy. The 'carers' are likely to encourage the needy person to stay a victim. It is in their interests to do so. This prevents the needy person from maturity and fullness of life. It probably also has to do with the carer finding it easier to relate to needy people than those who are more free and whole. This unhealthy interdependency is often named as 'love'. Love is seen as something which does not ask any hard questions and sympathetically goes along with whatever feels most comfortable to both carer and victim. Christians are sometimes tempted in this direction because we like to be 'nice' to each other and to other people. A colleague called Ron contributed a great deal to my understanding of this dynamic.

As one who has always looked for approval of myself in personal relationships, I have never found the rigour of real love an easy thing. This is partly because the rigour of real love invites honesty in both directions. It invites gentle, but clear 'Do you want to be healed? Do you want to move beyond being a victim? Do you want to grow up and live?' questions.

Those who dare to ask those questions of another must, of course, expect the same questions in return, as well as the honest and fearful responses of those who are faced with the cost of freedom. And yet, for us all, there is no real life and love which avoids the freedom and cost of growing. To encourage ourselves and others into staying a victim is to offer less than the truth and less than hope. It is to sell them short.

The moving on involves deciding that, in response to the victimisation, we will be responsible for making moves to reclaim our life. This can take many forms. It may involve the facing of another person with what they have done and inviting their appropriate response. It may be a matter of formally complaining or charging someone with an offence, either within the system of a work environment or with the police. It may mean becoming part of a general protest about a broader cultural or systemic situation — writing letters to editors, lobbying politicians, demonstrating. Whether the action is direct or indirect, it is still a part of moving from being a victim.

Sometimes the response in ourselves to this activity can be immensely healing and gratifying. Even an apology from the source of our pain can be amazingly restoring of life and freeing, not just to us, but to the other person as well. Reconciliation is achieved and we can be respectful and sustain our self-respect. This is not to say that we never feel like a victim again — healing from wounding is rarely so simple and comprehensive. A new journey to freedom has begun, however, and we can often return to the moment of healing and reclaim its power for our life.

Even if our action is part of a larger picture of oppression and we can see no real and immediate results of our efforts, it is still surprisingly helpful to have acted in some small way. It is about a sense of having made our point, of honouring the significance of our life, and of the reclaiming the ground of justice for our life by occupying it and raising our little flag of protest. Of course to sustain the process without results for a long time is another issue, which I will discuss in a later chapter.

But, what if the perpetrator/s don't care, won't respond as we had hoped, or are beyond our reach, even dead? We can do one of several things. We can go on being a victim. At this point we, the victims, begin to actually give power to our oppressors. We give them the power to obsess our life, to dominate our thoughts and feelings and to destroy our relationships. We have forgotten that, even if the perpetrator/s of our wounding are not prepared to, or cannot heal us by apology, or some other act of reparation or resolution, there are choices which we ourselves can make. Usually these choices are very hard to make alone.

The initial choice is to decide to lay down the power of the oppressor and take up our life as though we refuse to be a victim of anyone. Maybe a person with a very strong sense of self and inner life can carry out that choice alone. I have always found that people need to have caring 'hearers' and supporters for that choice — people who say, 'You can do it! We raise our glasses and coffee cups to you! We will be here for you when you slip back from the choice.'

Often I have found that a ritual which symbolises and marks the moment of choice is helpful — if that fits with the style and spirituality of the person. The ritual, in effect, says that this is a very important and impressive moment in someone's life. It involves the presence of others who agree that it is important and who commit themselves to share with the person in the next days of life lived as a non-victim. The wounding can be named and symbols of grief, anger and protest can be there alongside the symbols and ritual acts of being free to move on. The person can be given something from the ritual to take with them and put in an obvious place to remind them of the celebration of their courage and the commitment of support.

In the liturgy section of this book, I have included such a ritual for someone who had been betrayed by the church. This was written for a woman who had been sexually abused by a priest, had named that for herself, owned that she was a victim of abuse, raged, grieved, complained and acted. The church did not on that occasion respond with appropriate repentance and so the person decided to move on in her life.

As I said, some people can do all this alone. Some find the strength, healing and courage with friends or family. Others invite the company of a higher power. If you think about it, groups like Alcoholic Anonymous are amazingly successful in moving people from being victims of alcohol (and whatever led to that victimisation) by a mixture of self-honesty, group support and the invitation to connection with a Higher Power. It is left to the person concerned to decide the nature of that Higher Power. I have always found it significantly empowering to believe that the resources for my moving and living are beyond myself and what I can see.

In most of us, of course, there is a fear of freedom. For those who live with a sense of power, it is hard to imagine being afraid of freedom. For those who have never experienced being a victim of something or someone, it seems entirely unreasonable that anyone would consciously or subconsciously choose to stay being a victim. But, of course, life is never as simple as it seems to be.

Over the years of relating to people who have lived as victims for a long time, I have noticed that when we can see a glimpse of our freedom, a couple of things are likely to happen to us which inhibit the claiming of that freedom. Often, as long-term victims, we have developed ways of relating to people which are dependent on our being needy. We may have lost, or forgotten, how to relate to others as peers, as those to whom we can give as well as those from who we will receive. So we are at a loss to know how to reinstate ourselves in healthy and self-respecting relationships. We also may find that others also don't know how to make the change in relating to the new person that we are trying to be.

This whole situation should be taken seriously and we can ask the help of groups and people in learning how to create new ways of relating. One of the best ways of dealing with the changes that I have experienced is to be quite transparent, to say to people, 'I am going to make some big changes in my life. It's not easy for me to work out what this means when I relate to you. I am trying to be more interdependent in my life and relationships and that's a bit scary, so bear with me. I don't want to ask things of you all the time. I would like to be supportive of you, as you have been to me.'

I can also remember conversations with people who are making the change to living as a non-victim and they say, 'When I show people that I am stronger and more independent, they disappear from my life and I am afraid that I will be alone. At least when I asked things of people, I felt as though I had friends.'

As I watched what was happening, it was relatively clear to see people, of whom much had been asked, pulling back in relief when the needy person showed more independence. Again, transparency helps, like saying, 'You must be so relieved that I am holding my head up and trying to empower my own life. It will be great not to ask so much of you, but please hang around so that I can feel I still have caring friends as I make the changes. I might even be a better friend than you have ever known!' Of course, not everyone has the confidence to be so up front. However, sometimes someone who is watching what is happening can have a word with the friends so that the previously dependent person is less tempted to go back to being a victim in order to sustain the loving attention.

Those of us who enjoy the Monty Python film *The Life of Brian* will recall the 'leaping leper' who was healed without being consulted and followed Brian around trying to reverse the miracle. He had begun to find it an advantage to stay unhealed — uncomfortably close to the truth for most of us in some way.

VICTIMISATION can be personal or systemic and/or cultural. My own experience of being a victim has mostly been as a victim of a system and culture. As a woman who for thirty years has been part of the Women's Movement, I remember well the early struggles to emerge as equal participants in society. In my case that meant struggling to be an equal participant in my own culture of the church as well. We used often to image ourselves as birds in a cage who had never experienced what it would be like to fly free and we reflected that, for some, the cage was a comfortable place.

We found that as we began to fly free, at least two things happened to us. Because we were challenging the power of those who were occupying the ground of life which we believed should now be shared with us, we experienced various forms of 'punishment'. Sometimes the punishment was clear and unambiguous. We were quite directly attacked as aggressive and pushy women. Sometimes the punishment was more veiled. It took the form of whispers about our life: 'maybe our sex lives were not satisfactory' or 'maybe we couldn't get a man' or we 'had problems'.

Very often it was expressed as ridicule and, when we didn't laugh at the 'jokes', we were asked if we no longer had a sense of humour.

Sometimes it took a more seductive form. We were 'rewarded' when we did not claim our freedom and it was demonstrated in front of us that other women who were not like us, were to be more loved, found more attractive and generally given approval. Sometimes women who were more 'cooperative' and silent were given places on decision-making bodies. They could be pointed to: 'There, you asked for women to be given these places and we have done so. What's your problem?' We all knew the game that was being played. To stay in our cages was made a very attractive proposition.

The other temptation to stay in the cage came from within ourselves. It came from the fact that, as we emerged, we began to experience the burden of responsibility. If we claimed our life as mature people we then had to be responsible for it, to be accountable and to bear the consequences of our choices. We had to share, with men, the challenges that came in response to our decisions and policies.

Also, because we were often walking unchartered territory as 'new' women, we had to walk into the unknown. We had few models and, even though we analysed situations, debriefed with others, reflected on the possibilities, in the end, we didn't really know where we were going. In our past, at least the pathway was relatively predictable. The hardest thing about this was that we often found ourselves vulnerably separated from many other women who had either chosen different pathways to their liberation or had decided to stay in the known place.

We used to sit together and ask ourselves whether it was worth the cost to claim our freedom, to decide to begin living as non-victims. While we tried to be gentle with each other and to respect our own timing for change, we always knew that change and freedom were indeed worth the cost. We almost always found that, having glimpsed freedom, it was more costly to go back than to go forward.

I often think, as I watch some men begin the process towards their own liberation, that they will need to go through the same process as women. In the end, you can only liberate yourself. Others can create a helpful environment, but they can't do it for you, and staying a victim is never the road to freedom.

I WILL finish with a story. This is not, as it might appear, a story about people being much worse off than most of us. It is a story about the amazing resilience of the human spirit as it claims its ground of dignity and life. An Indian friend once took me to visit a community of people who were his friends and with whom he was working. They were the poorest of the poor and lived in holes dug into the bottom of an old rubbish dump. They had no sanitation and their nearest water was about two kilometres away.

Every day, the women walked that distance to get a small jug of water which had to last their family for the day. Their food was mostly gained by scavenging and, every day, they dragged the dead from their 'homes' for burial.

So confined was the life of these people to their small area that their children had never seen a white woman. As I walked among them with my friend, the children shrieked and ran away. The people had not been in the tourist areas of their city and had not seen people beg from tourists, so nobody begged from me — not one person in the whole community of people, who numbered several hundred. As we walked around, with my friend pausing to talk to people and introduce me, I saw with wonder that these deprived and impoverished people, even in their desperate struggle for survival, still saw themselves as people of dignity and worth.

Everywhere I saw the signs of that. I saw it in the way the women would be carefully tidying around their little cave homes. I saw it in the way the men were having important conversations together as they planned the life of their community. And then, after I was introduced in a manner (given that I could not speak their language), a woman took me by the hand and signalled an invitation to go into her home. As we entered the dim hole in the rubbish, she pointed with delight. There, on the mud floor was a dog, suckling several new puppies.

I suppose, if you were an economic rationalist, you could say to yourself, 'Why was she happy that there was another life struggling to survive in that poverty, and a less than useful dog at that?' What I saw was a beautiful human being who, in the midst of her own struggle for life, had retained the dignity and freedom to celebrate the life of another part of the creation. I was also deeply honoured that, as a stranger, she invited me into her home without apology at its poverty and assumed that I, too, would delight in the power of life to survive. What I took away with me, for my own life struggles, was the amazing power of a human being to rise above being a victim and to survive as a remarkable human being.

We could all share our stories about the rising in power of the dignity of human life, generation after generation. That is the true glory of the human journey.

Living Life under Attack

THERE are many different ways of living life under attack. Firstly, however, it is important to decide whether or not we have to stay in a place where we are attacked, and to explore very carefully what is at stake for us in staying where we are.

Attacks in personal relationships

I have known people, mostly women and children, who have for so long lived under attack that they seem to perceive that life as normal. In response to the attacks, they go to extreme lengths to mollify the attacker as though they themselves are responsible for provoking the attacks. Attacking people in a violent manner has, for all concerned, become a semi-appropriate way of relating and the only issue is whether each attack was in some way 'justified'.

The reality that needs to be established, or re-established, in this sort of situation is that violent attack in personal relationships is a crime. It is never justified and there are support systems in the community that have been set up to help people end living under attack. These support systems are rarely good enough, but some of us are working hard to make them better. The only way of life which is a good response to this sort of attack is to take action so that the attacks cease or to leave the attacker and find a safe place for all concerned. We are never due for less than this and we collude with the attacker if we believe we are. Certainly this sort of suffering can never be justified as God's plan for us.

One of the grave dangers arising from the religious beliefs, which some people hold, in a God-given arrangement for men to dominate women, is that it can give subtle and not so subtle 'permissions' for violence and attack. It is all too easy, if one starts from a right to dominate somebody, to justify violence against that person if they refuse to submit to your domination. Even in predominantly secular communities, the fact that some religions do uphold the belief that men should be in control of women is often used as a conscious or subconscious reference point to justify violence against women.

As a community, we still have a long way to go in ensuring that people who suffer this sort of close-in violence feel confident in asking for help. Things are gradually improving but we need commitment and vigilance in seeing that they continue doing so. We also need to understand that domestic violence and various forms of rape and sexual assault are not primarily about sex, but about power. Underpinning this is an illusion that relationships involve a 'cake' of power which is split between two people or members of a family. Therefore, it follows that if one person's life is empowered, the other's loses power. Somehow we need to find a way to move from that paradigm of relationship and see that, while there are negotiations in relationships, there is also a possibility of maximum powerful life for each person, without taking life from the other.

Attacks from outside

There are situations where the attacks come from sources outside our personal control. If we look at this on a macro scale, we can see war zone situations. Here people live their daily lives never knowing where and when the attacks may come. The nearest I have come to this was in visits to Palestine/Israel, Lebanon and Sri Lanka. None of these countries was engaged in an all-out war like that of the Second World War, but they were places where people lived with an awareness of danger and conflict — with military checkpoints, helicopters overhead and many members of the armed forces visible in their streets.

I recall walking the streets and wondering how everyone around me could just live on in a normal fashion, doing their shopping, taking their children to school and planning life as though nothing special was happening. When I talked with local people about that, they said, 'Well, what else can we do?' and I realised that not only was this a good question, but that their response to the threat really was the only viable way to go. The more normal life is in the face of threat, the more people are able to survive, not as a denial of what is happening but because they decide consciously, or subconsciously, not to let it stop their life.

I had a personal experience of this closer to home when, for two years, a group of racist and homophobic people decided to attack me and the parish of which I was minister at the time. The group may well have been anti-Semitic as well, given that at the time of their most obvious activity on the other two issues, there was also a rise in attacks on Jewish people. Some of their leaders had a previous history of identifying with the swastika symbol. In the period to which I refer, however, the group did not make obvious reference to Jews in their pamphlets.

We never really knew why we became the focus for the attacks, but they began after we held two rallies for Archbishop Desmond Tutu of South Africa and had been given publicity as people who tried to wipe out racist graffiti around the city. We first knew we were under attack when several men carrying a flag marched into our morning service and placed an attacking and hate-filled pamphlet on the lectern and then distributed threatening sheets to the congregation as they filed out of the church.

The attacks came in many different forms — pamphlets and letters, threatening phone calls in the early hours of the morning, the graffitiing of my house with offensive words, the throwing of foul-smelling matter around my house, knocks on the door in the middle of the night and, finally, a life-sized effigy of a woman burnt on my front doorstep. This last attack was accompanied by those responsible sending a photo of themselves in army gear lighting the fire to a major daily paper and an open letter saying they would end my ministry. The activity around the parish involved threatening phone calls to members, handing out of hate-filled leaflets, racist stickers put inside the church and the regular dumping of offensive substances at the doorway of the church.

We had to make decisions about how to respond to these attacks and I had to decide how I would survive them and live well in the face of them. We reported the attacks to the police, who took note but seemed to do little in response. We remained silent in relation to the media because we didn't want to give publicity to our attackers. This made no difference to the level of attack, but we hoped would give little satisfaction and encouragement to the attackers.

After a while, we became angry and also decided that to say nothing was lacking in self-respect and, as well, gave no opportunity for decisions by the wider community about an aspect of its life. Without being overly dramatic about our small situation, we remembered how the church had sometimes remained silent in response to Nazi activity and how that had given encouragement to the forces of hate and destruction. So we sent an open letter to the group concerned through the letters page of the local daily paper. In it we outlined our position on the issues concerned and said that, no matter how long they attacked us, we would not move from our position of support for an inclusive community and church.

This action produced more attacks, but three other things happened. We felt that we had the initiative and decided to expand on it. We put up a huge banner across the front of our church inviting people to a rally to celebrate the unity of humankind. Hundreds of people came to the rally, where we had several community leaders tell stories of human unity and then invited people of different ethnicities to come forward and offer the gifts of their culture into the Australian community. When they did that (and more than sixty people offered their gifts, all from different ethnic backgrounds), the assembled gathering said together that they received the particular gifts.

At the end of the offerings, an Aboriginal person came forward and said that the gifts of her people would be fully offered into the community when justice prevailed. It was a powerful and moving night and we were all energised and encouraged. At this time we also began to develop our own little rituals for healing and strength. Each time an attack took place, we sang a song which became our own theme song: 'Do You Hear the People Sing?' from the musical *Les Miserables*. When the Nazi national anthem, which is sung to the hymn tune 'Austria', was played through the phone to me in the middle of the night, we reclaimed it for ourselves and sang it as our hymn, 'Once to everyone and nation, comes the moment to decide'. All the time, our own energy and consciousness of commitment was increasing.

The second thing that happened was that many hundreds of people in the wider community began to show us support. People lobbied the police and parliament to encourage action on their part to stop the perpetrators. One morning we came out of our service and found many people gathered outside the church carrying posters saying things like 'If the police won't defend this church, we will'. This effort had been organised by some journalists from the daily newspaper who had been impressed by the stand the church had taken. This is not at all common in a city like Sydney. It was interesting that the media, which was often quite hostile to the church in general, had a respect for a church which would try to take a stand for others. Many people wrote letters of support to us from other churches and from the community at large, urging us to hold our ground.

The third thing that happened was that we suddenly made connection with other people and groups who had also been attacked by the same group. Many of these people were isolated individuals or members of ethnic groups, each of which had not known how to gather support around them. We formed a loose-knit coalition, pooled information and began to work out strategies for supporting each other and stopping the attackers. We brought together much more information to take to police and politicians to encourage action against the illegal activities. We also supported moves to bring in anti-vilification legislation — this later happened. We gave interviews to media and generally acted to oppose discriminatory activity in our society.

In the end, we succeeded, at least in relation to the particular attacking group. The police in charge of the case were changed and a number of people were arrested and charged. The group lost its leadership into prison and things were relatively quiet. In the process, community awareness was raised, a number of groups and people learned how to act in the face of attack by getting together and our church probably had the finest period in its life. This was because we were focused, we found we could stand at some cost to ourselves for something we believed and that there were many different ways in which we could support each other.

I had a particular journey of my own in all this. I had not lived with continuing fear before, particularly fear of something that seemed outside my control and which was unpredictable. In the first months, my life was largely taken over by this fear. Each day was lived thinking about when something might happen and with a dread of going home in case I was attacked that night. Although I was apparently continuing with my life and work, the predominant thought in my mind was surviving things that might happen. The attackers, in a very real sense, had control of my agenda and power over my living.

At this stage, a number of things happened. I began to share my fear with more people. I prayed for courage and liberation from the power of the attacks. Others prayed with me and for me.

People offered to come to me in the night, no matter what the time, to support me and/or help me clean up. Quite suddenly, I was free — it was not that I was not afraid when things happened — it was that my life was no longer lived in dread of what might happen. I did not imagine what the night might be like all through the day. In fact, I hardly thought about it and was quite shocked when something happened. I became less self-sufficient and learnt that, to accept the help and support of others enhances life and relationships. My life was no longer determined by the hatred and power of others — it was a liberation.

Another very beautiful thing happened to me at that time. In the middle of all the events, I went on my first trip to Scotland, the part of the world which I most recognise as the land of my family origins. I visited my clan ground in the highlands near the Isle of Skye. I read the stories of my clan's life of struggle and its capacity to fight for causes in which it believed. I read that my people were famous for producing the finest Gaelic poets and priests in early times and felt a sense of being a small part of something larger. They were also famous as fierce fighters who stood and died on hilltops defending their causes. Just by chance, I found the clan graveyard and standing among the McRae graves I said to myself, 'How did they survive?' Immediately I felt their energy, courage and strength flow into my body from the ground while an inner voice said, 'We survived and you will too.'

I returned home and reclaimed my clan name. My son Robert dyed some wool and wove me a long scarf of the clan tartan, with some bands of the tartan intermingled with the colours of the Australian sun and sky. I wrapped it around myself, pinned on my clan badge with its motto of 'Fortitude' and felt strong and linked with a courage beyond myself.

Not everyone is as privileged as I am. We can't all travel to the land of our forebears and many people don't have supportive groups and friends around them. In sharing these stories I am saying that to live with others and share your vulnerability with them is the secret of survival. I am also saying that for some people like myself, we are supported in survival by claiming strength and courage and liberation from forces of love and energy in God which we believe lie outside ourselves.

I NOW live under attack again, a different sort of attack, as an openly homosexual person. I will write more about that in a later chapter. However, here I will say that I remember, at the time of the earlier attacks saying to people, 'I am not as afraid of this attacking group as I am of the church.' It was partly because I knew that the next battle was on its way and I would then find myself attacked from within my own community. To be attacked by your own is much more fearsome and wounding than to be attacked by outsiders. It feels like a betrayal within a family.

I am able to separate the attacks into three categories. There are those who respectfully disagree. I am aware that this is to send towards me no more than I am sending towards some others. In claiming my life, I am respectfully disagreeing with many of my church family and must expect an encounter with them. Then there are those who attack to wound because they are shocked and hurt by my existence. They often feel powerless to 'do something' or get anyone 'in power' to do something to stop what they consider is my sinful and damaging activity. I understand their attacks on me, even if I find them wounding. I sometimes wish we could talk together and try to cross some boundaries of understanding, but that is rarely possible.

The last group is the phobic and/or the hate-filled. They attack to destroy and are without mercy or the remotest interest in a dialogue of any sort. They often send you things without any name or address attached, which is a sure indicator that they are not really interested in any response which you might have to them, or to their ideas. They simply wish to threaten and harm as far as possible.

I try not to give this group too much power, by committing their letters and other material to the wastepaper bin as soon as I realise its nature. If they will not put their name to something then I don't need to read it, I believe, because it is not a genuine conversation. It is simply abuse and, as far as possible, I refuse to collude with abuse.

Because I learned many things about survival and support and self-respect in the first experience of attack, I am better prepared to face these, even if they are, in many respects more painful. All of this has made me far more conscious about how many people are dependent for their well-being on the way we sustain our life as an inclusive community. We may never meet them in person, but they will be affected by the stands we take, the values we uphold and our preparedness to be in solidarity with them against those who would attack.

ONE of the things which became obvious to us during those years of being attacked was that while extremist groups must be accountable for their actions and people protected from their violence, it was respected community leaders who gave 'permission' for the extremism to emerge. There is, of course, in any human community the capacity for varying attitudes and activities to come to the surface. The reality that they are not usually so obvious does not take away from the reality of their existence. At each point in time, however, we give signals to each other about what is generally acceptable and what is not. A person like Hitler has an astounding capacity to persuade a community of mostly ordinary, decent people that it is appropriate to reject, oppress and even kill in the most appalling manner those who he decided were 'different' and not to be valued — in Hitler's case Jews, homosexual people, gypsies and some people with disabilities.

At the point in our society when the attacks on us occurred, it only took two men — an academic and a leading politician — in espousing mildly racist views (if there is such a thing) to lift the level of racist violence in our streets, school grounds and, finally, in extremist activities against particular people and groups. This was well documented at the time and has recently happened again in Australia. The upholding of the right to free speech is not an adequate response to the expression of destructive views by another. It can only be justified as a human right if people of care and justice will themselves exercise the right of free speech in rigorous and immediate reaction against those who would destroy others with free speech. In other words, free speech is a responsibility as well as a right.

For these reasons, we believed that there were high stakes for us and for our society in the stand we took in our church. I believe the same in relation to my present position. We believed that we had to express, as clearly as possible a counter leadership to that which was being given. Even as we entered the struggle, however, we knew that our brief time of encounter with the forces of hate was as nothing compared with the daily struggle of those whose race, colour, lifestyle and culture cannot be changed. It was these people who really lived under attack and they were counting on us to make the society a safer and more welcoming space for them and their children. The stakes were high indeed.

Was it worth it, and is it still worth it? Yes, it was and yes, it is. To live in a way that produces attack in order to live more truly (as against choosing martyrdom), is to live with passion. To stay holding the ground in the face of attack is to find one's life refined in a way which puts many things in a new perspective. The trivia, the pettiness often falls away because life has taken on a new significance. Even as your energy is poured out in staying the course, your health and strength can be renewed, because it is not a self-consuming passion. I would never choose to live under attack, but I will never regret living in ways which sometimes make it almost inevitable.

Living with Your Own Truth

MOST weeks I spend a day watching my grand-daughter, who is just two years old. Since the day she was born, I have marvelled at how quickly a child learns how to make her or his way in the world. I watch her learn about responses and behaviour that are rewarding, that gain attention and approval. I see her little mind tick over as she decides how she will relate to me and to others. I hear her chattering away to me from somewhere and then there will be a silence. Like her parents, I have learned always to investigate silences. Usually they mean that she knows that things are not as we think they should be. She has spilt or broken something, or she is busily filling her mouth with the whole of what is on her plate, all in one go. Or she is otherwise engaged in something that she suspects we would stop if we were there. Already, and even before she was two years old, she understands a little about hiding things, even though she has lived in a very gentle, accepting and rewarding environment all her young life.

In this conversation, I am not discussing dishonesty in the usual sense. I am reflecting on areas of our life and thinking which stay hidden because we suspect that, if we reveal them to those around us, we will be judged or rejected. M. Scott Peck, in his book *A World Waiting to be Born: Civility Rediscovered* (Bantam, 1993), writes about 'pseudo community' which is the corporate version of the fear of honesty. He is referring to situations where people live and work together as though they are having honest relationships, but in which everyone knows the unspoken 'rules' that sustain things as they are.

Certain issues and situations are not mentioned, because that would create conflict or rejection for the person concerned. Certain people or attitudes are given credibility because of their power in the group, even though many people are not happy with them. Or it can be that a majority of people thinks all is well and a minority believes that it is not, but do not feel safe to express their concerns. And so, everyone trickles along pretending that everything is fine. We smile at each other, refer to each other as good friends and tell ourselves, and others, that we are a happy bunch of people who relate well and travel along together splendidly. Deep down, most of us know that this is far from the truth.

As individuals we can do this too, in relation to our own truth. Even as we are in a state of chronic depression, we smile (often too much) and refuse to face what it would mean to be honest with ourselves, let alone with others. Obviously we don't do this to punish ourselves, well not normally anyway. It just feels too hard, too painful, to do otherwise. Sometimes we might be surprised at how easy it would be to be honest in our situation, but often it really is hard and costly. We are not imagining things. Perhaps it is not surprising that the people from whom we hide things are often those closest to us. After all, their responses to us matter greatly, therefore the risks of disclosure are high for us. The withdrawal of their love for us would have a critical impact on our lives. Again, this can be so in relation to groups of friends or in individual relationships.

I have a strong memory of being part of a group of friends who decided to meet and discuss relationships between women and men. We met for a number of years, every month. I have no doubt that other members of that group, like me, wondered at the reality, or otherwise, of our apparently intense and frank conversation. I used to sit in the group and ponder all the things that I knew were happening to people among us and which we never mentioned — even if speaking about them would have changed the conversation entirely. I also used to feel like saying something that was important to me but I'd worry that it might not be acceptable.

We clearly enjoyed our time together as we met year after year, but it could have been an entirely different group life if we had been just a little more honest with each other. In some way, deep down, we had agreed to the 'rules' of the group and were afraid to cross the boundaries which we had consciously and subconsciously set for ourselves. In the end, we decided that the group should end, not so much because we had achieved our aims but rather, I suspect, because group discussions are like life. If you are not going forward, you tend to go backward. If you are not authentically living, then you start to die.

The cost of silence

If the issues that concern us are minor, we can usually move past them with minimal cost. But, let's face it, if they are really insignificant, we would usually have a go at bringing them into the open anyway. The things we hide most are usually very important to us. They are about who we are in some critical way. We do not forget them in the rush and tumble of life. They keep coming back to us.

One cost of silence is that the silent things possess us, they will not leave us alone, and they often begin to take over our life. When they do this, others realise that something is going on for us and wonder what is wrong. Our often-smiling face does not convince them and they have a sense that they do not know us and that we won't trust them. This makes life lonely for us and for them.

The reality is that if an important part of us is hidden from others who matter to us, we can never believe that we are really loved. We always have a sense that if people knew more about us, they might reject us. Therefore, the love we experience from them is conditional and partial. It is possible to live confidently like that, especially if we love ourselves, but to be known and still loved is obviously a real longing that lies in most of us. The hidden part of ourselves lies dying within us with fear and pain around it.

At this stage, I would like to tell a story about a person who taught me a great deal about being true. His name is Jim and I met him at Pitt Street church. Jim was a survivor of the terrible experience of the building of the Burma Railway as a prisoner of war in the Second World War. The integrity he saw in his very honest mother and the atrocities he witnessed and experienced on the Burma Railway meant that his own faith journey had to be born out of very tough and honest questions. He attended church regularly but made it clear that he was agnostic about many things and preferred not to be described as a 'believer'. He, and his lovely wife Priscilla, who has since died, were very much part of our church community. One day he was asked to become Assistant Treasurer of the parish and, as was our tradition, we arranged the usual ritual for installing a person into an office, but without adequate careful remembering on my part.

By coincidence (or not!), I preached a sermon that morning which called us all to be honest in our dealings with each other as part of the authentic search for truth. Then I called Jim to the front of the sizeable congregation and said, 'We are now about to recognise Jim as one of the officers of this parish.' I went into the ritual and said, 'Jim, do you affirm that you believe in Jesus Christ as Saviour and Lord?' There was a silence.

Then Jim, who was not normally a man given to public pronouncements, said, 'Dorothy, if you had not preached your sermon, I might not have raised this, but now I have to remind you that no, I cannot confirm that.' Dear Jim. A man of courage and truth who invited us to celebrate him as he was, not as he was not. (We still made him our Assistant Treasurer, of course.)

My own experience of deciding to live with my own truth

Perhaps I should now share the story of my most significant experience of deciding to live with my own truth. This will be a more extreme story than most people would have in their lives, but because of that it has been a very stark and clarifying one for me.

For around thirty-five years of my life I was searching for this truth. I looked in many places and explored it in many ways. Always I was trying to understand why it was that I did not feel right in my male–female relationships, especially my marriage. When I look at the situation in hindsight, I wonder at my lack of insight and self-awareness. I was a woman of my time and culture, however, and that meant that the concepts, language, right questions and models were simply not before me. Maybe, in some inner space, I was hiding the truth from myself, but I am not aware of that.

When I finally knew my own truth, I certainly did not want to know it. There I was — a married woman with a husband and four children, all of whom I loved. I was a woman minister in a fairly high-profile parish in the centre of Australia's largest city and a member of many of my church's state and national councils. I represented my church in national and international ecumenical circles. I was a minister's daughter. I had a certain standing in secular society — the State Library had just asked for permission to gather and include in its files my papers and letters. I was around fifty years old. And I was a lesbian. This was not a welcome truth!

I firstly decided I could not change the truth

I could see a number of possibilities in front of me. I knew that there would be people around me in the church who would believe that to change from being a lesbian was both possible and desirable. I came from a family where my mother and one of my brothers had a gift of healing. I had seen miracles around our home where people came into our house in a wheelchair and walked out. I had seen, in my own ministry, miracles of inner change in people who had been open to the love of others and the love of God.

Two things moved me away from this solution. The first was that I had been on a thirty-five-year journey since my adolescence years to that moment, open to the challenges from God and others. I had sincerely offered everything I had into a long marriage. Quite apart from the authenticity of that journey, I had been through a number of agonising months as I faced the truth — what felt like a descent into hell, a waiting in the tomb beside the Christ for more than the three days and an openness to a resurrection experience. In spite of all this, I had found that my new life still had within it the truth about my sexual orientation. Any thought of going back into the old 'truth' I experienced like a death.

The second thing was that I had both encountered and read about those who claimed to be 'healed' from homosexuality. My reading included information from around the world which suggested that less than 1 per cent of people of homosexual orientation ever respond to forms of therapeutic or healing attempts. I also read the story from the US founders of the religious group 'Exodus' who, after years of leading their movement — which claimed to heal homosexual people of their orientation — left the group. As they did this, they stated that, in all the years since they founded the group, they had not seen real healings, only people who for a time were enabled to be celibate.

By this time, I had also met many peaceful, healthy and often Christian homosexual people who looked in much better shape than those who claimed to be healed. Even before I faced my own sexuality, I had met many troubled souls who struggled to move away from their orientation. They were often suicidal, breaking down psychologically and generally in a mess. I am not saying that this is always so. I am saying that those people I met were like that.

Also because I do not believe that God mocks us, I felt that if I was on the wrong track, I would soon know. I believe in an honest God, where what you experience is what you get. In other words, I believed that if I was making the wrong choice then I could count on feeling uneasy, losing a sense of peacefulness and being challenged by people I respected as wise and trustworthy about life and faith. In the light of all these things, I decided that at that moment in my life, the truth could not be changed.

I then decided not to deny the truth

There was a temptation to go on living as though the truth was not there. I had lived for many long years in my marriage. Presumably I had always been who I was and I had survived without falling apart or seeming to do too much damage. Was this also not part of my truth? Or maybe I could try to live with that old truth and the new one put together — sort of 'have my cake and eat it too'? The trouble is that there really is no such thing as two truths about the same thing: old truths are indeed old truths and the new ones take the life out of the old. Mostly it is an illusion to think that you can live in the old way once you have stepped onto the new ground. The fact was that I was no longer the person who had made that journey in marriage.

The other thing was that my decision to pretend that I was not who I was deeply affected my husband and family. What a patronising thing it would have been to decide that, knowing I was a lesbian, I would care for my husband by trying to pretend that I was not. In spite of the agony of his facing that truth, did I not owe him the chance for a new relationship with a woman who was heterosexual? And did I not owe my children the possibility of seeing their father in a proper heterosexual relationship and me as a full and free human being?

Quite apart from all that, I knew that if I tried to carry out a basically less than honest relationship in any sense, I would fall apart as a person. While I am no more honest than the next person, I like to live relatively wholeheartedly, to offer myself with enthusiasm. To live a lie to that degree would destroy me and probably those around me also. I longed for a ray of light to show me a way forward that would be good for everyone concerned. But it did not happen.

The last factor was that, even though I had somehow grown up thinking I was not really due for much, and even though I had been taught to live with endurance in the face of the stresses of life, to be self-sacrificing, I decided that this was the time to live in freedom and joy. I decided that after half a century of life, the God I believed in was inviting me to fullness of life, to a new courage and adventure.

So, with a trembling heart and an agony of soul and mind, I acted. In claiming my truth I was going to hurt other people, and they were people I loved who had done nothing to deserve this pain. It was the hardest thing I had ever done. I felt as though I was walking over a cliff and would die at the bottom and carry my loved ones with me. With the loving care of others around us and, I believe, a God who grieved with us, we all survived. I have no doubt that everyone concerned will always carry the wounds of that moment. I also have no doubt that in the awesome and awful complexity of life, if I had my life over again, I would still do the same thing.

I watched my husband marry again in two years' time and saw him happy with a wonderful woman who my children tell me is much better for him than I was. (And I wholeheartedly agree with them.) I watched my children shake in their lives, in their different ways, as they too faced the truth and grieved the ending of a marriage. I saw us all lay down a hope of a future with one mother and father at the centre of Christmas gatherings with our children and grandchildren.

I wept as I laid down forever the image of myself as a 'respectable' married woman and a person who holds to the vows that she makes and can make things right for people. All of that was the first part of living with my own truth. It not only reformed me into a person who believed she was due for a totality of giving and receiving love, it also reformed me into a very human being who could make major mistakes on the journey of life, who had to live with that and own that and who found this could sometimes make her into a more real human being.

To live with the necessity of grace and forgiveness — the grace and forgiveness of others and of God — sometimes makes us into more accessible human beings. In acting to end my marriage, I had now lived with my truth to a large extent. Because of the nature of my particular truth, however, there was still a tough journey ahead and other decisions to be made.

Next, I trusted who I trusted

There are some people around who assume that homosexual people cannot live with their truth unless they tell it to the whole world. They exist in both the heterosexual community and the lesbian and gay community. I do not agree with them. To those in the lesbian and gay community who demand that we all be open about our sexual orientation I would say three things.

The first is that in the environment in which we live, we never know what is at stake for others who choose to remain hidden. Many people are very vulnerable within themselves — their inner resources, for a multitude of reasons, are very fragile. Many others have minimal support around them. They have few friends; they live in threatening environments where their survival depends on their remaining hidden. We do not all live in cities where there are communities of supportive people to connect with. We are sometimes within hostile cultures. We are not all able to survive the loss of jobs or housing or friends. For all these reasons and more, our own timing for openness is due for respect.

Secondly, some of us refuse to cooperate with the determination by other people to define us by our sexual orientation. We are more than that. Heterosexual people do not say as introduction, 'Hullo, I'm heterosexual.' They do not do this because they are more than their sexuality and they assume it is not part of everybody's business anyway. The obsession that some heterosexual people have with the sexuality of others is not to be encouraged. Sometimes, part of human dignity and maturity is to understand that while we might like to live with honesty and openness, this does not mean that we need to go around naked in all company.

Thirdly, as an oppressed group of people there are sometimes situations where to be open about one's sexuality is to collude with one's oppressors. All of us have the right to decide on our own agenda for the struggle and to determine, preferably in the company of others, our own strategies for the way in which we will be part of the bringing in of the changes. Sometimes these strategies may not make sense to the onlookers, but the decisions about that still belong to the person concerned. We are on a tough and costly journey towards justice. We need to honour each other's choices as we go.

To those of you who are heterosexual people, I would say, even to those of you who are friendly, do not presume to know what my journey is like, nor that of other homosexual people. What seems appropriate and honest to you may cost me dear. What seems easy to you may be unbearably hard for me. You have never walked in my shoes and you never can. You have never felt the vicious hatred that comes towards homosexual people — the turning away from you, not in disagreement, or even disapproval, but in revulsion.

And do not underestimate your own journey in relating to me. There is often a very long journey for you between tolerance and acceptance of me. There is an even longer one between accepting who I am and celebrating my life and love. You probably don't even know the difference between all these stages in our relationship with me, but I do. Unerringly. For that reason, I will decide when to trust you with my fragile self.

To those who are not friendly and who, for some reason, seem to feel that this means I really owe you honesty, I would say I actually owe you nothing at all. You are not my friends. So why should I trust you and put my neck under your foot? I find it fascinating that the very people who accuse homosexual people of deception when they remain hidden, are the self-same people who wait to try and discredit and destroy them when they are honest. 'How could you not be honest?' they cry.

Well, look into your own hearts, sisters and brothers, and see the plans you have for people like me and you will find part of the answer. You don't share with me the inner truths of your life, sexual or otherwise. If you are in the church and feel that because you disagree with my view of God, Scripture and faith, I am due to be open with you, then I say that I will choose my moment to make myself vulnerable to you.

I will do that because I believe that I am living from the prophetic edge of the Gospel and that I will know the moment when I believe God is inviting me to take up the task in full. I would also say that I usually find that you are people with whom I would have many disagreements about God, Scripture and faith but I live with you respectfully in the diversity of the church. I am rarely confident that you would offer me the same respect and therefore I choose the time when I feel able to pay the price of your attack on me.

※

HAVING reflected in this way, I decided to 'trust who I trust'. I also decided that I would be honest if asked questions, and I held to that. Trusting who I trusted involved taking risks, but I never regretted deciding to go that way. I am a person who lives best with a reasonably high degree of transparency. I like to trust as many people as possible because that is a good and hopeful way to live. In this particular situation it was even more important for me to be somewhat open, because I needed people to both support and celebrate my new-found life and love.

It was interesting, to say the least, to see how people responded to my trust. The fact that so many people said they were moved, confirmed my view that people still assume that lesbian and gay people are right to live in fear.

When someone says to you, 'I am moved and honoured that you would share this with me', they are really saying, 'I am moved and honoured that you would feel safe enough with me to take this risk'. Sometimes I would feel sure that the person had guessed about my sexuality, so I would quite casually confirm it, only to find that they had not had the faintest idea!

There was one funny occasion when I was a staff person in a national church council. The chairperson was leading us in a get-to-know-you exercise. We were asked to get together with someone in the group and tell them one important thing that had arisen for us in the last month. I looked at the man with whom I had 'grouped' and thought to myself, 'Why not?'. After he had shared with me his important experience of the month, I said something like, 'Well, I have decided that I am now preparing to share with our National Assembly in July that I am a lesbian.'

He, understandably, had not expected such a deep level of sharing in a relatively light moment, but, being the man that he was, he rose to the occasion marvellously and we had a warm and moving discussion. While we were engaged in this, the chairperson suddenly said, 'Now, everybody, form into groups of four people.' We all dutifully followed her instructions. 'Now,' she said, 'share with the new members of your group the important event from your partner's month.' Fortunately my friend was a quick thinker!

The act of sharing with those you trust invites many things from you and brings many gifts. If the person is trustworthy, they will give a genuine response to you so that a good and wise human encounter takes place. In sharing, you have invited feedback about you and your life. Some people will do this with courage and honesty and care — an enormously valuable part of relationship. Because you have shared in vulnerability with another, that person usually experiences an invitation for them to share their life more deeply with you, and sometimes this follows. Relationship becomes more real, more authentic, closer, more true. This is a gift beyond imagining.

As a lesbian, of course, all this matters more than it would for other groups of people. Although racism, sexism and ageism are alive in our society, the fact that you are of a particular race, gender or age is not normally, of itself, something of which society disapproves. When you are homosexual, you always live dangerously. You can never assume that you are with people who accept you. Indeed, you have to assume that someone around you may hate you with a level of hate beyond that which they reserve for any other group of people.

It has always been shocking to me to find how profound this hate can be and in whom it can be found. I never believe that people who are otherwise open, just and loving could be homophobic, and yet you find it over and over again. I differentiate here between those who disagree with a homosexual lifestyle and those who are homophobic. Phobic hate and disagreement/disapproval are light-years apart. Even though I know that phobias are not related to reason or to the normal range of response to something, to experience phobic hate is frightening and always puzzling. I can never understand why someone's inclination to love a person of the same sex invokes such hate in another. There is nothing that I can see that is particularly threatened.

The heterosexual family has always survived and no one is stopping anyone else from being heterosexual, which is the dominant and strong instinct in most of the human race. I can understand why it would offend people in the church who regard people like myself as being disobedient to God's will. However, hate is not a solution to that and, at worst, even in the view of my accusers, I am simply being a sinner — which is not an uncommon human condition! I can understand that some might think that a person like me brings shame on the church, but the church can deal with that in its own disciplinary processes.

Anyway, for a period, I simply trusted individuals and some small groups of people with my truth. The wider the trusted circle became, the better it was for me. I lived less and less as a hidden person. I could celebrate my relationship with others — a normal expectation of life.

Most of the time I didn't even think about my sexuality because it resumed its normal place in my life as a part of me, instead of a dark, fearful, obsessive secret. My parish ministry blossomed and flourished. Our congregation in the ten years that I was there added around two hundred people to its life. This was not all my doing, of course. We were a team of people who pooled our gifts and created a church together. But, in it all, I felt whole and free. My life took on a powerful sense of thanksgiving and joy from which I could offer many things — not as a duty, but as an overflowing of my own thankful life. I do not believe that this was an illusion, whether in its inner or outer reality.

I knew, however, that my truth could not, in the end, be adequately expressed in this way. As time went on, I was faced with another decision. Would I now offer my truth in a public way — if you like, to the world? This would mean offering it to people in whom I had no trust and to those I did not know at all. It would also determine my future life and career.

Finally, I offered my own truth to anybody

I thought about this in a relatively focused way for about two years. As is my habit when I am going to take a new risk, or make a key decision, I 'rehearsed' what I would do with my partner and many good and patient friends. As we would say, 'We had many coffees.' I worked on what I would say and when I would say it. I tried to imagine how it would feel and how many friends I would have around me at that moment. I tried to plan how I would respond to what I suspected would become a media event. I could never make moves in my life if I didn't have lots of friends with which to do this rehearsal, over and over again. My partner is my greatest friend in this. You can never really prepare yourself for such a moment, but at least you have enough love around you to walk down the path towards it.

While I would never for a second compare myself with Jesus, the life of Jesus has always informed and encouraged me. I imagined him walking the road to Jerusalem. I understood why he needed supper with his friends where he tried to share, as he did on a number of occasions, his decisions about his life and his imaging of where it would go. He too, needed his rehearsals with friends.

Any big decision about living with your own truth involves

something that feels like a walking towards your death. And so it felt to me. The timing for my sharing of truth was determined by the fact that my church, the Uniting Church in Australia, was to have a focus and debate in its National Assembly on issues of sexuality. These would arise out of about five years of work with the church by a task group on sexuality.

We all knew that the key issue in this debate would be whether it was appropriate to have lesbian and gay people as leaders, including ordained ministers, in our church. By this stage, about ten years after I had ended my marriage, I was Director of my church's largest National Commission — the Commission for Mission. The commission covered a number of areas of work — Partner Church relationships with overseas churches, Youth in Mission, Human Rights, Social Responsibility and Justice within Australia, Cross-cultural Ministry, National Mission and Evangelism and ministry and services to remote areas in Australia.

I knew I would have to live openly with my truth at this stage, for my own integrity and also as an invitation for the church to look at the recognised and long-term ministries of a person in its midst. When the church debates the issue of homosexuality, it often conducts the discussion as though homosexual people are not already there and in leadership positions.

I had carefully prepared what I would say. I knew that I would have no more than sixty seconds to say it because that was the way the sexuality debate was to begin, with the invitation for as many people as possible to open up the debate with a sixty-second speech. I thought I had worked out a very clear statement, but when I showed it to a couple of our church media people they said, 'Are you planning to "out" yourself?' I said that I was and they said they thought people would not recognise that clearly in my prepared statement. They challenged me to go beyond subtle words and own my truth in a way that would leave no doubt in people's minds.

It was salutary to face that even at that late stage, hours before the Assembly entered the debate, I was still really trying to avoid doing what I had decided to do. As I changed what I would say, I was watched over by those two media people, whose eyes told me that they cared, that they had some idea of the cost and that they were surrounding me with their strength.

The debate was to open on the first Sunday afternoon of the Assembly. I had been invited to preach at a local church in the morning and went to do this with the small group to which I had been allocated for the duration of the Assembly. Most of the members of the group were people I had not met before. As I stood to preach, I wondered what the congregation and my small group would think when they heard my speech in the afternoon.

Indeed, I wondered if it would be the last sermon I would be invited to preach in the church of which I had been a member for more than sixty-three years. (That is, the Uniting Church and the Methodist Church, which became part of it at union.) I felt as though I was preaching the sermon of my life at a time when my energy was almost non-existent. If ever I depended on the grace and gifts of God, it was then. On the way back to the Assembly, I visited two Quaker friends who gave me of their calmness and care.

The session opened with a presentation of the report on sexuality. I recall listening to it as though I was somewhere else looking on as an observer. The president invited delegates to offer their sixty-second input to open up the issues and instructed us to line up behind the microphones to save time. I lined up with the others, knowing that as I rose to do so there were many loving friends and colleagues who knew what that meant. My whole body was trembling, but inside I felt a profound sense of peace. This was the moment when I was going to live with my truth, in full. I said:

As we discuss the question of whether or not lesbian and gay people may be ordained, I want the Assembly to know that my own ordina-

tion is in question. As I do this, I ask myself, am I, by my very nature, a person who can never be the bearer of word and sacrament?

Are those of us who are homosexual people perhaps those who the early disciples would have said are 'not following us' but are casting out demons in the name of Jesus, those of whom Jesus said, 'If they are not against us, they are for us?'

Are we the true or false prophets?

Jesus knew it would not be easy to answer that question, not as easy as quoting laws or texts, not as easy as identifying those who say 'Lord, Lord'. 'By their fruits you will know them', he said.

So all I can do is to ask you, my sisters and brothers, to make your judgment by looking at the fruits of ministry, of life and of faith. An Elder in Terrigal (a little town in New South Wales) prayed recently, 'Dear God, may we only find each other as Jesus has already found us.' That is my prayer for us all.

I sat down and experienced the love of God, of my partner and my friends washing over me. I felt emptied of everything else, as though I had given my whole being into that moment and it had not yet returned to me. I felt like that through most of the rest of the Assembly — a sort of amazing lightness of being. Because I was Director for Mission, I had reporting and presentation responsibilities into the Assembly. I found myself doing this as though nothing else had happened — simply resuming my role as Director. People remarked upon that, but I thought that this was quite consistent with my own profound sense of truth. I was a Minister of the Word, Director for Mission and also a lesbian. That was all true, and I believed it to be a good and faithful truth.

For a number of reasons, the Assembly deferred its decision about lesbian and gay people in leadership and committed itself to further discussion, at least until the next Assembly, which was three years away. This would give time for members from different cultural and language backgrounds to enter the discussion more fully. It also gave more time for the church at large to go on reflecting. There was no decision possible that would have pleased everybody. It was abundantly clear in the Assembly meeting that consensus could not be reached and it was impressive that no one moved to a formal and divisive vote. Had someone done so, I believe that the more radical options would have prevailed. However, and rightly, the consensus processes to which our church is committed at least allowed for a sense of satisfaction that everybody had been heard and that their views were respectfully considered.

For me, it was the finest experience of the church I had ever had. It was real people sharing real things, looking each other in the face and searching for the truth and almost always treating each other with respect. It even makes you believe that the power of God is there helping people cross the boundaries of their own convictions to listen caringly to others — a miracle! You can't get a finer experience of the church than that.

The representatives of all types of media relentlessly pursued me, of course. The news went spinning around the country and even beyond that, in these days of the Internet. After facing that the safest way to deal with that was to deal with the media personally in order to give myself a sporting chance of accurate reporting, things went rolling on in seemingly endless interest to them.

Meanwhile, I found that living openly with one's truth inevitably means that you either challenge or affirm everyone else's truth and that many people are likely to respond to that with messages, phone calls and letters. I was moved and surprised to find how many people sat down and wrote six or more page letters to me, pouring out their lives to someone they had never met. I guess it was about one claiming of truth inviting another.

The effort of trying to respond to this outpouring was heavy, grateful though I was to receive it. In fact I still have not done justice to those people, who became an instant community with me. Of course, I also received letters and messages of challenge and sometimes hate. I did not personally receive many of these, most of them went to my supervisory colleagues who were asked to dismiss me or stop me in various ways. They bore that load for me at a time when their energy was almost as thin as mine.

At a later point in the Assembly, I had informed everyone that I would carefully monitor the viability of my position in the church, as I realised that the effectiveness of my job depended on the level of confidence which the church sustained in me. This turned out to be a necessary caution for myself and the church.

Within a few months, I had resigned my position as Director of the National Commission for Mission. No one directly required this of me and it was accepted after much discussion. Having said that, I knew that it was required of me, given the pressures from a significant section of the church. I had no doubt that to stay would have been to distort the ongoing discussion and risk the work I had been doing, work which was very precious to me.

I had found that if people feel powerless to change the decisions of the church, they often protest by attacking any person who has become a symbol of the unwelcome decision. As one who had been in the church for the whole of my life, none of these responses surprised me. Like the rest of the community, the church is diverse, and also as human. One of our diversities lies in our view of the nature of the authority of Scripture and that has always had a significant impact on any discussions about sexuality. Many people have asked me how I can accept my sexuality in the light of the Bible and maybe I had better briefly answer that question here.

All ministers in the three churches which formed the Uniting Church, the Methodist, Presbyterian and Congregational Churches, alongside other similar mainstream churches around the world, have been training their ministers in a non-literalistic view of the Bible for more than half a century. Unfortunately, and possibly irresponsibly, the clergy of our church have not yet passed on to much of the church this learning about twentieth century biblical scholarship.

It is very hard to sustain a literal view of the Bible. There are texts in it which contradict each other. For example, there are two quite different orders of creation in the first two chapters of Genesis and varying images of God in relation to vengeance and warfare. There are instructions for living which will not stand up today because of their ethics or in relation to new understandings of truth. For example, the Bible affirms slavery, it states that women are unclean when they menstruate and that women are saved by the birth of the child, among many other things.

These things, along with other issues about varying theological themes that run through the Bible mean that the church and individual Christians have had to work out what sort of book it actually is and what sort of authority it has. We have also had to live with the recognition that we all interpret the Bible. None of us has the provable and actual truth from it, not even literalists.

I regard the Bible as a rich and astonishing collection of the testimony to people's experience of God down many centuries. It is inspiring and inspired because of the power of this collection and the sense of God which, in my view, breathes through it. I love wrestling with it and searching within it to see what new truth and life flows from it. It is a marvellous mixture of myth, fable, history, personal stories, theological reflection, poems, songs and symbolic writing. I give it authority precisely because, for me, some profound understandings of God and life leap forth from it.

In among the testimonies of their experiences of God, the biblical writers have also given us accounts of the way they ordered their life in response to God, as they understood God at each point in history — their rules for human behaviour and life together. You would have to say that some of their ideas are rather strange. Others have stood the test of time. I do not believe that we should receive their ideas any less critically than they did those of their forebears. For example, they did not sustain the idea that their kings should have numerous wives, nor that their leaders should have concubines on hand. They did not, in the Christian tradition, uphold the Jewish rule to refrain from eating pork and other things. We most certainly do not say in our sermons or letters, as did Paul, that slaves should obey their masters and masters should be kind to their slaves.

There are passages in the Bible that appear to refer to homosexuality. Several of the Old Testament ones are ambiguous. Paul says some clear things about obviously promiscuous homosexual activity around temples. There is nothing anywhere about loving and responsible homosexual relationships and Jesus says nothing at all, which is remarkable, given the strong feelings of the church on the issue today. People like myself would say that there were many issues operating in the formation of the sexual mores of the past. The survival of the tribe was a paramount issue, therefore taboos against non-procreative relationships, like same sex relationships, were understandable. It was likely then, as it often still is today, that quiet and faithful relationships between people of the same sex were hidden.

Even though we still don't understand a great deal about the formation of human sexuality, we know enough to at least suggest that there are more genetic and physiological connections than we had thought. The formation of gender is more complex and fragile than people would have understood, even a few decades ago. Although our information is not complete, in many respects we know that sexual orientation and its mysteries are at least up for discussion, rather than about certainties, biblical or otherwise.

I add my interpretations to the debate from a viewpoint of one who now identifies as lesbian. This gives me no more bias than those who are heterosexual. We can each only offer ideas from our own experience. In the Christian tradition, we will add to our general life experience our understanding of the nature of God from our lives and from the authority which we give to the Bible. After that, as I said in my speech to our church Assembly, we have no option but to look at the 'fruits'. Does life or death arise from our positions? How will we know what life and death looks like? All I can say now is that given the flow of decision in the mainstream churches of the world in this decade, people like myself are the ones who are going with the tide of history.

As I faced the opposition to me, I also knew that possibly most of the church had been moving along in what they thought was a long tradition of not ordaining homosexual people. A sudden change was disturbing and shocking and many people naturally had a sense of outrage. Changes of attitude on matters like this take a long time in any institution and we are not helped by our lack of biblical scholarship, nor our limited personal contact with people who dare to be openly homosexual.

After the Assembly, I faced a disciplinary process because someone, representative I have no doubt of many others, made a formal complaint against me of 'grave conduct unbecoming a Minister'. After a very careful and respectful process, the responsible committee of the church issued a report which concluded that one person's ordination was not the real battleground for deciding issues that were still being debated by the church. It sustained my ordination, for at least as long as it takes the church to decide on the matter in principle. That was a very special gift to me.

One day the church may face that the 'tradition' had probably never been in place in reality. I believe that the church has always ordained us. It has preferred not to make that clear. If everyone now, and in the history of leadership in the church who is of homosexual orientation stood up, the church would have to live with its own new truth and old hiding of the truth. We are everywhere, including in the priesthood and ministry of all the mainstream churches. We have been quietly and faithfully offering our creativity, our talents and ministries, in large numbers, into the church and community for centuries.

One day, and not much further on, I think, the church will have the courage and honesty to live with its own truth and it will be a better place for doing that. We can see this in a number of churches around the world which have already agreed that homosexuality is not a bar to ordination. My church is not at that point. In the meantime, we will go on having some brave conversations together.

Some months after my sharing of my life with the Assembly, I was approached by our national television broadcaster to be the focus of a half-hour program called *Australian Story* — a program which features aspects of an Australian person's life. I was told that it would be an intrusive process because it would involve interviewing my family and friends. With some anxiety, however, I agreed to proceed. I told myself that we were all adults, quite capable of deciding what we were willing or not willing to do. I said to my partner, ex-husband and children that I felt quite relaxed about whether or not they participated. That was my truth about the situation.

In the end, they told me that their truth was different from mine. My partner, Ali, decided that, if anything, she would just stay in the background as a very private person and one who did not want to invite voyeurism concerning our relationship. In reality, as she made clear in the end, if my ex-husband and all my children participated, she had no option but to be interviewed. If she did not, it would make our relationship appear less significant than the other relationships. It did not please her to be interviewed, but she did it for me and for her own self-respect.

Also, while she didn't face me with this, I realised after the program had begun that my ex-husband's participation would affect his wife. I had not even considered that. My children also said to me, 'Come on, Mum! If one of us is interviewed, we all have to participate whether we like it or not, otherwise people will wonder why we are not there.'

Anyway, because they are all gracious and brave people, everybody was interviewed. They all spoke their own truths about me and about the church and that made somewhat riveting viewing, to say the least. My children had a necessary conversation with me before they told the nation what they thought of me in both negative and positive terms. I was so proud of us all, because we were true, in our own authentic ways and, as it mostly does, truth brought us closer together.

Later again, I faced another challenge to the nature of my own truth. I was invited to be a speaker at the launch of the Sydney Gay and Lesbian Mardi Gras. The festival is a month of artistic events — music, art and theatre which celebrates the creativity and life of the homosexual community. It culminates with the Mardi Gras parade on the streets of Sydney, which is watched by around 700 000 people. Selected parts of the parade are shown on television. The parade features many different sorts of floats and groups of people marching along.

It is most unfortunate that because of the sensational nature of the Mardi Gras parade, most of the public who are not at the parade see only a small and unrepresentative section of it. They don't see the groups of Catholics, Quakers and sometimes Anglicans marching quietly among the rest. They don't see the numerous ethnic, including Aboriginal groups who are simply there marching, waving and celebrating that they exist, without doing anything particularly sensational. They don't see the hundreds of volunteers who give part of their lives every week to people with AIDS who march in a big group, nor the large group of parents of gay and lesbian people who usually receive the loudest cheer of all as they go past. This means that to associate the church with the parade is, in many people's minds to associate it with the more sensational images which could offend some people.

There were a number of things and ideas that influenced my decision to speak at the launch. The Director of the festival, in his invitation to me said, 'When we decide who to invite to speak at the launch, we ask ourselves who has been important to the lesbian and gay community in the past year. We decided that you were one of those people. Your statement about yourself has been important to the church, but it has also been important to our community.' The person who passed on the invitation to me before I spoke to the Director had also said 'Maybe you don't realise how important this has been for the way gay and lesbian people feel about the church and God, whether they are Christian or not.'

Even though I knew that I had considerable support in the church, in accepting my resignation and retirement the church had put me in a position where, at the very least, I could never assume that it wanted any part of my ministry from me. This was countered a little by the sustaining of my ordination, although in the next hours I was to learn that there was an attempt being made to appeal against the decision to sustain it and a new formal complaint.

In the invitation to speak at the launch, I experienced a sense of being invited to take my place as a Christian in the homosexual community and bring to them a gift of life and hope as I understood it. As I said to the media, 'These are my people, warts and all, and I am one of them, warts and all.' I knew that what I said to them would affect the way they saw God. Even those of us who are supportive of homosexual people have never really faced the pain and destruction that Christianity has brought, and still brings, to homosexual people. People literally die because they believe that they are an abomination before our Christian God. Just recently, I spoke with a woman whose son had hanged himself for that reason. People live in terror; they have breakdowns and become unemployable; they live rejected by parents who never speak to them again; and they are spat upon and hated. Christian parents live in grief and pain as their children cannot stay beside them in the church because of the judgment and rejection. Very importantly, most homosexual people decide to have nothing to do with God, because of the way God is represented by the church.

I decided that I could not always wait on the long, good time of the church as it goes through its careful and cautious processes of decision making. Jesus Christ never waits for that — Jesus goes before the church and the church catches up. The slaves heard the great hope of freedom long before the church decided that slavery was a sin. The South Africans heard the truth long before their main church heard that apartheid was a heresy.

As I was trying to live out truth and hope with my people, because I love the church and needed it to change for the sake of their freedom, I committed myself to try to be careful about what I do and not hold back the church. Nevertheless, I decided that the primary imperative for me would always be the truth itself and, if the church could not bear for me to stay with it as I carry what I truly believe to be that truth, well, so be it.

I reflected on the issue which confronted me as I considered associating part of the church with the Mardi Gras parade — the association with some activities and images and lifestyles which we might not support. In some ways, I believed that my speaking at the launch could give me more chance to make clear the nature of my place in and among the Mardi Gras. Coalitions are always ambiguous, and this one in particular, but I would have to say that I have mostly been a coalitionist. I, with other Christians, have joined communists in marches for peace. I have walked alongside women on International Women's Day who had different agendas from my own. In both these situations there have been critics from within the church because of the ambiguities of association.

On the other hand, few people seem as concerned about armed forces chaplains associating themselves with parades of people who have often shared in the killing, maiming and sometimes raping of other people, many of whom were innocent civilians. Perhaps we realise that war is, indeed, ambiguous and that there are heroic and just things in there beside the destruction of life and environment. It is certainly no less ambiguous than other associations that we make.

In most cases, I believe that the Christian calling is to be there among those who suffer, or in particular causes, stating the nature of our participation by our behaviour, offering models of hope, faith and love. Rather this than waiting for the 'pure' occasions when the church can be unambiguously itself, because it is on its own. I also believe that sometimes we need to build relationships if we wish to open conversations with people about lifestyles. Why would you ever open a conversation with people who see you as dirt and an abomination and who keep themselves well away from you?

A few years ago, a group of Christians carried out a 'cleansing' of the suburb of Kings Cross in the centre of Sydney from the sinfulness of homosexual people. At the time there was little public protest from the church in response to this activity. The people who were the subject of the cleansing mockingly carried as an effigy the head of the leader of the cleansing group on a plate in their next Mardi Gras parade and did things like dressing themselves as nuns. 'How disrespectful!' cried some of the church, without doing much thinking about how disrespectful it feels to be regarded as someone's dirt for the cleansing.

In my speech to the launch:

- I honoured Aboriginal people and the fact that the land on which we were standing belonged to them.

- I reminded homosexual people that they had a responsibility to other oppressed people.

- I claimed that gay and lesbian people are not some strange people to be stereotyped, but that we are everywhere, including in the church and the priesthood or ministry.

- I invited us to believe that we could be whole people, not defined by our sexuality alone. (This was a gentle critique of those of us who do define ourselves that way.)

- I claimed our right to celebrate our loving relationships.

- I told a joke.

- I announced that God loves us.

- I called us to claim our hard-won celebration and to live from it.

As far as I am concerned, that was a careful and gentle sermon. It was deliberately careful and gentle because I carried with me the history of an oppressive church and I knew that I had to respectfully ask for my place among these, my people. To pull back from this journey, because some people in the church had a problem with my understanding of the Gospel, was not something I could do and be true to either myself or to Jesus Christ. However, I remain committed to being as respectful as possible of the church as I go.

To carry the divisions in the church into a public arena is a serious thing to do. It is also a very grave thing not to do that, if you believe that people are believing that God does not love them because of the hate for them that is protected in the heart of the church. Even a few months ago I might not have used the word 'hate'. I would have used words about genuine differences and division among us. Even now I am not referring to all those who disagree with me.

If I have changed in this, it is because I have now experienced hate myself, real and vicious hate from people who claim to represent the loving Jesus. Since I have resigned my church position, the hate mail comes directly to me. I have also heard and read the stories of many more of my lesbian sisters and gay brothers who live with violence and hate, much of which is coming from the church. Whatever our position on the issue, we have a grave responsibility to denounce hate in all its forms — in each other, in the church, both publicly and privately. Sometimes the only convincing way to do this is to take your stand among the hated. I am grateful to those heterosexual people who stand with us.

In conclusion

One of the things I have learned in all this is that if you try to live with your own truth with a small amount of courage, then many people are likely to believe that you are, therefore, a tough person. They image someone who is rebellious, defiant, uncaring of the views or feelings of others and who is probably not easily hurt herself. Indeed, some of them feel free to attack you with minimal regard for your feelings. I believe the only human journey worth living is one that is largely undefended, except by the power of perceived truth, the love of others, of God and with innate self-respect. If you develop defences against anticipated attack, then you must create for yourself categories of people who are your enemies. This categorisation will allow you to prepare your return attack, or even to attack your enemies before they strike you. You take from others their capacity to reach you, even with their contrary views and shield yourself from what might be new truth. This is too high a price to pay for your own perception of truth.

All this means that you do not become toughened in the struggle. In some ways, you become even more vulnerable. Probably most of my opponents would not believe that there are some days when I cannot bring myself to open my mail. I have to wait until I feel a little stronger to face what might be waiting there for me. This happens, even though I know full well that there is unlikely to be any new bullets there, just more of the old ones. In all this, I would unreservedly stand for the appropriateness of challenges to my truth, just as I feel free and even responsible to challenge that of others. I just wish that we did not need to be so wounding of each other in the challenge, even as we hold some things very precious. Maybe one day, we will find a kinder way.

In it all, I do not regret this journey of living my own truth. One of the loveliest things that happened to me after coming out was an invitation to contribute a meditation to be included as part of a performance of Haydn's 'Seven Last Words of Christ' in the Sydney Opera House. I was given the words of Jesus 'I thirst' as the theme for my meditation. I found myself writing: 'I thirst… as a bird whose spirit flies free in resurrection life, while its body groans and bleeds in the costliness of its flight.' I knew as I wrote that it described my own experience as I tried to live with my personal truth. I also knew that to turn back from the flight to freedom would be to begin to die.

Living with Failure and Forgiveness

NORMALLY, I suppose we think of failure as related to lack of achievement, mostly the lack of achievement of some goal, which was set by ourselves or somebody else. Some people call various failures 'sin', although this has another dimension which is related to wrong-doing. Nevertheless, I suppose that all failure has to do with not achieving our best, in somebody's estimation.

When I do something wrong, I fail to achieve my own expectations, the hopes and expectations of others and, if I am religious, the expectations of my God. I also sometimes fail to live up to the hopes a whole society has for itself, because I am a contributor to the general life of that society. If I am simply inadequate in some way, do not have the resolve, the gifts, talents, intelligence, resources, information or support that are required for succeeding in what I am trying to do or to be, I fail. I do not achieve the particular goal that I set for myself or that was set for me.

I am not here focusing on those who deliberately do evil, although there are complexities even around that — of cause, of personality formation and genetics, of environment and of alienation — which blur the lines. Be that as it may, for this conversation, I am rather reflecting on situations where people have a profound sense of their own failure, through either inadequacy or what they believe is wrong-doing. Most of us find our own failure so unacceptable that we would rather pretend it hasn't happened. I am expert at this myself.

In fact, my strategy is to immediately work very, very hard to make things 'right'. I am so good at this that people are sometimes actually quite grateful for my efforts, even though it was me that caused the problem in the first place! Others, fortunately for my soul, are not so easily fooled. They are my real friends and they invite me to dare to face the fact that I have failed. They do this because they love me enough to try to teach me that people who fail are simply part of the lovable, normal human race. They probably also do it because they are not afraid of me. It is always good to have people around who are not afraid of you.

I remember once getting up before a large group at a women's conference and saying some things which I wished I had not said. I was filled with guilt, grief and remorse. I had attacked my friends in public. How would I ever face them again? I lay awake at night thinking about it and wishing I could go back in time. I felt depressed during the day, as though I was carrying a hidden load. One of the friends, Betty, came into my office. I poured out my sorrow and fear to her. I said I had made a terrible mistake, which I deeply regretted. She looked at me lovingly and calmly and said, 'So, you have failed, Dorothy. Well, you have just joined the human race.'

I remember thinking that it would be a lovely thing to really feel part of the human race — that there could be a wonderful bunch of people somewhere who just did their best and assumed that we would all make mistakes. I felt as though my friend lived in that place and that I had just been included as one of the ordinary, honoured, makers-of-mistakes and a truly human person. I felt as though this human person would be especially attractive, because 'saints' somehow make everyone else feel inadequate.

That made me realise that I had been living somewhere, other than this good place among the human community, for much of my life. My world was a place where I had to be 'special', where guilt and punishment survived well and where in order to gain membership you made as few mistakes as possible. Some of this world was my own creation. Some of it came from the experience of being a minister's child, and some of it related to being part of the church.

I have pondered this realisation over the years. Why is it that the community of faith — which takes as its God a Jesus whose primary message was about free, unconditional forgiveness and grace — is so often a place where it is fearful to acknowledge failure? Maybe it relates to the tendency in Christianity to believe in a God who offers us a set of rules for living and then calls us into relationship with the God who gives the rules? The concept of a personal relationship with any God is rather daunting anyway, to say the least. It is very easy to add an idea that involves withdrawal of this relationship if we don't measure up to the set standards. Human parents, at their worst, sometimes do this.

I don't think that Jesus actually imaged a God who punishes or condemns us if we fail to obey a set of rules. If, however, we see Jesus as one who gives us a vision of what life might be like and a God who is our parent, then it is all too easy to convert that into a view of ourselves as people who aspire to be very special indeed. Then, to please this God, especially the God who is presented as dying for us, we may well set our standards very high.

When you add to that the corporate nature of Christianity, then the pressures to seem excellent and unfailing alongside our sisters and brothers can become very heavy. We also, as Christians, speak and write about 'being saved' by Jesus Christ. If you ask Christians what they are saved from, you get many different answers. The stock answer is that we are saved from our sin. But what does that mean — that we sin less than others do? Few of us would dare to claim that. Or are we saved from the consequences of our sin? If it does mean this, it puts a punishing God there somewhere who, because of the special 'pleading' or sacrifice of Jesus, lets us off that punishment.

Whatever your explanation of being saved involves, it is hard not to distort your view of yourself when you fail. Being the 'saved' so often takes on a false meaning, the idea that we are less likely to fail, instead of its true meaning which should teach us that even when we fail, we are still loved. In all this, I am not suggesting that all humankind should not aspire to great and good things. I am suggesting that aspiring to the heights of human endeavour, coupled with a longing to please our God, often sets the stage for a false sense of what makes a beautiful human being.

We forget that the whole point of relating to a God who enters human life is that this God, rather than living in distant perfection, has actually shared our life and understands, better than anyone else, the struggles we face, our temptations and weaknesses. This God lives within us, between us, around us and beyond us. Do we not think that if someone could enter our own life like that, they would usually understand our failures? How often, when we have failed and received the judgment of others, do we cry out in our hearts, 'Oh, if only they knew what I have been through!' Could we not imagine that if we were able to enter the life of others like that, we would be far more forgiving and understanding of their life journeys? How often do we make judgments against each other and then, on meeting with the person and hearing the story, withdraw or modify our judgments?

I also observe that even people who have no association with organised religion, may still feel a punishing 'god' waiting somewhere for them and still enter the throes of continuing and disabling guilt and remorse. Often they have no way of dealing with this. I am thinking here about a guilt that stays with people beyond their appropriate efforts to apologise and/or make recompense for their failure.

What is guilt?

There are many pains in the human journey that are hard but not destructive. I believe that guilt is not one of those. Guilt is not a creative pain. It does not carry us forward. In fact, it usually paralyses us and stays like a debilitating deadness within our life. The sustaining of guilt shuts us off from the healing power of forgiveness. We are not open to it. We have decided to stay as an unworthy person, unworthy of love or respect, defined by our failure. It is a self-inflicted limit on the taking up of our life again and restoring ourselves to the status of an ordinary, humble human being who could, nevertheless, still aspire to go on to new things.

Of course, all of us feel guilt when we know we have done wrong, especially if it hurts other people. It is the initial form in which we own responsibility for what we have done. The development of guilt into a positive form of response is, in my view, grief.

To go to ourselves, or to those we have wronged, with real grief because of what we have done, or not done, opens up for us all, I believe, the greatest opportunities for moving forward in life. Grief is no less powerful than guilt, but it allows for us the possibility of receiving healing from others, our God if we have one, and in the end, from ourselves. This, of course, happens all in its due time.

Some people suggest that shame is a more appropriate response to failure than guilt, but I am not so sure, given the social history into which this idea may enter. In my experience to 'shame' someone is to put them in a corner and display how bad they are. I once had a teacher whose favourite form of punishment was to put a pupil out the front of the class for the rest of the lesson with a wastepaper basket over his or her head. I identify that as a way of shaming someone through humiliation. Shame might be a helpful alternative for some people, however. It can be interpreted as the painful accepting of responsibility for something, which is the first step to affirming that we are human, have failed and will face what that might require of us for our own healing and the healing of others.

The process of receiving forgiveness

To receive forgiveness is often as hard as it is to offer it to others. Many of us, no matter what we believe about God, believe that we should be punished for failure and can't really accept forgiveness until we have been punished to the level which we feel compensates for what we have done. Of course there are exceptions to this — people who live as though they have no responsibility for anything they have done — but I am thinking about people who live within the normal range of responsibility towards themselves and others.

I recall talking with a woman who had come to me, as a person who saw herself as representing the church, to quite explicitly receive forgiveness. She sat and told me the story of her failure in life, which was real. Then she told me of many years of painful remorse and endless efforts to apologise to those concerned and to make compensation to them. She told me of a life seriously disabled by guilt, of doctors and therapists, of medication and illness. She said, 'I have come to you for forgiveness.'

After talking with her for a time, I said, 'I can see that this is a significant moment for you. Let us make this quite formal. I invite you to kneel down.' She did that. I anointed her forehead with oil, placed my hands on her head and said, 'In the name of the God who is your loving Parent, in the name of Jesus Christ who has shared our life, and in the name of the Holy Spirit, our Healer and Comforter, you are forgiven. Rise up and live in freedom.'

She stood up and said, 'That was too easy.' I said, 'What is too easy?' She said, 'Forgiveness can't be that easy?' I said, 'Are you telling me that your journey to this moment has been easy? Were you hoping that I would lay out further punishments for you, like penances, so that you can earn your forgiveness?' She thought for a long time and agreed that, although this had not been a conscious thought, deep down, she was looking for something like that.

It is easy to see why penances have had a role in some parts of Christianity. Whether they are due to God, or anybody else, they often make people feel as though they have 'done something' to make things right. (All of which does not mean that I believe penances are a good thing.)

We reflected that those whom she had wronged had forgiven her. She had done all that she could do to make things right. We asked ourselves who was due for further offerings from her? She was not a particularly religious person, but we agreed that there was possibly a God hovering in the background. In a way, she did not want to be beholden to this God by accepting anything which could be interpreted as free forgiveness. She wanted to make the full payment. It was interesting to decide that, if there was a God, she wanted a self-respecting and debt-free relationship with that God. She also wanted the same sort of relationship with herself. In other words, she could only love herself again if she paid in full for her failure.

We thought about that for a while. What would ever be enough for this payment? She, in fact, found it hard to see when her debt to herself would end. I asked her what payment she required of people who had hurt her before she restored the relationship with them? It turned out that she was gentle and forgiving with her friends. She understood that people made mistakes and regretted them. I asked her whether, given that she required endless reparation from herself for her failures, she might not be acting in a patronising or paternalistic fashion with her friends? Why was she easily forgiving with them and not with herself? Was she being the 'lady bountiful'? At this point, I confessed that her journeying was one that I recognised well, as it was often my own. To cut a long story short, she agreed to kneel again, I forgave her, I claimed God's forgiveness for her and then she said, 'I forgive myself. I will now try to live as if I am forgiven.'

In moving towards the receiving of forgiveness, most people go through a similar process. We confess to ourselves that we have failed: that is, we say to ourselves 'I am responsible for doing this.' Even if we can see why we might have done this thing and that there were many complexities around it, we have moved away from blaming someone else ('They made me do it'). We experience the pain and grief of the acknowledgment that we are responsible.

If it is possible, we go to the one/s we have wronged and say, in effect, 'I did this to you. I can see that I have hurt you and I am very sorry I have done that. Will you please forgive me? I will understand if you can't forgive me yet, but is there anything that I can do to make things right?' At this stage, it is important to believe that, even though we are asking for forgiveness, which is the right thing to do, the other/s may not be ready to forgive us. In the work I have done for the past five years, I often came across non-indigenous people who had made a point of apologising to the Aboriginal people of our country. They assumed that more than two hundred years of oppression and suffering could be wiped out in a flash by their apology. They felt that they had 'done the right thing' in apologising and the least that Aboriginal people should do was to receive it with gratitude.

An apology is our first move towards asking for forgiveness. We then wait respectfully for the response. We are not due for that. We are asking for grace from another and that is a costly thing for them. They may not be ready to offer it until more healing takes place. They may never be ready to offer it because their wounding is so profound.

Sometimes there is no one to go to with our apology. We may be feeling guilty about something we have done which lets ourselves down but is not related to an action that directly connects with someone else. Sometimes the person we have wronged has died or is not available to us for some other reason.

Then some people will only pretend to forgive us. They will say the words and then require payment for those words in a multitude of ways. That is playing games. Real forgiveness is free. This does not mean that there are not ongoing consequences for what we have done. It has to do with the reality, or not, of the restoration of the relationship as we face those consequences. The relationship is not really reinstated if people keep 'playing with' our apology as though they have not received it. By this, I do not mean that sometimes the wounded person will not authentically remind us that they are still wounded. Most of us can tell the difference between genuine forgiveness and a phoney one which simply uses our apology as a weapon against us.

Of course, in asking for forgiveness we take the risk that those involved will be unable or unwilling to forgive us at all, and will tell us that. When this happens, our mood of penitence often turns to indignation. We have gone through all this agony of heart, we have humbled ourselves and asked for forgiveness and we are rejected! How dare they do that! Well, sometimes others are not very forgiving people, for all sorts of reasons. Sometimes they have never learned the power and freedom in forgiveness. Sometimes, the pain of our wounding of them is too great and they cannot find enough grace to forgive us.

Sometimes people are mixed up, even disturbed people who have been damaged by life and they are unable to understand the nature of forgiveness. Sometimes our act against them is the last in a whole line of destructive experiences for them and, in order to survive, they are saying to themselves, 'This time I will not be gracious. This time, I will stand and fight for my life.' That is their right.

So, have we wasted our act of inviting forgiveness? No, we have not. The decision to ask for forgiveness was for the good of our own soul, our own life, in its onward journey. It was not just for the sake of the wronged person. In deciding that we did wrong and that we will ask for forgiveness, we have moved our life along. We have lived with honesty, courage and sorrow and we have invited a gift from another. That is a life-giving human activity.

But who will forgive us if the person we have wronged will not? If, for any reason, those to whom we apologise are not able to give us their grace in forgiveness, how will we be forgiven? Will we ever be forgiven? I believe that although it is usually difficult, it is possible for us to receive forgiveness from someone other than the person we have wronged. I say this, believing that going to someone other than those whom we have wronged is never a substitute for dealing directly with those whom we have failed.

Some people can simply forgive themselves, and this is required anyway at some stage. In doing this, we look upon the wronged person, understand that they are unable to forgive and decide that we will not give them the power over us that is involved in lack of forgiveness. We claim our own grace and move on past them. This is the hardest forgiveness, but some people are able to do this. They usually need to share with others that they are doing so — not to ask them for forgiveness, but to affirm their freedom to move on.

Some people find it helpful to make their own private apology, in the form of a confession, to their God. They experience a genuine forgiveness in that relationship. They believe that even if human forgiveness is not possible, a God who is not directly involved, but who can see the whole picture, will be able to offer forgiveness. Some people like to go to someone whom they believe has a sort of 'authority' to forgive, like a priest or minister. They feel that the confession which they make, and forgiveness which they receive, is more affirmed than if they simply personally address their God.

Many other people prefer to confess to a friend, or friends. This may take place as they share the whole story with the friend. The good friend acknowledges that they have done wrong, rather than trying to convince them that everything was all right — unless there is real reason for giving that assurance — then hears and affirms that they are truly sorry. The friend gives strength to the belief that, even in the face of the inability of those whom they have wronged to forgive them, people can move on in their life. This friend, or group of friends, can help people to keep reinstating the forgiven state, which is often necessary.

I suppose that these other agents of forgiveness offer it on behalf of God, if that is meaningful, or on behalf of the human race. In either case, it is a matter of shifting the issue onto a wider front. In doing this we are saying that 'Yes, the person you have wronged cannot, or will not, forgive you. That is sad, but you are now offering your apology into a wider community, or to God. Both these agents are capable of a wider view of things and can affirm that you are forgiven.' Forgiveness like this is always harder to receive, because obviously it is not so satisfyingly direct. But it can be powerful. We each choose our own way of inviting forgiveness.

To genuinely receive forgiveness is often not easy. It invites us to receive a gift from someone which we cannot at that moment repay, and may never repay. As possibly proud people, we are metaphorically kneeling before someone else, owning that we have failed them and waiting for a response to be given in grace.

The sign that we have received forgiveness is that we take up our lives and move on. We dare to believe that we are people of essential worth, who can look life in the face again and restore our dream of what is possible. In Christian language, 'We are made new.' This does not mean that we cheerfully forget the past. The pain of our failure becomes a salutary learning within us, a wound that is part of our life, a humility that can make us a better and wiser person.

Offering forgiveness

Christians, at least in theory, give a good deal of importance to the requirement to be forgiving. As we are forgiven by God, so we are called to forgive others. This is obviously a good, generous and healthy way to live. I recall on one occasion, however, a young woman coming to see me. She was in dreadful distress. Two nights before, she had been raped. She had reported the matter to the police and had then sought comfort from the Elders of her church. They had heard her story with sympathy but their first response had been to say, 'Now you must forgive the man who raped you. That is the Christian way.' She had fled the room weeping. She had come to ask whether she should be able to forgive.

My immediate response was to say that to forgive at that moment would be a further violation of her desperately wounded person. We sat and asked ourselves where we thought our God would be in it all. Would this God be among the Elders asking her to forgive? Or would this God be sitting with us, outraged that she had been raped and wrapping her around with cherishing, healing love? We imagined that had she been run over by a car and injured to the same degree that her body, mind and soul was injured by the rape, she would be lying in intensive care in hospital. The medical staff would be caring for her every need. Her friends (and the Elders) would be phoning and visiting and bringing flowers. No one would be asking her at that moment to forgive the driver of the car. Their only concern would be for her and her healing. We decided that God was with us. We remembered that even Jesus, as he hang dying on the cross, did not forgive his enemies. He asked his Father to do so.

Neither of us believed that one day, forgiveness would not be possible and even desirable. We were seeing that, while some people have an heroic capacity to forgive, most of us need some time for healing before forgiveness can be genuinely offered, especially when the offence against us is grave. I would have to say that I rarely believe in the heroic capacity to forgive. Watching what happens to people who are heroic, I observe that many of them may not be facing the level of their own pain in the situation.

There is an honest and healthy self-respect in acknowledging the degree of one's own real pain. As a sometimes heroic forgiver myself, especially in the past, I am less likely to rush in with forgiveness these days. I wait to know a little more what I really feel. Quite apart from the health in doing this, I have to admit that my 'heroic' acts of forgiveness often turn out to be far less real than I had imagined. I find the reality of my unforgiveness emerging in all sorts of subtle and unsubtle ways. I find myself doing smaller and larger nasty things to the person in gossip, in little vengeances and other acts of power.

Having said all that, long-term refusal to forgive others sits, at least, like a stone in our lives, weighing us down on our journey. At worst, and commonly, it is more like a slow-burning fire which consumes our energy and joy of life from within. Slow burning or fast burning, rage saps energy like nothing else. The strange truth is that when we decide not to forgive someone, we give them more power over us rather than less. They become enmeshed in our life, holding us into the power of their offence against us. We think we are being powerful in not forgiving them, but the cost to us is huge. Often they go on without our forgiveness anyway, while we are stuck in our incapacitating unforgiveness.

The power to forgive does, indeed, come with time and healing. It is helped by 'debriefing' with friends — having them say, many times usually, 'Yes, how terrible! You were wounded by this person. We see that. We are with you, not with your attacker.' The validating of our experience of wounding is essential. That often takes a lot of the power out of it. It is then, as I have said earlier, a matter of deciding not to be a victim.

This is an act of faith. Sometimes the moment of announcing

forgiveness is not something that you feel you are ready for. It is almost a ritual act. Indeed, it can often be helpful to make it a ritual act. You decide that you need to forgive, to release yourself from your wounding and the power of unforgiveness. You make a time for announcing that you forgive and, surprisingly often, forgiveness is given to you as a gift. Who knows where it comes from? I say from God. It may be from the loving energy of your friends or from your own inner courage and determination.

The gift of being able to forgive is experienced by most people as the power to love, freedom from rage and obsession and a great energy for moving forward in their life.

Corporate apology and forgiveness

Australia is, at this time, debating whether or not it should apologise to its indigenous people for past wrongs. Some people are strongly for that and others say, 'We were not responsible for the wrongs. Our forebears did the wrongs and many of them were not aware that they were doing wrong. They meant well.' Some people suggest that the best way forward is to improve the lot of Aboriginal people now by giving money for health and education: 'Let's be practical and make a difference, rather than apologise.' Others even suggest that it behoves Aboriginal people to forgive their oppressors after all this time: 'Look, some of them have done well for themselves in our culture. What are they complaining about?'

I believe it is not appropriate to expect forgiveness if you have not said you are sorry, although some people are astonishingly gracious. The fact that a few Aboriginal people have survived the wounding of their people and achieved success in our system is a miracle, and makes little difference to the fact that the majority of their people have not been able to do that. Most prominent

Aboriginal leaders are leaders precisely because they choose to use their success for the betterment of their people, unlike most of us.

Then, to say that we will make things right by giving money for changing the condition of Aboriginal people fails to face two things. The first is that to bring health care and education of Aboriginal people up to the standard of the rest of us is nothing more than simple justice. They are owed that, like every other citizen. It is not magnanimous on our part to offer them this, it is simply beginning to right a wrong.

The second issue is that those who suggest this option fail to understand the nature of reconciliation. It involves, if you like, kneeling before the wronged people and confessing that we have wronged them. This gives the wronged people the power and dignity to then negotiate with us what it would mean to restore the relationship. This is not something we can decide upon on their behalf. We must wait respectfully and humbly for them to tell us what is required. An apology actually changes the status of the relationship so that they are more able to tell us what would restore us all to a new relationship.

Finally, are we required to apologise for things we did not personally do? The truth is often only seen in hindsight, therefore apologies can often only come later. Sometimes they can only come when the consequences of what was done are seen in the tide of history. We are the generation that can see those consequences, rather than most of our forebears.

When we are dealing with corporate situations, those who see, those who know, are the ones to accept the responsibility for the apology. Who else will do it? Certainly not those who have long gone. All nations move on in their life carrying with them the glories and good from their past. If they do that, they must also carry the sins and pains of that past. Otherwise the celebrating of the glories becomes an offence and a mockery.

Yes. We assume responsibility for the wrongs of the past and apologise. To do less will mean that we carry forward into our life a cancer in our heart which will never leave us. It will also become a continuing of the wrongs that were committed in the past. For the sake of our own heart and soul, not just for the sake of Aboriginal people, although that should be reason enough, we must acknowledge what has happened, express our sorrow and grief and ask for forgiveness.

It is not an onward and upward journey

While some people do experience both forgiving and receiving forgiveness as an onward and upward journey, most of us do not. We have our ups and downs, our returns to being unforgiven and unforgiving. In spite of this, the line has been crossed into a new space and mostly we like that gracious space enough to return to it and believe in it.

Living with a Bigger Dream

To live with what is, and imagine nothing more, can be quite satisfying. It is entirely possible to decide to do well that which is obviously your task, and to be the person you know yourself to be, without further aspirations. To live with a level of excellence in an uncomplicated way, can be a life well lived. Maybe the dream in that case is one of excellence itself, rather than unknown wider possibilities.

We each make choices all the time about the approach we will take to living the life which seems to be before us and within us. Perhaps here I had better explore the differences between personal ambition, competitiveness and having a bigger dream, because I believe that they are rather different. I see personal ambition as related to a desire to gain more power, status, recognition and/or money for yourself. I see competitiveness as trying to defeat and prove yourself superior to others in the pursuing of your personal ambition.

The 'bigger dream' lifestyle I see differently. For me, it is a matter of looking out on one's world, small or large, and imagining that it could be expanded in helpful, just and creative ways. The bringing in of this dream may involve quite small changes or it may be no less than an attempt to transform the universe. Having seen your dream, you then choose whether or not you can contribute to it, and in what way. As you choose to participate in the bringing in of the dream, your life moves from being passive, from being formed by others and by life itself, to being active and even passionate. You become a universal participant (even in your small place) rather than an individual who views life by looking into yourself and your own interests.

Of course, if you are working towards the bringing in of a bigger dream, you may become known as a person who takes initiatives, who thinks widely and is capable of assuming responsibility. This may lead to promotion or other forms of recognition, but not for their own sake, or for your own profit.

The capacity to live from a bigger dream is not related to age or degree of capability. I remember a very old woman, whose health was precarious, sitting in a group of people who were dreaming about things that they might like to see happen. She felt excluded by her age and health. Then she thought, 'What would I like to see change around me?' She realised that the potplants in her church were constantly looking droopy. She decided that her dream was to keep them watered. And so she did. In doing so, she helped to create an environment for everyone else which imaged sustained life and energy and she offered ongoing life to a part of the cosmos. She became part of her own bigger dream and participated in a bigger dream with others.

Another very incapacitated person who couldn't even leave her home and who was dependent on others for almost everything, tried to think how she could share in the life of the world. In the end, she decided that she could listen carefully to the radio and pray for something each day, remembering the needs of the person or situation and sending forth her love and caring. Because she became better informed than most, by her listening, she also began to share her concerns with those who cared for her, encouraging them to write letters, make their views on the matters known and join her in caring. None of us will ever know what that old woman achieved, but I suspect it was more than any of us recognised.

I do know that she lived with power and participation, that she respected herself and that others were filled with respect for her.

Obviously, we each have to decide whether there is anything more to life than we can see before us. I believe that there is always a dream, a vision of something new which can be found in every situation. I observe in history that it is the imagination and dreams of people which have carried us forward in every generation. People not only do adventurous things like reaching the moon and climbing high mountains because they are there. They also live in poverty, slavery and oppression and believe that justice could prevail. If you like, they begin to climb the high, almost impossibly high, mountain towards justice, because they believe that justice is there and it can be reached. With no signs that this could be possible and against enormous odds, they hold to their dream and they change the world.

Who could have imagined that in our time, apartheid could be ended and the Berlin Wall brought down without total warfare? Having said that, the ending of apartheid, in particular, was a very costly dream from which to live. Who would have believed that Mahatma Gandhi could have led the Indian people into independence? I visit India today and see the millions of people, members of a culture where there seems to be multitudes of strongly held theories about everything. I remember that he did not have the advantage of television to transmit his views, nor much literacy in the population, and yet he did it and independence was achieved.

Who could have imagined that the people of the Philippines would overthrow the Marcos regime, even if that has not yet brought in more than partial justice? Everything seemed stacked against them in power, in military might and in powerful international friends. Because I had some friends in that struggle, I saw the remarkable developments of ordinary people clustering in sectors of employment, class and interests and organising themselves together to be a powerful force for justice. I saw the coalitions of the groupings of people, who joined in absolute and costly determination to end the oppression.

I do not idealise any of this, of course. There were power struggles within power struggles and sometimes some ruthlessness, even on the part of those who stood for justice. But, with all that, some change for the good was achieved. So many people, known and unknown, have lived lives larger than seemed possible.

Not all of us are prepared to be captive to what is sometimes defined as 'the rational'. Those who do not encourage larger dreams sometimes refer to themselves as having that quality. But are they really rational? Or are they simply pessimistic or cynical? I think they are the latter because a truly rational — that is, based on the facts — view of history and humanity would tell us that bigger dreams and their living out are often possible. It is actually irrational to underestimate possibilities.

One of the most underestimated possibilities is that human beings can be inspired to new heights of compassion, generosity, justice and reconciliation. So many institutions and governments preach us bad news about ourselves. They offer us a doctrine of scarcity. They convince us that we have little to share with others, that we can't cope with differences in others, that we can't afford equality and that our neighbour at home and at work is our enemy who is trying to take what belongs to us. This makes us believe that compassion, kindness, justice, generosity and openness to diversity are scarce in us and that meanness is a virtue. 'Charity begins at home' they say, as though it is a biblical quote. In fact it is not and it is not the whole of the quotation. 'Charity begins at home, but does not end there' is the full quote.

Of course, many of us then, in response to this leadership, believe that nothing more can happen because it is in our interests to collude with this low view of ourselves. But humanity and its soul is never fixed. One decade we are killing Jews, disabled people and homosexual people in gas ovens and in the next we cannot imagine ourselves doing so. One day we are telling ourselves that we have nothing to spare and how dare any government think of raising our taxes, and in the next minute we are finding millions of dollars in our pockets for others in response to some catastrophe.

In our country, we will always remember our soldiers who went up a cliff face to certain death on foreign soil in response to the order of a country other than their own. At that moment, bizarre though their reasons may seem to be now, they acted as people who believed that they needed to offer their lives for something bigger than themselves. They found in themselves courage and preparedness to pay a price greater than they ever could have imagined. However their dream looks from the vantage point of history, they had one and they were prepared to die for it. We honour that, because we know that disinterested good, love for other which calls us to offer ourselves at cost, is the highest form of human life. Fortunately, we are not all called to die for that.

How is the dream discovered?

The beginning of discovering a dream is to decide to live as though we are looking for one. That may seem obvious, but I don't think it is. Lots of people don't, and are surprised when you suggest that they might. This is understandable if life is a struggle for survival anyway and has not appeared to offer anything beyond more struggle. Some people genuinely live with very little hope around them. Having said that, hope is infectious. It can sometimes be a gift from those who have time for looking and whose lives are a little more privileged. Maybe it is a responsibility of the more privileged to bring dreams to the world, as long as we are prepared to pay the price of them alongside those who have more to lose.

That is definitely not to say that dreams do not lie among people who are disadvantaged. Nor is it to say that the privileged bring in dreams for those who cannot do it for themselves. It is simply to say that those who have already experienced hope, and their power to make changes, are more likely to imagine that these hopeful things can be repeated in another context. It is also to say that the task of the hopeful may well include a handover of knowledge and power to those who have less hope. That is part of the bigger dream for the privileged as it enhances our own life to do that.

When the bigger dream emerges from those who we believe could not dream because of their circumstances, then it is powerful indeed. Recently I was in Zimbabwe and visited a quite poor church whose people were mainly refugees from another African country. We sat on the concrete strips that were the 'pews'. A little girl came and snuggled up beside me. She took my hand with confidence and peered with earnest curiosity into my white face, which was obviously very interesting to her. We listened to the magic of a group of young men whose choir singing would have been worth paying to hear in my country. They sang of hope and a new world where things would be different for all people.

After the service, one of the members of the choir asked if I could put them in touch with a youth choir in my church back home. I thought for a while and then had to admit that I didn't know of too many youth choirs in my church. The young man looked amazed and said, 'But what do they do?' He was really asking me how we could live without singing? My whole visit to that church was a challenge to my lack of hope because their hope arose from seemingly hopeless experiences of life.

Certainly, those whose lives are not lived in constant struggle for survival, often have clues about influencing systems which they can contribute to the corporate bringing in of the bigger dream. There was a period in my life when, as a woman who dreamed of change for all women, I became a token woman on many committees and councils of both the church and a political party.

If I gained the position of 'token woman' on all these bodies, it was partly because, with a lot of support from others, I had developed the confidence to rise to my feet and say something. I was also a rather formidable person in a debate. I suspect that was because I was one of five children, with a father who did not like overt anger but encouraged vigorous intellectual debate on political and religious subjects. We five fairly bright children became very quick and sharp thinkers in our debating demolitions of each other and our parents.

Anyway, in participating in the decision-making bodies of the church and a political party, I learned a lot about systems, how they worked, how to use them to the advantage of my cause and what political strategy for change was all about. In all innocence, I became a power broker and gradually, without my seeing it, a negotiator for my own power.

Fortunately, I had honest friends who challenged me with this and, to cut a long story short, I went through several years of downward mobility in personal power. At the end of that process (although the consciousness of the need to watch for oppressive power within myself will remain with me until I die), I realised that I would often have skills to bring to change processes, because I had some understanding of institutional power and systems. In working to change the world for those who are less fortunate than myself, while I cannot enter their suffering, I can sometimes bring these skills.

In developing dreams, one can sometimes try to do it alone, but even if that is your plan, it is always wise to test your ideas with others. They may have real insights to offer. They may challenge what turn out to be flaws in your dream, perhaps due to inexperience or lack of imagination or information. They may also give you support, or not. Having said that it is good to listen to experience, I am always cautious about taking the comment, 'Oh, we tried that ages ago and it didn't work' at face value. It may come from someone who tried to stop the last effort.

You need to look to see if the original effort was well planned, well resourced and well executed. Maybe there are different balances of power now? Maybe you actually have a better way of doing it? Or maybe it is something worth trying to change over and over again — for as long as it takes. That must be your decision.

I always think that group efforts to bring in a dream are by far the best idea. There are so many checks and balances in a group and so many resources for debriefing and sustaining everyone in the effort. My most significant experience of this was in the early days of the Women's Movement. We were a small group of feminists who were trying to bring change mainly in the church, although we had wider agendas than that. When we began, we were twelve women. (Very appropriate, we thought!) After a few years, we had a group of about twenty active women. Most of us had significant family responsibilities and the others were mostly in full-time work.

International Women's Year, in 1975, was approaching and we heard that our government was going to make grants to women's groups for projects in order to acknowledge the year. We decided to apply for some money. We couldn't decide what sort of project would be likely to get funding, so we decided to dream a large dream and apply for money for lots of projects, with the thought that the odd project might be funded.

My memory is that we informed the government department that we wanted to hold an International Conference for Christian Feminists in the Pacific and another for Australian women and to bring out an internationally known speaker for these conferences. We wanted to hold a series of seminars on women's issues at Sydney University and publish the papers from them, to prepare a series of 'popular' pamphlets on a number of issues, and to publish a book on the unwritten history of women in the Australian church. All of this we planned to do in one year. We thought big and asked for $35000 to fund our projects. We expected to be granted something towards one or some of these suggested projects. Instead, we were given the first grant and we were funded for them all!

And we carried them all out — only publishing the book ran through into the next year. I must say, we were rather quiet for a long time after that! But we did it, and many good things flowed from our energetic and large dreaming. We learned that a few women can carry out big things, if their dream is large enough. Some years later, we were influential in the formation of the beginnings of the Uniting Church in ensuring that the old pattern of token representation on decision-making bodies for women was ended. None of us who was in that group ever doubted that we could go far beyond our perceived energy and hope and that things could be changed, by us.

What happens if differing dreams emerge in a group? A lot depends on what sort of group it is. Maybe the group is loose knit and is not worried about diverse dreams. Most groups, especially church and political groups are, however, rather disturbed by diversity. It is as though the unity of the group is dependent on negotiated consensus on the dream. Sometimes differing dreams are experienced as a critique, one of the other — and, of course, they often are that. However, unless one dream is a violation of the other, breaching the understood ethics of the group, it can be possible to stand back one step and put everything on a larger canvas for reflection.

There were times in our Sydney parish when we needed to stand back and tell ourselves that the vision for a new world was so far beyond our achieving and understanding that there were worlds of room for different initiatives. We could decide to spend more and more time debating strategies, or we could free each other to 'have a go' and see what happened in response. We decided that to endlessly reflect was self-indulgent and that the task was to encourage each other to take on the task, however we saw it.

We did, of course, make helpful and sometimes less than helpful comments, but the general idea was to be supportive of each other in moving. It was at times, remarkably freeing and exciting.

Some people did public things like wiping our racist graffiti or holding demonstrations or vigils, others were always collecting signatures for petitions or letters to editors or politicians. Some people organised seminars or concerts to raise funds, others did hands-on acts of serving people in the community or visiting the lonely. Some people opened their homes for group discussion and prayer or support and others were active in their workplace or joined groups like Amnesty International or a political party. The stories of all these activities were shared with everybody over morning tea after worship so that the whole group could encourage each other and newcomers could join some activity.

This freeing of diversity sometimes challenges the concept of living from an ideology. I am by nature and experience a person who has been attracted to living from ideologies. Just as I like to struggle with theology, ethics and world views on things in general, so I like to try to formulate coherent ideas about how systems work for the good of the world. I am less sure about that approach to the bigger dream than I once was. I have seen so many ideological believers turn into fundamentalists, of the right and of the left. On the other hand, I would want to sustain the analytical thinking that produces ideologies. A continuing analysis about the way systems can be changed, who they sustain in power and who they disadvantage is, for me, essential for those who work with bigger dreams.

Can non-religious people have dreams? There should be no need to ask this question. If I ask it, I ask it from within the institutional church in order to acknowledge our frequent failure to respect others. Of course non-religious people have dreams for themselves and for the world. In stating this, I am not about to say that God works through non-religious people, whether they know it or not, although I would always claim that God is active in the world outside the church, often in ways which the church does not recognise.

My experience is that as we stand alongside each other as human beings, we bring our own truth to, and from, our view of the world. Our claims for the source of our dreams are somewhat irrelevant, although interesting and challenging. The question that faces us, as we live alongside each other, is more about the truth of the dream than its source.

If it is a good vision of what might be, there is no reason why we can't support each other in sharing in bringing it into reality, whatever our religion, non-religion or ideology. After all, even if we believe in a commitment to God, surely only fundamentalists would believe that God is a not a coalitionist.

Some of the most insightful and creative dreams I have been part of have come from people who had no connection with institutional religion. If religious people wish to challenge the dreams that lie outside religion, in order to convince people of the existence and worth of their God, then their dreams must be seen to be more just, true and loving than others. I am not suggesting that this becomes a competition, but that the denial of the authenticity of other people's dreams is not a worthwhile occupation.

Sustaining the living of the dream

I remember a conversation I once had with a leader of the struggle for justice in the Philippines during the Marcos regime. He had been visiting a 'radical' group in Australia and had shared some time with us. I might say that the group thought it was rather excellent in its commitment to, and action for, social justice. He said to me, 'Changes will be hard to make in this country.' I asked him why and he answered, 'Because you work for change as a hobby. When you get tired of doing it, you go on to something else more interesting.' He added, 'You mostly seem to like the romantic and exciting but more comfortable bits. You don't see that change often comes through faithful commitment to the boring tasks and also preparedness to pay the price of change.'

We agreed that if you live in a country where oppression is widespread and obvious, the need to commit yourself to change, or otherwise, is a much sharper and more daily question. Many people can live in countries like Australia and never even hear critical questions of justice, and others of us can feel quite heroic and virtuous when we make an even minor commitment to a bigger dream. It is always hard to sustain the dream when you are relatively comfortable. Having said that, it is much, much harder to sustain it if the cost of sustaining it may be your life.

Perhaps we could sustain our efforts for longer if we invited all sorts of people to share in our vision. We could involve people who are good at being faithful in small things. Some people, because they don't feel competent at writing or speaking and don't want to engage in all sorts of activities like protests, feel they are not worthy to join movements for change when, in fact, there are many layers of things to be done. It is also good for the souls of those of us who are elitist, to find that talking or meditating over endless and seemingly mundane 'hackwork' can be a valuable thing to do!

Before I reflect further on sustaining the work to bring in the dream, it is important to recognise that sometimes bigger dreams lead to nothing more than frustration and disappointment. We all know people who live all their lives believing that they should have done better, never measuring up to their own, or someone else's, expectations. Perfectly competent and good people can feel a depressing failure in that context. Very often this feeling of failure is related to someone else's ambitions for the person concerned, as against a dream for the wider good.

I remember, during the struggle for the ending of the Vietnam War, going to visit a young man who was threatening suicide, in fact he had already made a serious attempt. He was a truly beautiful young man, handsome, with lots of friends, successful at school and his father was a millionaire who was also concerned for justice and peace. The young man was gravely concerned for the peace of the world. He had a deep and painful longing for justice. He believed that neither of those hopes would be realised, no matter how hard he tried to bring them in. We spent a great deal of time with him on that night, reflecting with him on his hopes and fears. He lived for that night but, not much later, he successfully committed suicide.

The way we move beyond this risk, and the way we sustain the work towards the dream is to continually reinstate life as corporate. If you image the bringing in of the dream as individualistic, with yourself at the centre, then you are most likely to feel either a failure or unable to continue because you are discouraged and exhausted. If you can see a picture of yourself as a little, but unique speck in the great continuum of human endeavour, stretching into the past and into the future, then you will see yourself in perspective. Of course, because it is unique, then your tiny little contribution matters, but the bringing in of the dream is not dependent on you.

This gives you permission to rest, or give to yourself a smaller dream for a while. When I do this, I always imagine myself being carried along on a soft cloud by the other dreamers, while they keep walking the journey. This means that I am not left behind, or rejected, but respectfully given a break. I don't just assume this is happening. I tell my friends that I need them to do that for me. This gives me permission and understanding and them permission to ask the same of me at another time. It also leads to a healthy sharing between us about the going being tough.

One of the best freedoms I experienced in the struggle for women was the moment when I decided that I didn't have to fight every battle. Even if there appeared to be no one present to take up the struggle, I could leave it to someone else, somewhere else, even in another generation. I could let someone call women

'men', or forget that they had no women on a committee without rising to my feet and protesting. I could decide that I was saving my energy for a bigger issue or acknowledge, with self-respect, that I had no energy for any struggle at that moment. What a liberation!

It was sometimes not easy to live with that degree of liberation, but I found it infinitely renewing and so much more self-respecting. What I also found was that people, usually men, often came up to me afterwards and said, 'I thought you would be on your feet about that [whatever the issue was], Dorothy?' It gave me some satisfaction to respond by saying, 'Well, obviously you saw the issue at stake, my friend. So why didn't you take responsibility for challenging yourself? Or do you believe that only women struggle for justice for women?' It is perilously easy to become the one who is seen as strong enough to continually fight all the battles while others sit on the sidelines. Even though they sit, their cheering (more often than not, silently, in my experience) is not a healthy situation for you, or for them, or for the cause.

Of course, to change from fighting every battle personally depends on moving from the belief that you are the Messiah, the saviour of the world. I lived for a while having some thoughts about myself which were not far from that. When you articulate it, the idea sounds absurd. But if your life begins to move as though nothing can be solved without you, then the question about who you think you are is firmly in front of you. It is a great thing to move way from being a closet god. Probably makes you a more pleasant and human person too!

The sustaining of balance in living life on the way to a dream is critical. I will discuss the concept of play in another chapter. Suffice to say here that balance is part of wholeness. It sustains everything better, including the journey to the dream and holds us into humanity.

Another common response from those who are messianic in their endless and relentless pursuit of the dream, is burnout and despair or cynicism. These ideas about sustaining struggle for a dream relate to groups as well as individuals. The world is permeated with radical groups that are corporate saviours of the world. They are often very grim and boring groups too. Many of them collapse in a heap after a while because they either rip each other apart or give up in sheer exhaustion.

Some of their members decide that the development of their inner life in meditation, or something like that, is the only way to go. In this last, they are partly right, as long as it is not a permanent escape from the dream. I exclude from this conviction those people who seem to have a calling in life to live in seclusion and contemplative life. They are often very highly informed people who give their inner energies to a different sort of contribution to the dream. That would not be my choice for a whole life, but it may well be for others.

AN imaging that I find valuable in moving from a messianic view of myself is one which I find in Christianity — others may find it elsewhere. It involves a belief in the ultimate victory of life and love, in the Christian view, a victory which is already won for us. This idea is often referred to as the living from a new world which is 'now, but not yet' and which Christians see as part of the paradigm portrayed in the crucifixion and resurrection of Jesus. It involves living 'as if' something is already in place. In other words, you live with justice, even if justice is not yet brought in. You claim the ground for it by the way you live, but you do not see yourself as a single agent for change, just one who demonstrates a change that will one day be visible and in place for all people.

This theology is called 'eschatology'. I believe that at its most helpful, it gives us a sense that we are participating in a great and long-term effort to make real something that was always meant to be and always will be. This means that we are on the side of reality — a reality which says that the apparent victory of evil is only temporary, that there is, built into the universe, a more final statement of reality — that love and life are stronger and will prevail. We can be part of that greater reality, whether others acknowledge it or not and it gives us encouragement and hope, even when we cannot see anything change and our efforts seem to fail.

This is quite different from what is called 'apocalyptic theology', which has as its base a judgment, sometimes final and at other times simply at a future unknown date — a return of Jesus Christ (or someone else) who will come and punish the bad people and gather up the good for reward. This theology appears in the Bible in books like the Book of Daniel. It is also seen in history, often in two different environments. The first is when a group or nation of people live under such oppression that they can see no way to move in relation to establishing their liberation. Such is their despair that they live from a hope which they can only perceive coming from a dramatic intervention of their God when their enemy will be defeated and they will be saved. This formation of theology and world view is understandable and I would not presume to be its critic, not having lived in such oppression, powerlessness and hopelessness.

The second form is related to people who live in comfort and often privilege and who do little to bring in bigger dreams of good for others. They await an 'end of the world', when God will bring in all justice. This justice usually includes a reward for them as the chosen and punishment for all their perceived enemies. I regard this theology as having little to do with either God or justice, or responsible living, for people who believe they are religious. This is not the bigger dream from which we live, but the bigger dream of our own defining, when we believe someone or something else will hand it to us on some heavenly plate.

'Civil disobedience', which is a particular form of non-violent action often portrays the good demonstrating of the life which is the coming new life. This is not always so, as sometimes it is an act of freedom to protest and does not image the change. However, a good example of the demonstration of the new life happened when Martin Luther King led his people onto the buses, where the seats were segregated. They occupied any seat they chose and that was a re-imaging of equal and just public transport, even though the laws had not changed.

Another time it might be a matter of shifting your own lifestyle to, for example, an environmentally sustaining lifestyle, even though no one else around you follows your example. It is clear that your small action will not save the planet, but you are choosing to live as though that is possible. Sometimes actions like this also reveal the nature and malevolence of the forces which are opposed to such good change, and that in itself, can encourage others to join with those who have the dream for good. They suddenly see the end result of the activities of the forces against change, and the behaviour of the people concerned, in a radical contrast.

Sustaining a bigger dream is also about encouraging those who will image hope for us. These people are often the artists, the singers and musicians, the playwrights, the preachers and the prophets who rehearse, in inspiring ways, what a new world would look like. They also honour the pain of the struggle by symbolising it, holding it before us so that we know someone sees it. It is an irony that in hard times, in cultures like that of Australia, we are likely to reduce our support funding for the very people who would sustain us. We fall for the falsehoods of the 'rationalists' who tell us to be practical and save our money for more obviously material things. If you visit people who have really suffered, like the people of southern Africa, it is not difficult to be convinced that their songs and drums have carried them through their tough journey.

ANOTHER way of lifting hearts is, as we go on our personal journeys of survival, to consistently mark the times of hardship and the times of small gains towards the dream. This is to make significant all that happens to us. It affirms that we are on an actual journey, not simply standing in one place and that we are on it together. I have included a Christian liturgy of this type in the last section of this book. It can easily be adapted to suit other spiritualities and belief systems. The giving of gifts to each other is part of this marking. This is not only a generous thing to do, it also by its action states that we are not simply about very concrete hopes in our bigger dream — we are about life that is gifted, beautiful and gracious.

Life with a bigger dream is writ large on all fronts. It is painted vividly in many colours, to change the metaphor. We hope more strongly, weep more strongly, are more strongly afraid and we celebrate on a larger scale. This is the life for expanded people who are nevertheless not heroes. They know that to live a bigger dream is not about being brave, but about having a little courage, here and there. This courage arises, paradoxically, from the sharing of one's fear with other people who are also often afraid.

It comes from the recognition that ordinary human people can together find new things within themselves and can participate in the creating of a new world. It comes, for those of us who are religious, from finding that new things can also come from God, if we will wait expectantly for them. As we become participants in a bigger dream, we often receive the gift of seeing our own personal lives in a bigger perspective too, and this gives us a greater sense of hope about ourselves.

Living in Community

I BELIEVE that life is essentially — that is, of its essence — corporate. In societies such as ours in Australia, it is hard to sustain the essentially corporate nature of life. Capitalist systems are really based on the opposite value system. In this system, we have underpinning assumptions about our life, which tell us that we are in competition with each other. We are taught that this is healthy and the source of excellence. Individualism is highly regarded and personal autonomy is made a semi-sacred right. We applaud those who have made it on their own. Independence is the sign of strength and we are careful to try to owe nobody anything. (Except in formal arrangements with money!)

Some other cultures regard a lot of this as rather pitiful and strange. They see us as in a sort of breakdown of society and engaged in dangerous living. They view our efforts to survive in such a system as odd, while at the same time being tempted by the seductions of greedy living. I recall a young woman I found drifting around aimlessly in an Asian country which I was visiting. She had been funded to staff an international aid project by a well-meaning Australian agency to facilitate 'small group' work in this Asian country. No one had thought to ask the people there whether that was a needed project in their country.

When she turned up and tried to describe why she was there, people were truly amazed. Why did you have to teach people to work in small groups? They were always in small groups — over every family meal, in the village under a tree, in the local leaders talking, in the women as they gathered around their daily tasks, in their religious groups and political groups. What was there to learn and why would someone be paid to teach them? How could life go on if people did not talk all the time in small groups? These societies could not imagine acting without talking together.

They had almost no institutions for caring for the old, the disturbed or the people with disabilities. They had little welfare for the care of the poor and vulnerable. I am not suggesting that none of these resources was needed, but that the support systems existing in their corporate life were infinitely stronger than ours. This meant that they survived in the midst of truly terrible deprivation and oppression.

Another face of a corporate view of life which works well in terms of supporting the vulnerable, exists in some of the Scandinavian countries. There it is assumed that good citizenship and community life involves a high level of taxation so that the majority of people are cared for by everyone. This is widely accepted and people believe that everyone benefits from such sharing of financial resources in a universal covering for need. This is what good citizenship means and it is not appropriate to do tricky things to avoid or evade one's share in supporting the community system of care. While I am sure that even there, some people are not so committed to the common good, the general populace assumes that this level of corporate life is part of their culture. I mention these things to indicate that what some cultures assume to be 'normal' is not seen as that in another culture.

As I have written this book, I am aware that at every point on the rigorous journey of life, I have not travelled alone, nor could I have done so and survived. Lonely heroism is not a virtue, it is a worry. Fierce and proud independence is actually neuroticism. Survival of the fittest is a ruthless and sick way to live for human beings. Coming through ordeals of life on your own is an aberration to be wondered at but not applauded as a way of life. Celebration is not really that, unless it is shared so that we all may be given hope. The greedy and cruel competing for the greatest personal profits in life is a destructive way to live, both to oneself and to those around us. It becomes addictive behaviour — why else do the multimillionaires need ever more money, far beyond an amount that anyone could conceivably need.

If we look at the cosmos, whatever its source of life, we can see its interweaving circles of coexistence. We can experience, to our detriment and that of the environment, the consequences of our choices on others and on the way everything works for good or for ill. When I hear discussion about extraterrestrial life, I sometimes marvel that any person could conceivably imagine that we are the only conscious life in the cosmos. Here we are, a tiny speck in one small planetary system set in a galaxy that is beyond our capacity to conceive, which is itself set in myriad other huge galaxies, and we could think we are alone! How incredible! How could we be other than part of something and among someone, however different from ourselves? Even in our very existence there is a paradigm of corporate life.

Having said all that, I am not in the least romantic about living corporately, especially in a society that is now so far removed from the sort of corporate life found in some other cultures. Nor am I romantic about some aspects of those more corporate cultures, which sometimes rest heavily on the exploitation of some of their members, particularly women and children, and whose pressures to conform to the accepted corporate culture can be very oppressive.

AT THIS stage in my life journey, I believe there are five great barriers to living in community and many other 'sub-barriers'. The five great barriers are class, race, gender, the war industry and global economics. I add to that list sexual orientation, but I have discussed that elsewhere in this book.

I became aware of class divisions when, as child and adolescent, I experienced a degree of poverty. There was enough poverty in our family for me to rarely have exactly the right school uniform and sometimes to have to miss class outings because we could not afford them. Fortunately, because we had a highly literate and literary environment in our home and a valuing of education, this sense of not being able to keep up with everyone else was significantly modified. I was also a reasonably good athlete and that helped a lot.

When I went on the big trip south from Ballarat to Melbourne to train as a teacher, I experienced the reality of the class system more powerfully. In those days, pre-school teaching was regarded as a desirable profession for young women from private schools, probably as a nice preparation for marriage. Melbourne, unlike Sydney, was a place where the school you attended was quite significant. People who attended the Greater Public Schools (very British) spoke with different accents and looked after each other when it came to employment.

I arrived at the Kindergarten Training College in Melbourne in the upper-class suburb of Kew, clad in my home-made dresses, wearing no make-up and having never been to a ball or a Head of the River Boat Race. 'What school did you go to?' I was asked about thirty times in the first hour. 'Ballarat High School,' I said, thinking I had gone to a good school. 'Oh!' they said in dismissive tones and turned away. I spent the three years of training feeling absolutely socially gauche and inadequate, but I cleaned them up when it came to exams! The experience sharpened my political and ethical interests. I decided before I left the college that I was probably going to be a socialist!

Then, for the first seven years of married life, we lived on the edge of a huge public housing area in Melbourne. About 75 000 people were settled there, in about seven years, by the Victorian Housing Commission. The people had been resettled from inner urban slum areas in Melbourne, separated from their natural support systems. They were required to have children to qualify for housing, but there were few schools provided. Most of the development consisted of virtually identical houses. There were no hospitals, pubs or social services in the area and minimal public transport. Few people owned cars.

In those seven years, I saw first-hand why the poor become poorer and the rich become richer. Everything was stacked against those people. If they missed one hire-purchase payment, their goods were repossessed. If we did the same, we were given another chance to pay. The doctors sent us an account for service, the Housing Commission people had to pay cash before the doctor would see them. Their employment in the big industrial companies nearby was always insecure. The depth of poverty was something I had never met before — they were generations poor in money handling, in home skills like cooking and buying and parenting. They had low expectations about relationship at every level, from marriage through to government. Life had taught them that they were due for almost nothing.

I saw how poverty could become systemic and reinforced through the life experience of many generations. I was fortunate to have as a minister at the time a young man called Bruce Silverwood. He did not see the solution to poverty as lying in welfare, although he saw the need for some emergency care. He saw the solutions as lying in the empowerment which comes from helping people to analyse situations and to gain strength from each other in challenging injustice, alongside education for living. Amazing things took place as we built relationships with the struggling people and worked together for justice.

In that experience, I was radicalised forever. I also knew that my class was not anywhere near the bottom of the heap. When, later, I was involved in international aid work, I saw even greater poverty but it seemed to me that what I had learned at Broadmeadows in Melbourne gave me insights into what sort of aid might really empower for change and what would simply create dependencies.

I also learned then that most people prefer nice, safe, welfare aid. They don't really want people to be liberated, just helped. Having said that, I now know I am not as radical as I thought I was. I too inhibit the liberation of others and have taken my place in the comfort of middle-class existence. However, I do know that we will never form real community in this world until there is far more justice between us, and I go on working towards that.

※

I AM not sure why I have always felt strongly about the barriers between people of different races. Maybe it was because we sometimes had people from Asia and the Pacific staying with us when I was a child and I saw what special people they were. As a painfully shy teenager, I fronted to my first school debate with trembling knees and shaking voice, simply because the topic of the debate was the White Australia Policy. I knew that I could not remain silent on this issue (and I was usually silent on most things).

The most powerful factors in taking up the race debate later in life related to two conversations. The first happened at an international conference of women who were working on 'A Woman's Role in Peace Education'. After a working group which was discussing race issues, we had to report back to a plenary session. I said to a South African woman in the group, 'Why don't we do a role play, only we will reverse roles. You play a white woman and I will play a black woman.' (I was not very aware in those days!) She said, 'I could never do that!' I said, 'Why not?' and she replied, 'Dorothy, every day of my life I have been taught that I am inferior to you. I no longer have it in me to play a white woman.' I was shocked and silenced and vowed to myself that I would not rest until apartheid was ended.

The second conversation happened in Nairobi. I was there for the Assembly of the World Council of Churches and went to visit an old friend of my husband's family. She was British and had lived first during the British regime in Sri Lanka (then Ceylon) and now as a landowner in Nairobi. Her large mansion was surrounded by parkland and she had armed black guards at her imposing front gates. She was a kindly woman who had a reputation for caring for local black children through her church. We sat at her elegant dining table and were waited on by her black servants. At one point in the meal she suddenly turned to survey one of the servants (a middle-aged man) and said to me, 'They are quite nice-looking people aren't they? They have good strong bodies and some of the women are rather beautiful.' The man stood there beside her, his face expressionless. I thought to myself, If I was that man and the revolution came, I would kill this woman first. And she would have no idea why I would want to kill her. So profound was her racism that she thought she was kind to blacks, but she had turned them into less than human beings.

Racism is something which resides in most of us, including me. I find myself using a patronising voice, or at least a maternalistic voice with people of other races. I find myself surprised about things they say and do — a sure indicator of my prejudice. When I visit Africa, I am acutely conscious of what the white race has done to its people, so often in the name of Christianity and 'civilisation'. I wonder at their grace and courtesies to us, their oppressors. There is a very long way to go before the curse of racism is ended, but we will never be a world community until it is gone.

I HAVE mentioned some things about gender injustice as a destroyer of human community in other parts of my story. My childhood life was really rather good in respect to gender equity. While there was a degree of gender role assignment, it was always assumed that the girls in the family would be as educated and were as intelligent as the boys.

I remember varying responses from people outside the family when my very clever sister, Carmyl decided to major in Physics at Melbourne University. It was not that she was stopped at any stage, there were simply points where discouragement took place and encouragement to do other 'more suitable' subjects. She, of course, went on to be a fine physicist.

My then husband, Barrie, was also committed to working hard on better male–female relationships in marriage and parenting. However, it was very clear to me that sexism was alive and well throughout our community at large and most certainly in the church. One of my most focused experiences of this was when, late in life, I attended a theological college to train for ordination. Often I was the only woman in the class in a field that had been predominantly male for centuries.

I would say something in class discussion and there would be a brief pause, as though there had been a minor interruption and the discussion would go on as if I had not spoken. I spoke more assertively and they would say things like, 'No one thinks like that!' Then, sometimes, I would do better than them at exam time. This seemed to produce a modest change in their view of me and they would engage with me a little more respectfully. After a bit longer, they seemed to decide that I was a sort of honorary male. They would even tell me awful sexist jokes from their male culture. Then they would realise that I was a woman and become either very excited about having a woman friend or run a mile or, in some special cases, have a normal friendly and equal relationship.

At one point the women in the college got together and compared notes and found that we each had very similar experiences. We called the men together and talked with them about our experience. Some were defensive and attacking, but most of them agreed that they had never really had friend relationships with a woman. They had girlfriends and wives (they didn't admit to lovers), but not peer friendships.

I think things have changed a little since then (about twenty years ago) and I hope that, quite apart from the justice issues which lie between women and men, we will learn to be friends in the human community. Maybe if we could learn how to be friends, we would move past the power struggles which so often give permission for violence.

THEN there is war. War is a truly terrible life-destroying and community-destroying activity. I can't believe that we think that anyone really wins a war. We are all losers. For much of my life I was an absolute pacifist. As with all absolutes, however, I found that this one too could not become a rule of life for me. When I saw the level of oppressive and devastating power under which some people suffered, I could see that sometimes, the only way to remain a human being with some self-respect may be to take up arms. I saw that powerful people rarely give up power. I would always hope that armed struggle would be a last resort, but I knew that the decisions would have to lie with those who suffer, not with those who watch in comfort from outside. As the South African leader Rev. Alan Boesak said, 'Only those who stand knee-deep in the blood of the people, have the right to decide what they will do.'

However, if I include the war industry rather than war itself in my list, it is because I believe that there is another force for evil which actually creates and sustains wars beyond the normal result of human conflict and territorial ambitions. It is not by chance that the nation of Iraq, which is now seen as a dangerous power in the Middle East, was in fact significantly armed by the war industry of the United States of America. The war industry has no concern for peace or for international ethics. I believe that it feeds off minor conflicts and generates them into major war. It sells its weapons of death to anyone who will buy them. It cares not a jot whether its weapons are bought by ruthless dictators or people who struggle against them. It is all for money, and that is what matters.

The war industry also has an evil curiosity. It wonders what new devilish weapons it can create. Can it develop bombs that kill people but leave buildings intact? Yes, it can, and how convenient that will be for those who prefer to have the property rather than people. Can it invent bullets that explode inside people like many bullets, instead of just one? Yes, it can. Can it make chemicals that kill off the environment for countless years to make it easier to see an enemy? Yes, it can, and who cares about the future.

We all would have noted that in the last round of perilous engagements with the Iraqis and near war, the Pentagon was heard to say, 'Oh, good. We have some new weapons to test!' Maybe next they can work out, as they have always wanted to do, how to create a real star war, a satellite bombing of our fragile people and our fragile planet.

I take all this very seriously as a terrible threat not only to human community, but to the planet itself. I took part in the struggle to end the Vietnam War, but before that I was marching in 'Ban the Bomb' marches, which was a movement calling for global disarmament. That movement would now be reasonably respectable, unlike then when we were all called traitors and communists and spat upon as we marched. Now we have conservative governments calling for an end to nuclear testing and weaponry. That is good, but I still don't trust the merchants of war. I believe they will go on working away on other weaponry and impacting upon our capacity, or not, to keep this world in peace, or at least negotiating for peace. I believe that there is a vigilance necessary far beyond where we are at the moment and that, as we struggle to control the power of the international commodity marketeers, we need to watch more carefully the marketeers of war.

※

IF I ADD to the barriers to human community the area of the globalisation of economies, it is almost too great a concept to mention. Some people would describe it as the takeover of the economic rationalists (or irrationalists, depending on your point of view). Anything I can say about it in a book like this is almost too superficial to be worth saying. Except, to say nothing would be worse.

The globalising of anything sounds as if it, by nature, should involve the breaking down of barriers. And, of course, in some senses it does. The takeover of the world economy by powerful financial and international corporation forces does indeed crash through cultures, national media, differing workplace agreements, nationally based environmental concerns and previously assumed public sector services and policy setting.

However, I see no evidence that any of this breaking through does other than destroy many forms of community. Rather, it subjects all agendas to its own overwhelming and relentless agenda to shift wealth to a narrow group of people who will try to control the rest of us. These people form the equivalent of a 'closed shop', in that they, firmly but informally, establish the 'going rate' for top executive salaries. They separate themselves from all other forms of workers by determining that they are due to earn millions of dollars a year and receive huge rises in salaries. Most of them also pay almost no taxes — a greedy refusal to participate in community responsibility.

The activity of this wealthy sector tends to divide and rule — to set worker against worker, rural against city, poor against poorer, indigenous against non-indigenous, technologically resourced against those who are not and the public sector against the private sector. It seems to me that, as this rationalisation continues, it is gradually making a fundamental shift in the balance of rewards between those who actually do the work and those who can afford to hold the shares. When the key agenda in life is based on greed, our commitment to justice and community is sorely tested and most of us succumb to its temptations to some extent. In the end, this system must surely implode and destroy itself, but it will take with it millions of suffering people.

Most of us are just beginning to perceive the enormity of the agenda and to feel the dimensions of our powerlessness against the forces that are prevailing in ways which are not answerable either to the people or to their elected governments. However, in the face of this, you can already discover the new networks of determined people of goodwill whose goal it is to reclaim a civil society where systems and people work for the common good, for the rebuilding of community.

Trying to form community

Having said that about these five huge barriers to world community, I would also like to say something about trying to form community in general. I have been part of many groups and institutions which have tried to live in more creative community, and I know well why they basically give up their dreams. In sharing the following stories of attempts and learnings, I will be drawing on experiences in my own culture. I would not presume to try to describe what I think I see in others, except as I have already done in pointing to more general impressions.

The nuclear family is one obvious form of community life. As others have said before me, it is a relatively recent development in corporate living. It is a vulnerable unit because it relies so heavily on the one pivotal relationship of wife/husband and usually mother and father. If that relationship is under pressure or breaking down then the whole small group is at risk. If one, or both, of the people at its centre are in trauma from outside forces and try to draw all their support for survival from the other central person, it can put a huge load on an already relatively stretched relationship.

One new factor that often challenges nuclear families is the prevailing economic necessity of having two incomes for survival. I am not here advocating the return of women to full-time work in the home. I am rather suggesting that, in a household where there are children, if both adults need to work full-time for economic survival, it sometimes puts intense pressure on the relationships, health and well-being of all concerned.

The weakness in any blood family grouping, in looking at the forming of more general human community, is that it tends to be exclusive and excluding. It is not really the model for human existence because mostly its boundaries are closed to others and it sometimes reinforces excluding views of life and relationships with others. It tends to 'look after its own'. This is not always so, of course. Those of its members that it rejects often don't find their place in the wider community because the blood family rejection is somehow one which defines their sense of themselves.

Sexual and physical abuse within the nuclear family — which is prevalent in our society — is something from which many people never recover, so great is the betrayal of the community unit. Many people stay long in this unit experiencing continuing abuse and violence because they need to try to make the family 'work' and there is little support outside it that they can see.

In saying all this, I am suggesting that most nuclear families would benefit from being connected with a wider community if they are to survive well. Maybe, instead of thinking that the nuclear family is the primary community within the community, we should see the wider community as the primary gathering and the nuclear family as a key part of it that needs a good deal of support to survive well. If the nuclear family has a healthy loving relationship at its centre and is surrounded by close relationships with others, so that the intensely focused responsibilities and loads can be shared and spread around at times, then it can be a good little life-giving group of people. It can also be the place in which forms of community are taught, including social responsibilities and human rights.

Contrary to some often voiced opinions, I would say that one of the tests of the health of nuclear families is whether or not those families feel attacked by the presence in the wider community of people who choose to live in other forms of community. This sense of being attacked by difference and the blaming of one's problems on another group that seems to be happily living in a different form of community is often a sign of vulnerability. However, to make scapegoats of others can often inhibit the seeking of truth about the problem, which may well lie within the original and accusing group. In other words, if nuclear families are breaking down as a form of human community, we need to ask what is going wrong within the life of nuclear families rather than feeling threatened by the emergence of other community groupings for living.

History has a way of evolving all societal structures and, those that are viable are likely to survive alongside others that are life-supporting and creative. I see no problem with other groupings of people for love and support — same sex couples, older people, young people, clusters of nuclear families, people with disabilities. And if any of these groupings can gather into their care others who need care, then why not?

If I reflect on the church as an attempt at community, it is because that is the attempt at community with which I am most familiar. One of its callings and one of the claims the church makes about itself is that it is a community of faith, the Body of Christ. The concept of the body has to do with corporately imaging the life of Christ in the world. It also has to do with each part having its good and equal function in the living of life, with each gift recognised and contributing to the whole, as in a body. Some are the arms, the hands, the eyes, the ears, the feet and so on. I fancy myself as a toenail, getting around a bit on the ground, small but needed and not very fancy. On the other hand, we encourage the thought that other people discern your place in the body. (Some might think I am the endless mouth!)

Another hope which the church announces about itself is that as a sign of the power of its God in Jesus Christ, the reconciling one, it will try to model a diverse and inclusive community which, nevertheless, lives in unity. This is a bold claim, if ever there was one. And yet, it is good that the church has the courage to point to this as one of its bigger dreams, and the vision of its God for humankind.

The body concept of human community is hard to sustain because of the profound temptations which beset us in relations to power and elitism. Even those who are the most ideologically committed, the idealists, fall before the corrupting call of power. Once power is present as an insidious and often unnamed factor in a group, then gifts begin to be arranged in a hierarchy of importance.

Who really, really values the person who cleans the toilets as much as the chairperson of the group, or the one who speaks for the group in public? Who really and truly believes that the women who make the tea are as great in status as the people who vote and speak in the debates of an institution? These demarcation lines of power are revealed in a multitude of ways — their public acknowledgment, or not, for a start.

When I was one of the 'good ladies who made the supper for us', nothing used to rile me more than the patronising votes of thanks we received. I am not talking here of some paid for and formal arrangement for catering, where someone is thanked for doing a good job. I am recalling times when people gathered for a decision-making meeting and, as usual, the women offered to do the supper. The important planning and decision-making went on without us and then we were called in and thanked for our efforts. No matter what was said, it was abundantly clear that the real thing was going on in the meeting and we were the 'auxiliary' function. We even sometimes called ourselves that: 'The Ladies' Auxiliary' (which means secondary or supporting).

This does not mean that there are not some people who enjoy catering or even washing up. It means that a truly corporate life involves bringing all such people into the formation of the life of the community, asking for their views, even if they don't want to take part in the actual debate and finding ways of making decisions which are not dependent on debating skills for participation. It is at the point where we engage in the forming of community life that we reveal who is included and who is not. Powerful people are not nearly so interested in who does the work as in who makes the decisions, and it is there that real community is formed or diminished.

Of course, there is a place for the recognising of gifts in moving the community forward in its life. I have been part of church and feminist groups where so much attention was paid to processes that nothing ever got done! One of the recognised gifts may well be leadership, especially facilitating leadership, and a rotating of responsibility in this may enhance the life of the group. Good leadership often elevates the participation of a wide cross-section of people in the community and enables a satisfying sense of moving forward and achieving goals.

The identifying of good leadership and the agreement of a group in inviting that leadership can be enormously releasing. Some of us remember well some experiences of trying to work in collectives, in the early days of the Women's Movement, where no one was the leader or facilitator and we were all equal. In the end, many of us longed for designated leadership so that the undesignated and unnamed power could be challenged. There were always people who had more power than others, whether we liked it or not. They had more knowledge, more charisma or more dominating styles. If we challenged them, they said, 'What's wrong with you? We are all equal here and you have just as much right to share in the decisions as I have!' The days of the good old collectives — those were the days!

So many movements begin as free-wheeling groupings of people, as associations with a vision for good which gives them purpose and energy, and then subside into being institutions where people struggle for power. Sometimes I wonder whether that is not the way things are, a sort of cycling which flings off movements at intervals while the institution tracks on and eventually dies.

In saying this, I am not saying that we don't need institutions. Institutions tend to create order out of emerging disorder in the life of a group. They short cut the time-consuming negotiations which are needed to sustain loose-knit groups and networks and they shoulder the considerable administrative load which is required to make things happen and deliver services. In some ways, they make it more possible for the energy for movements of change to exist.

They can also give coherence and power to a body of people who want to challenge systems of oppression — one identifiable body of power challenging another. In this sense, institutions can add to the formation of good community as well as taking from it in the negative power which institutions often exercise.

When we consider diversity, we need to face the fact that it is hard to hold together in diversity — diversity of cultures, views of life (or God and faith), diversity of lifestyle and of life experience. I can think of many groups and churches to which I have belonged. We thought of ourselves as tolerant, accepting people, inclusive in our style of community. The reality is, however, that once a group of people forms, they tend to attract people like themselves — which is a much more comfortable way to group, after all. Then another sort of person tries to enter the group. No matter how accepting or tolerant we are, that person is pushing uphill among us. If the prevailing attitude is one thing, then to express the opposite is hard and alienating.

❦

THERE is also the issue of acceptance of diversity versus your commitment to what you understand as justice. For example, how much diversity can you accept in relationships between women and men if you are a feminist? Or, how much diversity can you accept in gay and lesbian lifestyles if you believe that some of it is damaging to people? How much freedom do we accept between cultures if there is mutilation of children involved? There is no easy answer to these questions if we value our own freedoms alongside that of others. If we protect our freedoms, surely we should protect that of others?

Of course, each society draws some boundaries on freedom. We are not free to drive on whichever side of the road we like at whatever speed we choose, because it puts others in danger. We do put some limits on activities which involve physical damage to people. In our country, it is a crime to mutilate your child or bash or rape your wife, even if your culture says that these activities are acceptable. When it comes to other sorts of damage, or activities or attitudes that some of us believe are destructive to others, it is more difficult.

The only way I can find to honour both cultural differences and yet make it possible for cultures to be challenged by diversity in attitudes and values, is to be committed to the building of relationships across cultures. If you build genuine and respectful relationships across differences, so that honest conversations may take place and different ideas and lifestyles can be seen, then sometimes things begin to change. I believe, however, that it is the place of those within a culture to bring in the changes apart from changes to activities which are clearly criminal. For example, a Muslim woman and myself may get to know each other. As we share our lives, I may see in her culture something that seems good to me compared to the way things happen in my culture. It is then my responsibility to carry the challenge of the new idea into my culture. She may support me from the sidelines, but the real struggle for change belongs to me. And what if things don't change? Maybe, sometimes, I might then enlist her support as we both go public in our opposition to the situation that concerns us, but I make it clear that I have invited her to do that.

After that, you move into the whole process for trying to change something, which, I would hope follows the practice of non-violence. I understand this to be:

- discussing the issue with those most concerned
- if nothing is resolved, getting some helpful mediation between you
- if this is not helpful, advising those concerned that you need to take the discussion onto a wider front, such as inviting a discussion with a representative group, council, court of the culture concerned
- if this proves unsatisfactory, advising all concerned that you need to take the discussion into the public arena.

Obviously, this process only relates to situations where there is a very important issue at stake as we try to live with diversity. The fact that we do live with diversity, however, means that often quite critical issues of justice stand between us and the formation of genuine human community, and they are far from easy to resolve.

SOMETIMES, although the dream is always to try to live respectfully with diversity, it is easier for there to be groups of relatively like-minded people interacting in regular and short-term ways with groups of people who have different ideas. In other words, if we space out the interaction a bit, it becomes more sustainable. It is a bit like the idea of living in a community household. It seems a wonderful idea until you try it. Those that succeed often try for a less intense commitment to each other — they keep things relaxed and invite in others who are close enough in style to survive.

Most of us feel more able to sustain our interactions if we can 'go home' from each other to some place where we don't have to live all the time in such a high degree of diversity. I don't see any problem with this, provided we are honest about it and can see the beauty of a wide range of diversity on the spacious and cosmic front and find regular engagement with differences a place for growing, raising questions and expanding one's world. The problems arise when we decide that community is dependent on conformity and relative sameness. It is at this stage that we become fundamentalist and define some as 'in' and 'good' and others as 'out' and 'bad', simply because they are different from us. Many groups of this type seem to actually generate their energy for staying together by creating an enemy outside. This is a very different activity from that in a group which generates its energy by focusing on a bigger dream for loving and just life and works together towards that. It is a very fine line, of course.

I could give the example of those in my own church at the moment whose focus is on defeating in the church those who disagree with them on the issue of homosexuality. They would claim that they have the bigger dream of a church which is liberated from this sinfulness in its doctrine and leadership. Those of us who oppose them would claim that the bigger dream is ours. I don't think we want to weed out our opponents and deny them their place in the church in the direct sense, but of course they may well feel that our powers of persuasion and influence make it impossible to stay.

In the debate in my church, I would ask those who want to exclude homosexual people what it is that they think is destructive to the life of the community, either the church or the general community? Even when you use the Bible as an authority on godly community, it needs to make sense, not just be a rule which we are required to carry out because it is there. I can see antisocial behaviour in both the heterosexual and homosexual communities. In relation to anti-social behaviour in the heterosexual community, we work for transformation and only reject people from our community if they are truly destructive. I see no reason why the same approach should not be appropriate with homosexual people. I see no harm at all done to the life of the church, and to our community in general, if I live responsibly and lovingly with a woman rather than a man.

I WOULD claim that love, truth and the forming of human community always has a commitment to inclusiveness at its base. What if those who want to be included have a lifestyle of which we don't approve? I don't believe that the dream of human community can ever be defined by setting boundaries on who may live within it. Obviously there are times when someone becomes so destructive to the life of others that they must be set apart for rehabilitation before they can return. Unfortunately we know more about punishment than rehabilitation when we try to do this, so that many people who we 'set apart' are unlikely to be able to rejoin the community as changed people more ready for human community.

I believe that exclusiveness is often about not presuming to think that we know someone. So much excluding is related to stereotyping — knowing one thing about somebody and, on the basis of that, deciding that you can put that person in a box and dismiss them, or limit what you will offer them in being part of the group. Many are the times that I have been caught out in that myself. I see a person in a wheelchair and it never crosses my mind that the person could be in a senior management position. I am challenged by someone about my sexual preference and then am surprised when I find myself in a gentle and caring relationship with them. I am befuddled by someone with a greater brain than mine and unexpectedly discover that their part-time job is cleaning houses for people who can't do that for themselves. I try to assume that I will always be surprised if I wait to know someone better and that they will be just as surprised if they wait to know me.

It is very, very hard to form and sustain in close relationship a diverse and inclusive community. We can never assume that we have achieved even a glimpse of it until people tell us that it is their community of safety and reconciliation. No one can tell another what is community for them. We can only have brave conversations about that together and keep trying.

※

THE safest community, in my view, is the deeply human one. It is a group of people who make no pretence of being special and who with a degree of humour and vulnerability share the stories of their life journey with each other. It is often a place where people can have good arguments with each other because they trust the honest kindness which is faithful in the relationship. A safe place is one where we can be ourselves and know that people will not try to destroy us.

Safe places in community do not usually stay that way for long, of course. The test of the level of safety is how honest we can be with at least some of our community. I don't actually believe that it is realistic to think that we can find genuinely close and honest relationships with everyone in a large group, or even a middle-sized one, but each person needs to feel 'known and understood' by a percentage of the group. Then there is honesty about the nature of the life of the group itself. If the safety for that breaks down then we are reduced to M. Scott Peck's 'pseudo community'. The capacity for people to feel safe enough to be honest about group life brings us back to the problem of power.

Honesty often cuts through false and damaging power, but it is more often prevented from happening by that same power. It is often a very brave person who tells the truth into a group. The child in the old story who said, 'The emperor has no clothes!' was challenging power, in no uncertain terms. The fact that a child could do that, should give us a clue about where truth is often able to emerge. It can come more freely from the young, who are usually very perceptive about the real nature of groups. It can also come from the old, who are sometimes beyond being too bothered about how they are perceived by others. Both groups have less to lose than those who lie in between.

A highlight of my life with the children of Pitt Street Church came when I was asked to have a discussion with a group of about eight ten to twelve year olds. We were thinking that one day we would prepare them to ask of themselves whether they wanted to formally join our group, the church. I decided to approach the matter by asking them what sort of group they would like to join. What would it be like? This is what they told me.

Fiona: 'I think there would need to be trust so that you wouldn't need to worry about telling people things.'

Katherine: 'There are groups at school and if you don't have one of your own, you feel awful. When I don't have a group, I pretend I am going to the library. I would like to join a group where you didn't have to pretend you were going to the library.'

James: 'A school class is a bit like a group. Sometimes the teacher tells you to look after someone who is not very nice. We all pretend we will but nobody does because, if you play with that person, nobody will play with you. I would like a group where people still played with you when you looked after people who are not nice.'

Jessica: 'I have a friend who was playing up in class because her mum and dad were breaking up. We all knew that was why she was getting into trouble but the teacher kept punishing her. You'd think that if the children knew why she was playing up, the teacher would too. I'd like a group which didn't do that to people when they are in trouble.'

Katie: 'Lots of families break up. I think you need a bigger family when your small family breaks up.'

They continued reflecting in their wise way for a while and I listened to them and wished that more adults could hear and learn. When it came to finishing time, I hardly dared to ask them whether they could imagine themselves joining Pitt Street Church! However, I did ask and waited with baited breath for their response.

'Oh yes!' they said. 'We love Sundays after the service finishes and we can run around the church galleries...and, do you know Dorothy, don't tell anyone this, but while you are all having morning tea, we go right up behind the organ and there is this little window which we can open. When you hang out of it, you can see this big lake a long, long way down and David thinks he can even get out on the roof!' (The 'lake' was a great water-filled hole left by a developer about six storeys below the roof of the church.) They then mused on the quality and quantity of biscuits that were available to them. On the whole, they thought they might join us, especially if we lifted the standard of biscuits.

I gave thanks that these were ones who could be so full of

profound wisdom one moment and in the next be the noisy, sometimes mischievous, fun children of our hearts. I looked at their growing, restless bodies, their gangly legs and earnest faces and hoped we could go on receiving truth about community from them.

F O R some people attaching themselves to groups is not a good option. We are not all energised in and comfortable with life in a group. Most of us need reference points for testing ideas and receiving support, however. There are tight groups with high commitment and a greater sense of organisation, and then there are looser groups that people flow through. Maybe we need both, even in the church.

Much is made these days about the loss of genuine human community as we converse together electronically rather than face-to-face. Maybe there are risks that we will lose the capacity to engage in multidimensional conversations, where we not only see the words but hear the tone of voice, watch the body language, see the tears and smiles and sometimes hold the hand of the person who is speaking. However, I suspect that, for some introverted or people lacking in confidence, the Internet has opened up their chance for conversation.

There are some people who, for many reasons, are not easy to include in groups and who are the lonely in our societies. It is a romantic notion to think that everyone can find friends and sustain relationships. However, a group that is strong and loving can often share the caring for such a person — drawing clear lines about how much they can give so that the person is not given false hopes and promises, and simply being faithful in what they can genuinely offer. The resources for the survival of vulnerable people who are less easily included in human community are, I believe, not given to individuals but to groups.

In all my life in the church, I have looked for the above experiences of community. The church is a fragile, failing very human bunch of people, however, and most of us only catch glimpses of the Body, the unity and the image of Jesus Christ. As long as we own this, maybe we will not betray people so badly, but sometimes we pretend that we are who we are called to be.

The politics of community

Community life is not dependent on politicians. However, governments can diminish or enhance community. It is usually through our governments that we set up policies which indicate what sort of community we are. Are we a community which cares for its vulnerable and weak? Do we trust that the people in general can form our life or are we bringing into being a 'guided' democracy? Do we allow ourselves to learn and grow by our corporate mistakes and successes, or do we abrogate that right and hand it over to an elite? Do members of our community know their power and their ways of participating in the formation of community life, or are they imbued with a sense of powerlessness? Are we so trusting of our community that we do not have to store up personal provisions for all eventualities, or do we have a fundamental sense of being on our own?

A community which exists in reality is proud of the utilities, properties and services that it builds up for the common good. It understands that this adds to its life rather than taking from its individuals. I heard a lecture once from Dr David Wells of the University of New England in New South Wales. He spoke of the concept of 'The Commons' in England — the common property at the centre of many British towns and villages. When the commons were set up, people were concerned about who would care for them, but the people found that, if they each and all shared the responsibility, it was to the benefit of everyone.

This understanding of what lies at the centre of community — that which is cared for by each and for all — is one which is rapidly slipping in many societies of today, including ours. 'User pays!' we cry, instead of seeing that many things which we sustain together simply enhance our corporate life and turn us into truly civil people. 'Use pays' is, I believe, not a virtue in forming community. Assuming appropriate responsibility so that we can live peacefully, kindly and justly together is the virtue. The user may have lesser or greater resources to pay, for all sorts of reasons. The user may become a kinder person in sometimes paying for another, and the one who receives the generosity may become a quite special member of the community because he or she has received unearned kindness.

Yes, a minority of people will always take advantage of the goodness and generosity of others. This will not matter too much if we are good and generous for the reason that it enhances our own life together. If a few less deserving others benefit from our generosity, well so be it. If we are finding that more and more people are trying to avoid their due responsibilities in the social system, we might ask ourselves whether the social system is not breaking down. Why are so many people alienated, resentful and non-participatory in the well-being of society? Are there some basic injustices elsewhere that are hidden, or even affirmed, with no action taken against them, that these people resent — like the rich paying almost no taxes? Are they being told that they are bludgers and lazy layabouts during a period when they genuinely tried to find work to pay their way? Are they people who have been abused in ways that no one has dealt with or recognised? Was their education for life under-resourced and their youthful environment deprived? Are they generally regarded as inferior human beings because of class or race or lifestyle?

In response to lack of community responsibility, you can set up more policing of various types, or you can use the same expensive resources to try and engage in real dialogue with those concerned and repair the breakdown in relationships. Most modern societies go for the policing because it satisfies our 'righteous' anger against such antisocial people, it gets them out of our way and asks less of us in social responsibility. We all pay the price in the end though, because our community becomes less and less a civil and safe place for us all.

Professor Klaus Offe, of the University of Berlin, in a recent lecture on the Civil Society, suggested that community is based on a balance between the life of the state — the judiciary, the legislature and the administration of public resources and services; the markets — the commerce of life and the interchange of products and skills; and the community of the people in general — that is their gathered history, values, mores, religions, cultures and general perceptions of themselves. Academic and social commentator Eva Cox responded by saying that, in a sentence, 'if the state becomes too strong you get a Stalin, if the markets get too strong you get the Mafia, and if the community becomes too strong you get a Bosnia'. The holding of the balance is dependent on a continual discourse between people in all the sectors of life — checking how life is for all and sharing ideas for its betterment.

There are many other paradigms, which we need to keep exploring for the developing of human community. If there is one thing that is clear as we end the twentieth century, it is that the ideologies for the forming and sustaining of human community with which we entered this century have all failed us. Probably all of them had some truth within them, but not enough. How we carry forward the best things that resided in some of our failed ideologies is a question for us all.

How we preserve the necessary critical analysis of our life without trying to formulate fixed ideologies from our analysis, is another difficult question. It seems to be part of our human condition to try to describe utopia and the way it will be created for us and then insist that we know and that other ideas must be destroyed. Maybe we will know we are somewhere near a good idea about the way societies are sustained when the one we uphold does not need an enemy to destroy.

Moral and Ethical Living

MY DAUGHTER Melissa's philosophy dictionary tells me that the meanings of morals and ethics are not unalike. However, morals, which are linked with 'mores' are more focused on the ordering, the rights and wrongs for individual behaviour and often have a religious underpinning. Ethics has to do with 'ethos', is less likely to have a religious base and has more to do with the interrelationship of people in the enacting of, hopefully, moral behaviour. In many cultures today, including ours, it seems to be more attractive for people to claim that they are ethical rather than moral. To be moral has a more rigid, religious and dogmatic feel about it.

Maybe this is why in these days, in my experience, we don't hear much explicit talk of morality or immorality, except by people known as the Religious Right. In the past it was often mentioned, usually by those who believed that they were moral people. 'Immoral people' were likely to steal, tell lies, drink, gamble, commit adultery, visit prostitutes, be homosexual and be generally socially unacceptable.

Often the discussion was initiated by Christians who wanted to define sinners, or sin. There were differences of opinion about that, particularly across Protestant/Catholic lines. In my childhood and adolescence, if you were a Methodist, you were taught that drinking alcohol, gambling, dancing, and playing sport on a Sunday were wrong. These were things that Catholics did. If you were Catholic, you were taught that using birth control was wrong and that you should not eat meat on Fridays, among other things. There was some agreement, however. We were all, in the religious environment, taught that we should not steal, kill, commit adultery and have sex before marriage.

Some of the moral rules changed over the years, or at least were seen as more ambiguous than we had thought. Methodists were allowed to dance, drinking alcohol was viewed differently by many people, and Catholics ate meat on Friday.

These days, even if we don't often talk about morality as such, I suspect that we do mostly have some sort of moral code in our heads and we use code words to describe that. We might say that we are 'for the family' and most people will associate us with a whole range of moral values. We might describe ourselves as having a 'liberal' view of relationships and most people will assume other things about our moral stance in life.

I suspect that one of the reasons for the fairly radical shifting of views of morality in a community is linked with the possibility that few people ever describe or understand why the moral rules are really there. I sometimes think of the three generations of women represented by my mother, my daughters and myself. My mother would have been told that she should not have sex before marriage because she might get pregnant and because no man would marry her if she was not a virgin. She knew full well that both those personal consequences of such a fall from morality were likely to be true and that there would be other very powerful and punishing social consequences.

She gave me the same instructions and described the same consequences, which she assured me would be there for me if I was not moral in her terms. I thought about it all and realised that I probably knew enough about fairly primitive contraception to have a sporting chance of avoiding pregnancy. That would be a risk and I knew that a pregnancy outside marriage was something I would find impossible to face. I had also heard that it was not as easy to tell whether you were a virgin as my mother suggested. I believed, however, that most men would prefer to marry a virgin.

When my daughters and I discussed sex before marriage we had an entirely different conversation. I knew that neither of the reasons which had upheld the earlier view of morality on this issue would impress my daughters. They had access to rather reliable contraception, should they choose to ask for it. They had medical cover to pay doctors to get that advice and most doctors would hand over the information without moral comment. They knew that most of the men they were relating to would ask the same questions about their own virginity as they asked in relation to women — some of them would not find the issue an important moral one and others would believe it to be important. So my daughters and I talked about self-respect and respect of others, responsibility in relationships and not getting oneself into relationship situations that you are not ready to handle because of lack of age and maturity.

One of my daughters asked me what my response would be if she did become pregnant? I recall an earnest and somewhat anxious conversation on my part. I remember saying that, whatever happened, I would stand by her and we would look at all the options together, but I hoped that she would not become pregnant. I recall hearing her relating this conversation to her friend over the phone with some excitement. I remember imagining, very probably mistakenly, her friend then telling her conservative mother that my daughter was allowed to get pregnant!

Probably only in my daughters' generation was there a more general attempt to begin, in a modest way, to discuss why no sexual activity before marriage might possibly be a moral value, or not, as against simply warnings of punishing social consequences. This discussion mostly took place, if at all, in homes and small groups. It has still not been the subject of a broad and open discussion in the church, which is often the source of advice on this area of morality.

In the ten years of my life as a parish minister, I married only three couples who did not live at the same address prior to marriage. While I do not presume to make assumptions about that, I am sure that most of them were in a sexual relationship before marriage. Is this immoral? Maybe, maybe not. I do not intend to discuss that here. I would only say that if a new generation has moved past a moral stance of the church on this issue, it is not surprising. We did not really give morality a reason for being sustained. We seemed not to notice when the consequential reasons we were giving for obedience to our moral rule were no longer valid.

In all this I am suggesting that past generations mostly relied, and sometimes people today rely, on authority to enforce moral codes rather than the persuasion of reason or an appeal to some value or vision of society and relationships. When the old authority systems break down, the social mores based on morality, as we have perceived it, often change quite quickly. We should not necessarily blame 'the youth of today' or 'the breakdown' of the old family authority for this change. Most families had little understanding of why society and/or the churches held certain views of morality. They were simply trying to enforce morality without much personal authority standing behind it, apart from 'Do as I say' and a sense that the morality they were trying to uphold was somehow important for the common good.

So, how can we understand the building of moral systems and principles?

Even 'private' morality has to do with the ethics of a community, or a group/religious understanding of what is right and wrong. Sometimes this understanding is connected with general ground rules which seem to sustain community life, rather than being about moral absolutes. The Ten Commandments were such guidelines for the Hebrew people — a covenant agreement with their God which enhanced their life as a community and which they believed would be followed by the signs of God's blessing.

It is interesting that modern-day societies with an underpinning of Judeo-Christian influence, often refer to these Ten Commandments as though we are all clear about their relevance for our society today. 'Let us get back to the Ten Commandments, and all will be well,' we say. I suspect that few of us could recite the Ten Commandments and that, if we did know what they said, we might be surprised. For example, would most of us believe that God is a jealous God who punishes children for the iniquity of parents, to the third and fourth generation of those who reject God? Most of us do a few jobs on Sunday (let alone the Sabbath, which is a Saturday), and we expect that some of us will do paid work on Sunday so that we can travel, shop and have all the services we expect.

Slaves were presumably okay, because we were not to covet those who belonged to our neighbour, and wives were the property of husbands. Quite apart from what is there, we might ask ourselves about what is not there in the Ten Commandments — nothing much about freedoms or rights, as we would understand them. Nothing about racism or sexism. They were formulated for the people of the time and place. Some of them have stood the test of time quite well.

It is interesting that morality is nearly always registered as a prohibition — 'Thou shalt not...' Those who claim to be moral guardians for a community are often associated with stopping certain sorts of behaviour. I want to suggest that while the prohibitions may be worthy in themselves, this behaviour sometimes leads us to see morality as primarily linked with stopping the sins of others, and possibly controlling ourselves, rather than actively promoting broad aspects of good. It is not simply that people who devote their lives to the prevention of what they view as sin in others are 'wowsers' or 'spoil sports'. It is, rather, that morality becomes detached from what could be seen as the primary moral virtues such as kindness, understanding and compassion and rather become focused on the controlling of life. This detached controlling activity may be for the common good, or it may have little to do with that.

Such control also often becomes so focused on private, individual morality that corporate immorality can run unchecked and almost unnoticed. I would have to say that I don't think that this is always by chance. I observe that at times of high indignation about the immorality of certain groups, there is often cruel systemic immorality prevailing, sometimes well supported by the group involved in the moral outcry. For example, at a time when poverty is increasing and employment is decreasing, there is often moral outrage about some young person living in 'luxury' on social service benefits. At a time when there is a general breaking down in the social fabric, and a survival of the fittest, competitive social environment being encouraged, the focus will sometimes be upon 'wicked' teenagers who become single mothers. These people are seen as immoral, undisciplined and 'obviously' doing what they do to gain a sole supporting parent's benefit.

If you read novels or letters written in earlier days, this activity becomes even clearer. The 'lower classes' were regarded by their privileged 'betters' as full of unimaginable vice. This view of people is, and was, often related to those of other ethnicities and cultures. We are inclined not to recognise the morality systems that are different from our own. We therefore presume that people who are culturally different from ourselves are immoral. It is always easier to point to what we regard as individual immorality than corporate immorality. After all, discussions on individual morality usually involve pointing to the activities of someone else, rather than ourselves.

Ethical and moral living are closely intertwined

If I want to reflect on that intertwining, it is because I experience in many contexts the consequences of the behaviour of people who call for greater morality, but whose behaviour is what I would call unethical. While I am sure that all sorts of people are quite capable of this, I experience it often in connection with those whose fierce fundamentalist and moralistic view of life seems to give permission for the 'ends' to set free the 'means' from ethical constraints.

I think of people who are concerned about your perceived immorality. In order to expose this and try to make you stop what you are doing, they spread private information about you behind your back. What you are doing may well be immoral. What your attackers are doing is unethical. To be ethical, they need to speak with you directly, indicate their concern, invite change and await your response. If there is no change and they are still concerned, then they may tell you that they are about to make your private life public. Some would still regard this as unethical, but that would depend on the circumstances — the role you have in life and how much your private life impacts on the life of others.

I also think of people who give speeches about the need to get back to basic values. By this, they usually mean people working hard, not sneaking days off, paying their taxes and ensuring that their children are not taking drugs or breaking into someone else's property. At the same time, these people could be doing things like raising their own salaries, employing lawyers to minimalise their taxation, encouraging the reduction of services to the general populace and doing deals with media powers for their own advancement. They would still point to themselves as 'moral' because what they are doing does not fall within the simple definitions of stealing from others. It is all legal, after all, but is it ethical?

How are ethics formed?

Obviously the formation of ethics is dependent on your beginning point, and there are many theories about their formation. I will mention only three. If I do this, it is because I found it helpful myself to have ways of exploring the formation of an ethical view about something. It was also useful to see a little more clearly where others might possibly be coming from when I disagree with their point of view.

Natural law ethics

This approach to the formation of ethical positions on various issues is commonly used by parts of the Christian church in particular, but also by some other religious people. It can sometimes be the basis for people who see life as rather fixed in its beginnings, for whatever reason. The general idea is that there is a natural state of things in the universe which is there from its origins and from which moral absolutes can be formed. An example is that God created a man and a woman to live together in marriage. Once that marriage has been entered into, it may not be ended because it is ordained by God. In order to avoid being unmerciful, the Catholic Church, for example, has a relatively complex process of annulment of a marriage. This means that it is decided that the marriage never really existed, rather than being given permission to end in divorce.

Another example is that sexual intercourse is created by God for the procreation of children and, even though it is also pleasurable, it is primarily for procreation. Therefore, if you have intercourse, you are cooperating with God in possible procreation and you should not interfere with this by using contraception. God will decide whether or not the intercourse leads to procreation, not you. That is the natural ordering of things.

Or, God said 'You shall not kill', therefore you may not abort a foetus or participate in euthanasia. In earlier centuries, the church defined a 'just' war to allow for killing in warfare. This definition cannot justify modern warfare as it contains a clause that defines a just war as not killing civilians to any extent, but most of the church does not seem to have done much work lately in this area of ethics.

This approach to ethics has the benefit of being very clear. That is helpful only if you believe that the issues are clear and able to be appropriately determined from a system of absolutes. It also sometimes gives people a vision of what could be if things were ideal. In my view, however, they are rarely that. Unfortunately, it has the disadvantage of applying simple absolutes to very complex situations where one set of values is in tension with another. It can also, I believe, be rather unmerciful in many human situations.

Situation ethics

Most people are familiar with this approach to ethics. Indeed, probably most of us instinctively make decisions from something like this base. We believe that although there are some fairly basic principles to apply to life, such as 'You shall not kill', each situation needs to be carefully examined and judgments made on the basis of that particular situation, rather than in response to a fixed principle.

The fact that we mostly begin with some sort of basic principle, requires the situation to convince us as to why we should not adhere to that principle. That is, we say, 'I believe that you should not kill, but ...', and we outline to ourselves why we would want to modify or lay down that principle in the particular situation. In war, we might say, 'I believe that we should not kill, but it was a choice of killing or dying, or killing versus being dreadfully oppressed.' Pacifists, who hold to the absolute principle, would challenge with the view that it is better to die than to kill and that violence brings more violence. And so the discussion goes on.

In the case of euthanasia, someone could say, 'I believe we must not kill.' Another person would say, 'I do too, but my commitment to life involves mercy for this person. This person's suffering is not the way life was meant to be, in fact it is not really living.' Both people, if they were open to each other would agree that they are each trying to sustain important values — to life, and to mercy. In the end, they may still disagree but they will recognise that neither has the absolute right to claim the high moral ground.

So, situation ethics looks carefully at each situation and judges it on its merits. The strength of this approach is that the complexity of each situation can be recognised, and the competing values weighed against each other. In response to all these issues, the person or group then decides what to do, acknowledging that whatever is decided is likely to be a moral compromise.

One weakness in this approach to ethics is that such a decision is likely to be subjective. It can be affected by our own inclinations, ignorance and vested interests. We can counter this tendency if we do not make the decision alone. Another weakness is that, in reality, each situation does not stand alone in life. We may make a decision about something in response to a particular case, but that decision often becomes part of our life as a community — it contributes to the forming of community attitudes and mores.

A decision creates precedents, and precedents become reference points for the future forming of the social mores of a community. To complicate matters, what we do in a situation, the ethical stand that we take, may become detached from its 'situation' and formed into a guide for someone in an entirely different situation. That is why opponents of euthanasia talk about the 'thin edge of the wedge'. In following the example set in a merciful situation, will we take it as permission for the unmerciful killing of people with disabilities because their life is less than the way life was meant to be? This view can, of course, be countered with thoughts of careful guidelines and the invitation to trust that the community does not always degenerate into being followers of a 'Hitler'. Sometimes it has done so, however, and therefore the cautions must be taken seriously.

'Koinonia' ethics — the ethics which create community

A fine teacher, named Allan Loy, introduced me to the approach to ethics that I have found most valid. It involves the bringing in of basic principles which are not seen as absolutes but as guiding ideals. Then you look at all the issues and values at stake, as in situation ethics. After that, you ask what impact your conceived ethical decision would have on the life of the community.

You ask questions such as 'What if everyone, or many people did this?' and 'How will this action begin to shift traditional values and will that matter?' or 'What might become normal practice if I proceed in this direction and what would that do to the life of the community?' I also assume that even if nobody knows what we or you are doing, the change of values within the small group, or in the person, contributes to a shift in community values. Sometimes it can be concluded that the ethical decision is the right one for special cases, so people need to think of how boundaries are made around that action so that it stays restricted behaviour.

If we look at the tough question of whether abortion is appropriate or not, we can see most of these issues coming into play. Let us start with a woman who wants an abortion. We might say 'We believe that we should never take life' as a good basic principle. The following issues may be raised with us:

- This is not really 'life' as we know it, only potential life.

- All life is 'life', there is no such thing as potential life.
- This woman will have less life if this child has life.
- This child will not have a real life because it is not welcome and there is a scarcity of resources to support it, both in love and material things.
- The woman has a right to have control over her own life and fertility — maybe she was being responsible about this and her efforts at contraception failed.
- Maybe she was raped and this pregnancy is a sign of her violation — God would understand if this life was returned for a new beginning.
- Maybe this woman is poor and she had little chance of controlling her fertility.
- The question of the sustaining of life has only arisen at the point where the carrying forward of life costs this woman dear, not at the stage where a world or community cared about the carrying forward of life in poverty. She will have to bear the weight of this life while the world does nothing to resource her for this load.
- The woman can't face the social cost of bearing this life because of the community attitudes to a single mother. The community requires she bear that cost and it then punishes her for her perceived sin, and the child also suffers. The community does not punish the father in the same way
- Or, the community is compassionate in offering this mother good support in the bearing of this life.
- The father of this child is not owning responsibility now, or ongoing responsibility and sharing in the cost of this life.
- Whether or not the father is responsible and caring is irrelevant because it is the right of the woman to choose.

- Other children will suffer if this child is born, because there is not enough of anything for another.
- The health professionals who do this abortion are asked to participate in an ending of life and they do not want to do that, or they are prepared to be involved but this makes them and their professions subconsciously less concerned for the sustaining of life.
- If the community condones abortion then it becomes accustomed to ending life and therefore values life less.
- Women are using abortion as a contraceptive method, rather than being responsive with available means of contraception.
- If the community refuses to allow abortion then it becomes less merciful in its understanding of the complexities of the human condition and women's life struggles in particular.
- If the community allows abortion then it lessens its valuing of life.

We could all add more issues to this list, I am sure. An issue such as abortion or euthanasia is an extraordinarily complex one. So, given that, can you ever make an ethical decision in relation to subjects such as these? Is it not better to stick to the absolutes? When ethical issues are very complex, it sometimes feels a relief to fall back on absolutes. For example, in the case of euthanasia, it feels safer to state that 'We believe in the sustaining of life' and thus end the debate. While staying with absolutes may make some of us feel more secure and more moral, I believe that this is a dangerous illusion which often violates other people, many of whom are far more vulnerable than us. On the other hand, I believe that whatever decision we make about complex issues, we can never rest peacefully and claim that we are right without acknowledging the things that we inevitably hold in tension.

I think we can only humbly do our best to look at all that is involved, think aloud with many other people about our processes in doing that, and struggle towards the most loving outcome for as many people as possible. Absolutes may protect us from the experience of painful struggle, but they cost us and others dear because they are not founded on entering the situation but on separating ourselves from reality. Indeed, I observe that absolutes are often sustained by people who will never come near the situation in which other people are living and struggling.

As a Christian, I follow a God who was not afraid to totally enter every human situation. So when I make my tough decisions, in which I try to be ethical, I have full confidence that this God fully enters the struggle with me, can see and feel all the complexities and uncertainties, and journeys on with me. I assume that this is an important part of the human struggle and one that requires an ongoing reflection on the outcomes of our decisions. What impact is our decision having on the life of our community? What values are being weakened or strengthened? Are we becoming more just, or less? More loving or less? More honest about what is happening to us, or less honest?

Underneath it all is, I believe, the question of whether our processes in building an ethical and moral life together move us towards a deeper understanding of the human journey. Have we involved all concerned in this process, or was it a relatively costless process for people who have never entered the tough life that others face? In other words, is this struggle towards truth an authentic struggle or one which is about abstractions and theories and sometimes controlling people? Authentic human engagement can carry us into a new place in human community and can link us with a God who, I believe, never sees things simplistically nor without a deeply loving heart.

A moral and ethical community would, I believe, be regularly involved in this rigorous engagement on many fronts. It would also challenge those who, sometimes self-righteously, call for a restoration of moral values in ways which focus on private morality issues and distract us from a careful look at public and corporate morality. A community that has a strong moral and ethical base demonstrates its capacity for honest and transparent dealings in every aspect of its life. It challenges all clever use of power which cloaks unethical behaviour. It becomes a society of deep compassion for its most vulnerable members and walks in humility before the awesome complexity of human life.

Living with Power

NELSON Mandela once made a very significant statement about power in his inaugral speech as President of South Africa in 1994. He said:

Our deepest fear is not that we are inadequate.
Our deepest fear is that we are powerful beyond measure.
It is our light, not our darkness that most frightens us.
We ask ourselves 'Who am I to be brilliant?'
Actually, who are you not to be?
You are a child of God.
Your playing small does not serve the world.
There is nothing enlightened about shrinking,
so that other people won't feel insecure around you.
We were born to make manifest the glory of God that is within us.
It is not just in some of us, it's in everyone
and, as we let our own light shine,
we unconsciously give other people the permission to do the same.
As we are liberated from our fear,
our presence automatically liberates others.

Nelson Mandela is right. Most of us are afraid of our own power, both rightly and wrongly.

If we are rightly afraid of power in ourselves, it is because we have experienced destructive power in many forms: in ourselves, in others and in systems. There is the power to dominate, to determine what is acceptable in others and not acceptable, to threaten violence and to exercise it. We all know it is only too true that 'power corrupts and absolute power corrupts absolutely'. We know the seduction of that in ourselves and we often bear the suffering of that corruption in our leaders.

We are also familiar with the sort of power that sneaks up on us. We are just about to be true to ourselves and strong when someone, often someone we love, indicates by the look on their face, or a word on their lips that we are about to hurt or offend them. Our intentions turn to nothing and we live on, overpowered by the manipulation of someone else's emotions and their subtle power of disapproval, which may be appropriate or inappropriate.

We long to claim our own life, but someone near us tells us that if we do that, we will take life from him or her. We live together as though there is a cake of power and if one of us eats some, we leave less for the other. Women in particular are often told that. If girls do well in school they are taking self-respect from boys and are the cause of them doing less well. Some people believe that someone has to be the 'head' of a marriage — they ask, how can you have a relationship like that without it being clear who is the head, the one who has ultimate power?

In a nation, we are often told that we have to be very careful how much power the people really have, in case they make mistakes. In order to save us from our mistakes, 'they' will make decisions for us as our elected representatives, sometimes far beyond their right to do so without widespread discussion by the people in general. Then, even among the elected representatives of the people in government, it becomes apparent that some are greater and some are lesser representatives. The cabinet and prime minister are those who have the inside information, so the rest should accept their advice and give power to executive government. So a nation moves from democracy to guided democracy and most of us don't even notice it. We accept that we are foolish people who don't know what is best for us (we even voted in these politicians!) so it is best that they, or their representatives, decide as much as possible for us.

Not only that, but it is inefficient to spread power around. The fewer people we have making decisions, the smoother it will be, we are told. We can do away with all those people who used to share the power in managing things, pay the top people ten times more and still save money. Many disempowering activities take place in the name of rational efficiency, without most of us asking what the real cost in loss of power to a wider community will be. We rarely ask either whether this 'efficient' focused power at high levels is worth all the jobs that disappear and stop to add up the sums which the community pays to support them as unemployed.

Also, in many countries, we sometimes watch those who fought against entrenched power on behalf of the powerless people turn into tyrants themselves, even as they speak the rhetoric of freedom and equality. Some of us have walked that path as leaders ourselves, including me. I would never underestimate the seduction of power, nor my capacity to rationalise my engagement with it. Although I think these days I know a modest amount about how to live with power, I still often choose to turn it into power over others rather than the authentic power of being fully alive. In some ways it is easier and more exciting to live with that sort of power.

When the going gets really tough in a community of people, we can observe that people are easily deceived by the clever activities of the powerful. They can still teach us that some other unfortunate and powerless people are our real enemy and that they are to blame for our sorrows and deprivations. So the poor whites turn on the poor indigenous people or the poor immigrant people in rage and hate. All of these experiences of power are ours and many more, so how can Nelson Mandela, of all people, call us to lay down the fear of our own power?

There is a beautiful Japanese imaging of good relationship which I sometimes use when I am marrying people. They light two candles and stand them side by side. Then I move them closer together and point out that, as I do so, neither candle takes life from the other. The two flames of life burn just as brightly alongside each other. All that they do is to create a greater and stronger light in between themselves, which is the relationship. If only we could image life like that, instead of the cake of power to carve up between us, we might all live with a greater flame of creative and healthy power.

Of course, it is romantic to believe that to live alongside each other with power is a simple and easy thing to do. As Nelson Mandela recognised, we are afraid of doing that. It carries us into a far less passive and comfortable existence.

So, what is so frightening about living with power? Why do we choose to avoid it? I can only say why I often choose to do so. I find that if I live wholeheartedly, at full power, I engage with other people in ways which are sometimes likely to make them angry with me or challenging of me. I don't like people being angry with me, so I 'cool it', so to speak. I do this even though I know that, when I find someone, like my partner Ali, who is not afraid of my power, I could live at full steam and with glorious powerful, authentic life.

Living with power means, I think, that you put out into the open and into all relationships almost everything that you know, can be and long for. Naturally, that clashes with other people's power of life and all that they know, can be and long for! So, as powerful people together, if we are to go on in relationship, we have to engage in some rather heavy encounters with each other at times. We have to live with a degree of conflict and a very high level of trust. I suppose that it has to do with breaking through to believing that your life is not really trying to take life from the other, nor theirs from you, but that both lives are just trying to emerge in honesty, passion and freedom. It also trusts that negotiation and collaboration in giving maximum life to each other is possible.

Ali tells me, and proves to me, that this is possible. She has lived in the presence of anger before and knows it can be survived well, even as one licks one's wounds. She knows the difference between destructive anger — really a violence — and anger that is simply two human beings asserting in confidence their claim to live in fullness and openness. Sometimes I actually believe her. One day I will believe her more often. That is one of my callings if I am to keep growing until I die.

I also know that, all my life, I have discovered the most marvellous and magical gifts lying hidden in people, which only need encouragement to come forward. So many of us live at half-life level, like printers that are on economy instead of normal ink setting. We live as pale images of who we could be if we would only have the confidence to be seen, known and acting in our full colour and clarity. Many of us receive so many negative messages about our place in the scheme of things that we move with all these fences around our power and with voices inside us which say, 'Don't be a fool. You can't do that! You will look an idiot and make a mess of it! So don't even try, or start, or say it.' So we don't and the moment passes. We have lowered our life level again. It is a very hard boundary to move past because so many cultural messages reinforce our caution.

The only way through is to decide that it is a risky adventure and that most other people are as scared as we are and that we could all laugh together if things are not as we had hoped. Just imagine if we lived in a world where everyone lived as largely as that, where everyone had the trust in each other to offer all they were into everything without fear. What a rich and life-giving, life-sharingly powerful place it would be. What a world of colour and light we could create. That is worth struggling for, even at some cost.

Living in Our Landscape

I DOUBT that anyone would dispute that our landscape is important to us. Maybe it is more important to some of us than it is to others. I guess that the level of significance which we give to it is determined by our focus in life and from where and from what we draw our resources for living. I suspect too that when people have to move around a great deal, especially as children, they learn to adapt to many different landscapes and draw life from most of them, or learn to live within themselves with minimal need to interconnect with their landscape.

Some of us are taught by our culture to dominate, to conquer and to use our landscape. The gift of God in the first chapter of the Book of Genesis in the Hebrew Bible when humankind is given 'dominion' over everything has possibly encouraged some European-based and Anglo-Celtic cultures along that path. I suppose the Jewish people may have been similarly influenced, but I am not so sure about that. Whether the early creation story ever really had this concept of domination of the landscape at its centre in the environment and culture from which it originally emerged is, I think, doubtful. Later peoples have heard it differently in cultures which were more separated from the land in the first place than were the Hebrew people.

Those of us who come from these more landscape-conquering cultures may, I believe, never really enter the landscape relationship which belongs to those cultures who have never been conquerors — the people who are owned by the land. An Aboriginal friend of mine once asked me to feel a piece of bark and tell her what I knew and experienced from doing that. I felt its roughness and its smoothness. She described a whole range of relationships when she felt it.

I have been told that Australian Aboriginal children in their tribal culture know more than three thousand environmental relationships before they are seven years old. They learn to love and respect those before they learn anything else. All those relationships are their family.

In more recent days, in our country, some of us have been trying to understand and acknowledge this, as we attempt to build a more reconciled relationship with indigenous people and with the landscape. Even as we might make progress in these relationships, I think we need to be cautious about any suggestion that we can actually experience the entry into a relationship with the landscape which is anything like as profound as that of indigenous people — maybe one day, many generations hence. We are after all talking about about more than forty thousand years (maybe even sixty or eighty thousand years) of unbroken, loving, indigenous relationship with one section of land and/or sea. The relationship comes from people who always believed that they were formed from the land as their mother and who have never sought to significantly exploit it beyond their immediate needs for frugal survival.

※

Nevertheless, many of us do still know that our landscape is linked with how we feel about ourselves and our life. My father was born on a farm. His parents were never rich farmers. They toiled hard, with modest results and few amenities. My father left the farm to go to university in Melbourne when he was about twenty-three years old. After he graduated, as a minister he moved around in various parishes in Victoria and Tasmania. It was the practice of the church in those days to send young ministers to the country and then, if they did well, they had the opportunity to move to the capital city.

My father had a number of opportunities to make this move to the city, but he refused them. The nearest to the city he could manage was provincial cities and, as he became older, he gradually moved back almost to the area where he was born — near the Murray River and the farmlands of northern Victoria. When he was old, he reminisced more and more about this early life on the farm and the family's horses, which he always maintained were the most intelligent creatures on earth. He never felt right in a huge city and you could feel him unfold into life as he turned for home and the rural landscape.

I can still see him, every time we moved, almost within hours of our arrival getting out his spade and turning a sod in his back yard in preparation for his first vegetable patch. I can see his large red farmer's hands holding the spade and with energy and a sort of joy, sinking the spade in the soil. Then he would construct his compost enclosures with sure bangs of the hammer on rough wood and then turn to decide where he would have his chook pen. All these things were priorities, part of his making his home and connecting with his farmer view of his landscape. I recall being annoyed when he picked up the inevitable stray cats (which I was most certainly slipping some food) on the toe of his shoe and tossed them out. Cats are working animals, he would say. They belong outside catching rats. I would think, 'He's not on a farm now. These are my pets, not working animals.' We had a different relationship with our landscape.

My mother also loved the wonder of the landscape around her. She stopped and marvelled at almost everything, to the exasperation of her children at times. I remember us all, trundling along the road in an old Austin Tourer, going at our maximum speed of about 24 miles per hour while everyone else sped past us. My mother would say, 'I am sorry for those poor people going so fast that they never have the chance to see the view, children.' As most of us were being carsick jammed into the back seat, we were not nearly so grateful for the view! She would sigh with pleasure at almost everything she saw in the natural environment and give thanks to God for everything in sight.

She also had an intimate relationship with her landscape. She would rejoice in the fruits of my father's labours because they were his — her husband was a good grower of vegetables, strong and productive. She herself cherished each living thing around her as though she was its mother. I don't actually remember her doing much active gardening. However, especially in her later years, she would walk around the garden, exulting over the wonder of each bud and bloom, checking on its progress, stroking and encouraging. She did this in the early evening each day, usually with my father, who probably looked at each thing with a different eye, but who enjoyed seeing her delight.

On the day she died, very suddenly, I joined my father in their house and, when the evening came, he thought it would be good to walk around the garden together, as he would have done with my mother. As we looked at each plant that she had loved, we saw with amazement that every single bud and bloom had died overnight, not the plant, just the buds and flowers. Her garden was mourning for her, dying a little in recognition of the loss of a relationship. My father was in no doubt about this, although he was not given to romantic theories about such things, and we reflected on how little we really knew about our connectedness with the creation, our landscape.

IN SPITE of having spent my early life in rural towns and provincial cities, I would say that my primary life-giving relationship is the city. I enjoy a few days in the mountains, but as I come down the mountain road, I find myself seeing if I can glimpse the skyline of Sydney. After the initial shock of the noise, traffic and pollution, within minutes I am taking my place with satisfaction in its humming life. When I worked in the centre of Sydney, for the past twenty-two years, I would go out every lunchtime and feel its buzz and variety with a sort of elation. It was not just the moving diversity and interactions of its people, it was the total environment of a great city.

I love seeing how weeds grow on the sides of old walls, or in tiny cracks in concrete pavements. I like the interplay between older and newer. I am fascinated by the survivals of beauty and kindness in many little places and actions. I find the brashness of the city of Sydney endearing. I love its rather cynical humour and cheekiness. I love the vulnerability of most of its people, which they will let you see if you love them and get to know them.

At first, I couldn't believe it when I saw all the columns of our fine Town Hall wrapped in red plastic for last Christmas and a gaudy Santa plus children and large presents hanging all over it with a blow-up rocking horse on one of the towers. I laughed to myself and thought, 'How gross! Only Sydney could do that!' and felt an affection for our folksy style and our refusal to be elegant most of the time.

I love it when we stand on the foreshores of our harbour in hundreds of thousands on New Year's Eve and watch the fireworks display. The moment I wait for always is when the fireworks go up on the Sydney Harbour Bridge and it sounds as though the whole of Sydney says 'Oooh!' together with a sort of sigh of love and admiration — the 'icon' of our life is being honoured again. This year, when the fireworks went up on the bridge, we saw a great smiling face in lights across the bridge. Our bridge smiled at us!

Tears came to my eyes. Very sentimental? A bit corny? Who cares? It is our landscape and we are very homely people. I don't even know what my tears were about really. I think they were something to do with us being very ordinary people, who struggle along in messy ways and there was our dear bridge, smiling at us in warm encouragement. Still sentimental and corny? Probably, but what does it matter?

One of my greatest joys is the fact that at the back of our house now, in between the rooftops and our neighbour's trees, I can see a small patch of the city skyline with the distinctive Sydney Tower standing out. I look at it in every part of the day and in the night, and sense love and excitement as I do so. My city forms and feeds me, gives me energy and life. With all its ambiguity in its domination of the old landscape on which it is built, it is my landscape.

Having said that, I would now acknowledge that it is built on Aboriginal land, the land of the Eora and Gadigal people. I grieve that my delight is built on their blood, pain and dispossession. I apologise that my forebears were the invaders of their precious landscape.

THE only time I have had a minute glimpse of what that dispossession could have meant, apart from observing the terrible consequences for Aboriginal people, was when I returned to the land of my Scottish clan. This land was 'cleared' by the English landlords when they wanted room for more livestock rather than people. They burnt the homes of my forebears and forced them onto boats which took them far away to America, New Zealand and Australia. As I stepped onto that land for the first time, on the Isle of Skye, I felt a sense of homecoming and sadness — a tiny, tiny experience of dispossession. The particular light that I experienced on the West Coast of Scotland, the harsh sweeping mountains, the sparse growth over the earth and the rockiness moved me in some deep way. I picked a sprig of heather, dried it and framed it to capture a memory — a little bit of my old landscape to bring to the new. Remarkably, it's kept its beautiful colour as it hangs on my wall.

Numbers of people are, in this period of our life, reflecting more deeply on the way the Australian landscape might form the spirit and life of even its colonising peoples and those who have sought refuge here. I, like many others, am always clearer about this when I move into a foreign landscape and contemplate what it does to me and why it feels so alien. Australians have many different relationships with our massive area of land and sea. Aboriginal people are possibly the only ethnic group who have lived in harmony with all its varied spaces, right across its breadth and length. Maybe they too were attached to their particular part of it. Certainly there were distinct tribal boundaries and it appears that most of the desert tribes had large areas and that the coastal tribes, with the more fertile land, had smaller areas.

Maybe they were like the rest of us and had their historic preferences. Certainly, as with my parents, some of us cannot imagine living in the large cities. They are a minority. Around 85 per cent of Australians live in urban areas. Within those cities, some of us like being near the sea and surf, and others nearer the mountains or plains. Because our land stretches from the equator to the far cold south in Tasmania, we choose between tropical, subtropical, temperate and subtemperate landscapes. Our vegetation and wildlife varies from the west to the east — a great expanse of land that takes about six hours to fly across.

We all live under the southern sky, however. That unites us in this place, in spite of the wide variety of our landscape. It is interesting that as we discuss as a nation the possibility of a new flag, the polls indicate a wide attachment to the stars of the Southern Cross on our present flag. When I go overseas and into the northern hemisphere, even though I am not very capable of identifying different stars or clusters of stars in the southern sky, I immediately know that I am under the 'wrong' sky. It's funny how you know you are under the wrong sky — the northern sky looks too evenly sprinkled with stars — even if you are not an experienced identifier of individual stars. Where is our Southern Cross? Where is the Milky Way?

When Australians claim that their spirituality is connected with the 'wide brown land' it is sometimes challenged, given that so many of us cling to the fertile coast. While some of our claims may be a fantasy, a sort of romance, I would not dismiss them so quickly. Our forebears, on arrival, had a terrible struggle to survive. They died trying to cross deserts and mountains to get to the inland or to explore the continent. People still die of thirst in the desert. I suspect that while we may indeed mostly live in the cities, we live there in relationship to our awe, respect and fear of the desert. Living in anxious proximity to this landscape also shapes our life and our spirit.

※

MANY of us learn most about our relationship with our landscape when we visit that which belongs to someone else. I remember my first travels in England and Europe. Initially, I was overwhelmed by the green charm of the rolling hills of England — 'England's green and pleasant land' as the song goes. Then I was stunned by the sharp peaks of the French and Swiss Alps. I felt as though I was living in a fairytale, and, in a sense, so I was. It took me a while to realise that quite apart from my admiration of the spectacular beauty before me, I was also entering the land of my childhood story books, the land of the fairytales and castles, of Christopher Robin and Winnie-the-Pooh, King Arthur and the knights and countless others. That was special. For a while.

After a time I began to feel like someone who had eaten too

much — all that chocolate-box scenery. It seemed artificial, too bright, too perfect. Where was the real thing? Where were the grey-green gum trees and acacias with bits eaten out of them and scraggy shapes? Where was the oldness, the worn-downness? It was all a bit too damp, too fertile, too new. Where was the dryness, the sparceness? No matter what my original roots, I longed for my home, my landscape. I longed for my city skyline and the Harbour Bridge. I longed for the special light that we experience in this great south land, not some hazy greyness that makes you think it might rain any minute, when it doesn't.

However, it was not until I spent some time in New Zealand recently that I began to reflect on the way in which our landscape may not simply mean a great deal to our sense of well-being, or otherwise. I began to reflect that it might actually shape us. The people of New Zealand and their culture might be expected to be the nearest thing to Australian culture. We have a different indigenous base, but the same dominant British/ European culture from our colonisation and a developing multicultural society. This last is more obvious in Australia than New Zealand, but it is only a matter of degree. We all live under the southern skies and we are both living on islands — larger and smaller.

I soon realised, though, that we have developed into different peoples — the cultures have a different feeling to them. I saw football signs in New Zealand saying 'We are the warriors', and I knew that Australians would be unlikely to describe ourselves as that. I knew that the warrior concept probably came from the Maori image of strong people, but the rest of New Zealand could still live with that image for their football team. I found myself laughing as I imagined any Australian group having the warrior image of itself. We would have to dress up in something ridiculous to indicate we were not serious! I observed the vigorous culture of a people who aspired to and affirmed excellence, who were often industrious and entrepreneurial.

Then, as I travelled around, I saw their fertile paddocks that appear to be newly mown and with shampooed sheep grazing upon them. I saw the sharp, snow-capped mountains and the streams of water flowing everywhere. I had this image of a people living with a fertile, challenging mother — one who gave her people much and then invited them to engage with her sharp and often dramatic terrain. In all her variety from the north to the south, apart from her restless earthquakes she was still relatively predictable in her seasonal responses to her people as they came to know her. She was a rich and nourishing mother inviting her people to adventure and the scaling of heights. She was not like my landscape mother.

I thought about our Australian landscape mother. She too is varied, but often unpredictable. Her fertility comes and goes. Just when you think she is holding you safe, she sends her floods and when you are resting in her fertility, she brings on her droughts. Just as you think you will die, she sends the rain and grass again, mostly just enough to save you and sometimes too late to save you.

You cling to her most fertile breastedness, near the coast, and out of nowhere, she will ring you with fires — huge, mobile, devastating fires that often seem to come from nowhere. You move far from the dryness and then the typhoons race across her body and flatten your home there. And, in between all this, she will be your loving mother, very sparse in her gifts, very frugal in her feeding, with parties here and there and with her own special dignity of colours and contours.

As I say this, I love this land-mother with a fierce defensiveness. When a European looks at her and observes that she is like 'the other side of the moon', as I once heard while travelling from Sydney to Canberra, I feel like saying, 'Well who wants all that excess anyway?' I see us play games with our mother as we try to run across her deserts to see if we can survive. I feel our pride as we discover (mainly through Aboriginal people who know the mother better) that, in her mountains, we travel on the ridges rather than the blind valleys. I see us become people who live without a high expectation of anything, somewhat cynical and impatient with pomposity and other self-indulgences.

I recall a person at a conference once drawing a picture of two people standing under a tree, looking at a small plane caught in the branches. One was saying to the other, 'What's wrong with you, mate? We got it off the ground, didn't we?' Somehow, that described us, the children of the rather tough mother, who, just as we get off the ground, often brings us down again. Our conversation is typically understated in style, our emotions are there but subtle in expression, and we often laugh when we all know we mean to cry.

I am often reminded of some research that I did as a preschool teacher. I was doing case studies on children from relatively deprived households. One of our favourite children was a gutsy, rather cheeky little boy. He was always straightforward in his naughtiness and his tough and cheery exterior covered a generosity to other children, which was well recognised by them. Other children liked him, while being a little wary of some of his styles of relating to them. We often observed his mother, whose own life was hard, give him a good cuff around the ears for virtually no reason and we were concerned about her parenting. When I visited their home and watched more carefully, I observed that the regular cuffs were received as a sign of rough affection by the child and given in that spirit by the mother. This was a child who knew, without a doubt, that he was loved, even if love was delivered in ways which appeared strange and ambiguous to other people. There was an odd sort of health about it all, which was hard to describe. Sometimes I think Australians have that sort of relationship with our landscape mother.

Even as I share these impressions, I recognise that I am describing, predominantly, one part of the cultural response to this landscape — the Anglo-Celtic part. I believe that some of this 'rubs off' onto newer migrations of people, as they also link with the landscape, but I would not dare to suggest that I know what the relationship with the landscape looks like in all places, nor what it will evolve into being. Maybe those who have had a hard journey into this landscape from dangers and deprivations will find this land-mother a bountiful parent. I don't think it is helpful to do much generalising, but I do find it fascinating to have a conversation with others about their experience.

HAVING described some of my journey, I would still acknowledge that many of us non-indigenous people travel mostly on the earth rather than with it. Maybe our genes, our corporate histories, have taught us not to connect too deeply with a mother who might be taken from us. Many of us are uprooted people, at least if we go back a few generations.

The grief and dislocation of indigenous peoples comes from those whose roots are so deep in the land of their generations that they genuinely start to die as a people when they are dispossessed — to die in body, in mind, in heart and spirit. The very fabric of their existence as a community and as individuals is threatened.

Maybe it takes forty thousand years to become as vulnerable as that to the uprooting. Maybe it takes the centuries to develop our harmony in existing with the landscape-mother. A friend of mine, called Eddie, describes it as a reconciliation with the creation. He sees it like this because he thinks we must go beyond care and conservation of the environment. He sees a wounded planet, mostly wounded by humanity. To move forward together, we need a grieving for this wounding and a building of a new and reconciled relationship. This would involve love and respect, a careful 'listening' for what the planet now needs for health and a recognition that, as we do this, our own healing takes place. Then we can journey on together in as near to harmony as we can manage, giving gifts to each other on the way, attending to each other's needs and acknowledging our interdependence.

If I have shared my understanding of the way I live with my landscape, it is because I believe that there is an interesting conversation to be had together as part of the developing understanding of our life. It is also an invitation to live in the landscape that you live in. Some people don't live in it because they are longing for another. Even as they do that, they are being formed and having their life determined by their actual landscape and are choosing whether to live with it or against it. Most of us do that some of the time, but we could consider that there are ways of carrying enough bits of our old landscape with us to make the new one our home. We can honour our old love with pictures, images and symbols and sometimes revisitings. The landscape deserves this honouring, like our old friends and family.

If we do this, we can then sometimes bring ourselves to look with enough interest and love on the new place and find its gifts for us. A story of my own experience comes to mind. I had a friend, a man of deep spirituality, and we often shared poetry and ideas for the expression of our life in a relatively leafy suburb of Sydney. I moved to the city for my parish ministry and one day I had a call from him. 'Dorothy,' he said, 'I have found this beautiful poem. I will read it to you.' It was a poem about squirrels in the trees. I listened to it, objectively a beautiful poem. Then, I had to face that it no longer fitted into my landscape of downtown central Sydney and that my spirituality had actually shifted. I realised that I needed poems about the joy of grass growing bravely in the cracks of the concrete. That was my landscape.

Now that I spend most of my time at home, living with someone who loves creating a garden, I suspect there may be another shift. My city may well become a little more fertile than the grass in the concrete. It may have very small patches of plants and trees growing in fertility, if watered, with some birds flying around and nesting there. I may become a different person with this landscape mother. I look forward to that!

Living with Humanness and Fun

CHRISTIANS are encouraged to read this chapter.

Some years ago I was invited to speak on a worthy subject to a group of women in a suburban church in Sydney. The person who invited me told me to 'feel free to dress up'. She explained that the group had decided that at regular intervals they would dress up and bring food for a dinner, together with a speaker, because women outside the church did that and Christian women were not to be deprived of this fun. Sure enough, when I turned up to speak there were all the women in cocktail dresses (minus cocktails) and made up to the nines for the evening of fun. As a non-after dinner speaker (I have only one joke), I wondered how they saw listening to my earnest address as fun.

They did appear to enjoy their night together, but it seemed a bit sad to me that their fun was so serious — they even brought their own food. I understood what they were trying to do, as I have a long life in the church and I know that the church is not very good at real fun. At times I have found myself thinking, 'Come! Join us Christians for the good life — three serious meetings a week, a working bee to clean up the church and arrange the flowers on Saturday and church twice on Sunday with teaching of children thrown in.' What an attractive offer, how could anyone refuse it? Of course, we try to make life for our young people a bit more fun than that, but once adulthood sets in, we are really on the serious life task. Even for the young, we usually tuck the serious stuff in among the fun, just in case they get into the habit of enjoying themselves. Fun takes on a role of being like the honey you add to get the medicine down sometimes.

༄

I HAVE a delightful grand daughter called Brook. Her play, as her aunt Melissa observes, is really like psycho-drama. She uses her toys to replay her life. There is a Mummy Bear, Daddy Bear and Brook Bear who do things like sitting on the couch together, exchanging lots of cuddles, looking for their hats when they go outside in the sun, eating their dinners and patting the cat. Mummy and Daddy Bear go to bed, but Brook Bear stays up!

In the middle of all this serious play, however, we always have the joke of the day, which is identified by Brook. One day we will say, 'Where has the cat gone? The cat is in the car?' Then we roll around laughing because cats don't go in cars, do they? The next day we put a plastic chook on the block wall we are making and we say, 'Chook playing?' Then we laugh a lot because we don't think plastic chooks really play! Recently we have become more cheeky. As a careful listener for new words, Brook realises that Grandma, unlike others around her, seems to say 'Hmmm' in many tones of voice. So, next time Grandma says, 'Hmmm', a cheeky face comes around the bench into the kitchen saying 'Hmmm!' and laughing loudly. Once we have found the joke for the day, we repeat it a thousand times and we all laugh together each time. Brook, even at two years old, has a marvellous sense of the ridiculous.

Laughing is at the very heart of our humanness and the delighted chuckle of a child — in its innocence and sheer delight — is one of the most beautiful sounds we hear. I find myself wanting to create a world in which this child of joy will always find laughter, to protect her from things which take her laughter away and to receive from her the capacity for lightness of heart. I also hope that she teaches me and holds for herself that healthy sense of the ridiculous, especially recognising ourselves as faintly ridiculous.

But then I had serous beginnings. Life was an earnest affair. It was not so much that we never enjoyed ourselves, but that fun was somehow earned and planned. It was rarely a freedom and an intrinsic gift, a part of the essence and abundance of life. I think it was my relationship with a special friend called Jen which, when I was more than fifty years old, taught me to play as an adult, just for the sake of playing, as a value in itself. That was a great gift to me, a return to authentic humanness. Quite apart from a general sense of fun, Jen had a marvellous capacity to make a nonsense of my most pious and pretentious moments in the pulpit.

I RECALL a particular day when, as a parish minister, I faced the day in tiredness. I thought to myself, 'What I would really like to do is to get on a ferry and sail across the harbour and have fish and chips on the beach.' Feeling very daring, I thought, 'So, why not?' I left all the undone work and the worries and took off for the quay. As I sat on the ferry, I heard the voice of a God who said to me, 'What is wrong with you? I give you the wind on your face, the sun on the water and the birds wheeling overhead and you would consider sitting in your office?' I knew that this God was the one who deliberately created a world where play and laughter was built in for our health and fun. I also knew that for most of my life, I had been feeling faintly guilty about receiving those gifts.

I stepped off the ferry and strolled happily towards the sea-front. On the way, I saw one of those slot machines that challenge you to try to get a stuffed toy from it with a large claw. 'Why not?' I thought, and triumphantly emerged with two stuffed toys under my arm. (I had a program of getting stuffed toys out of this type of machine for quite a while, in fact! I might even start doing it again to add to Brook's collection. This serious interest developed when several of these machines lay between my church and the church offices down the street. I used to look at them when I walked past and think to myself that I was certain I could defeat the machine and get a toy out. Then I would decide that if I stopped and had a go, the General Secretary of the Synod or a ministerial colleague would be sure to walk past and see me. Now I don't care!) So, carrying my toys and my fish and chips, I sat on the wall by the sea, swung my legs and just enjoyed myself. To less serious folk, all this must seem quite a normal and usual activity.

A little self-indulgence, simple fun, doing nothing for its own sake, swinging one's legs in idleness is something that happens often for many people. And so it should. To have most conversations with no 'throwaway lines', to eternally seek the meaning of life and the changing of the world, to regard praying as a leisure activity and meetings as a way of life, is, I believe, to be less than human.

※

I REMEMBER during the height of the struggle to end the Vietnam War, being at a large meeting of anti-war activists who were hearing speeches and discussing their next strategies. One man dared to get up and suggest that we might buy large baskets of flowers and stand on street corners in the city and give them to people. There was a shocked silence. The debate moved on in embarrassment — clearly one of our leaders had lost the plot. In fact, the rest of us had lost the plot. We had become grim, humourless activists. To portray ourselves as the flower people would have been a radical breakthrough to a new day for us. The very peace we were fighting for had largely left our own souls.

There is a beautiful old song that calls upon us to 'stop and smell the roses'. Maybe, if we did this more often, the world would be a different place. What I have now learnt is that you don't stop to smell the roses in order to make the world a better place, but because the roses are there and you are a human being who simply enjoys the roses.

The people of Pitt Street Church were also people who taught me about all this. They actually often laughed in church. When I chose an Australian Christmas carol that had a line about 'drovers bright and gay', they laughed. When the rain came through the church roof just as I was doing a baptism and had pronounced that God parted the waters for the people of Israel, they laughed loudly. When I took myself very seriously, they found ways of saying, 'Come on, Dorothy, lighten up!'

When we decided as part of our anniversary celebrations to serve free drinks on the church steps and people ran away from us (because the church doesn't give out free drinks for no reason), we all laughed a lot at ourselves and at what the church had become. When I went to Pitt Street, they told me that they always went out to dinner together to celebrate their life on the last Friday of every quarter. They just took over a restaurant and enjoyed dinner together. It was a great thing to do. Much later, when we were under attack, we knew a lot about parties and celebrations, which had no prayers at the beginning or end and no quick sermons in the middle!

At the parish camp, we watched the film *The Life of Brian* and rolled around the floor laughing at the absurdity of religious people and the sharp eye of the Monty Python crew, who mercilessly sent us up. We watched ourselves in earnest discussion about sexist language and the right name for our latest protest group, we saw ourselves passionately debating and arguing about the exact wording of some resolution while the world died around us. We saw ourselves carrying the shoe, as the sign of our particular view of the God we were following in superiority, as compared to those people over there who carried the gourd as the sign of their saviour! We laughed at ourselves in healthy delight at our own absurdities. And it was not by chance, I believe, that we also did more actual creative activity than any other religious group of which I have been a part.

Sometimes I think the greatest sin of the church is to be boring. I have spent a lot of time in my life visiting and being part of hundreds of different Christian churches. Sometimes I have marvelled at the faithfulness of people who stay there, week after week, in such boring activities. To be boring is a form of dehumanisation. I am not therefore suggesting that we should create gatherings where there is a laugh a minute. There are few things worse than clergy who try to prove that we are really one of the mob by telling jokes. I am not referring to endless happy-clappy singing either. I am rather thinking of the real thing — laughter about ourselves as overearnest people, lightness of heart as we journey on the serious way, throwing everything up in the air and taking off for the ferry and the fish and chips.

Fun is not planned and contrived. It happens because you have a view of life that includes it. I will never be very good at that because I come from a long genetic line of Christian 'martyrs' who made self-sacrifice a way of life and endless work a virtue. Their eyes looked at the world and saw art as barely an aid to the main agenda, which was to personally change the world, or at least to help others. I come from a church whose originator, John Wesley, decided that walking together to London and talking together as they walked, was a waste of precious time. So he read his friends elevating books as they walked. Heaven knows why they remained his friends. However, having said I am not yet very good at fun, I will try for the rest of my life to claim it for myself and others, because I am a lesser human being without it and because, when I manage to have fun, it is great fun!

Hard Questions for God and Some Equally Tough Possible Answers

IN RESPONSE to the experience of living and to the brave and significant conversations that I have had with people, in direct relationship and from the past in their writings and art, I have formulated some hard questions for God. As I have reflected on possible answers, I find them almost, but not quite, as tough as the questions. The answers are only my own, of course. I am not one to pretend to have a 'hot line' to God. In formulating the answers, however, I am including many wisdoms that I have received from different people and the accumulated understandings that I have received from people who believed that they too were travelling in relationship with God.

Why would I bother to ask questions and try to formulate possible answers? I do so because I believe that we need to continually participate in this process in order to make enough sense for our lives. We will each choose our own framework for the reflecting. Whether we are conscious of it, or not, most people engage in this forming of a world view all their lives. I find it helpful to hear others think aloud about the way they understand life, so I am daring to do the same.

In my experience, while people have an astonishing capacity to survive severe difficulties in life they often find it much harder to recover from a shattering of their world view. After all, if nothing makes sense any more, how can you take up your life with any confidence? What if you are offending something or somebody without knowing and that power waits to descend upon you again? How can you live with meaning and purpose when life appears to be chaotic?

Of course, there are people who are simply fatalistic, who assume that life is chaotic and meaningless and that you 'live, eat and be merry' if you have the means to do so, until you die. Most of us can't easily live like that. Others, in sincere thoughtfulness, decide that there is no plan or answer except to live with others with integrity, courage and hopefulness, assuming that what we see is all that there is. That is still, of course, a carefully considered world view.

Most of us begin, as children, in believing that if we are good we will be rewarded and if we are bad we will be punished. That is our earliest understanding of how life works. Little children expect to trust not only their parents but also life itself. As children, even if we discover that we can get away with things without being punished and that being good is not always either recognised or rewarded, we are still likely to stay with something like that world view for a time, unless our life is seriously damaged or abused. How often do we hear a child say, with great indignation, 'That's not fair!' Children usually have a fierce sense of justice. As adults, we mostly try to sustain them in that perception because we know that, soon enough, they will discover that life is not quite like that.

As we grow older, the idea of 'good' is usually reduced to being 'reasonably decent' and the idea of 'bad' is likely to become more associated with relatively serious acts of which we disapprove. We have modified our view of the world, probably because we have a more realistic view of ourselves as well as of everyone else.

Even when we see rogues and vagabonds appearing to prosper while some of our friends seem to have a good deal of undeserved trouble, we are likely to cling to this simple view of things until life confronts us very directly with a challenge to our idea of inbuilt justice.

Whether we are overtly religious or not, many of us carry with us a subconscious conviction that somewhere at the heart of existence, either in its origins or its ongoing, there is a system that keeps things relatively neatly organised. This may be held in place and organised by God, or some higher power, an energy or a source of things. We may rarely consciously think about this ordering of life but, in the face of inexplicable tragedy or trauma, we find ourselves filled with a sense of indignation. Something at the heart of things has betrayed our view of what is proper. How can this be? Have we offended some power? Why has this happened to us?

Of course, religions and various philosophies are the attempts of humankind to make sense of reality. Religions, as opposed to philosophies, offer ideas and beliefs about the connections between the meaning of life and 'the other', the higher power or the God who is given many names and described in different ways. I will think aloud about that from a Christian perspective but one which begins with the questions about meaning rather than a belief system with its dogma and rules. In doing this, I appreciate that people from other religions and philosophies would have much in common with my thinking and also important differences. This I respect. I am one part of a conversation which is more exciting and enlightening when it becomes a dialogue.

Is there really any justice?

Only those whose lives have been almost trouble-free and who have not paid much attention to the real life of others, can sustain the concept of a universe which delivers justice to everyone. It is simply not true that we get what we deserve. Most of us receive far more than we deserve and many others receive far less.

Some things can be explained in terms of the human freedom to choose. We do have the freedom to be greedy, oppressive and careless of each other's well-being. We are free to hate, to discriminate, and to hold such prejudices as racism, sexism, ageism and homophobia. We are free to be irresponsible, violent, exploitative and oppressive. Much of human misery and injustice can be tracked back to our own activities, attitudes and decisions. We rarely like to face the real consequences of what we do. Indeed, we often defend our meaner activities as the right and justified way to live and complain bitterly when we receive back the consequences of our behaviour. This applies, especially, in the anger and attack which comes towards us from those whom we have hurt or oppressed.

Having said that, I think we don't often blame God for such events and situations, unless we move into full-scale war and ask ourselves why God doesn't stop it, or protect us from each other. Occasionally there are human events of truly terrible brutality and magnitude. Events like the Jewish Holocaust or the 'killing fields' of Cambodia haunt the human race for generations and invite a question about who or what is in ultimate power — an evil or loving force?

I think we can see why even such events emerge from the evil of human activities. The question we are more likely to ask is, 'Why didn't God, or someone, stop them?' If the violence is directed primarily against one group of people, such as the Jews in the case of the Holocaust, it is understandable if the Jews ask, 'Why us, in particular?' A level of human evil arising from racism or hate-filled prejudice can usually be found underlying such frightful activities, but the question still goes forth to God in some cases.

So, in forming our world view, we are invited to be consistent. If we decide that God is one who does not play us and control us, like puppets attached to strings, then we are frighteningly and gloriously free to do what we like. We may have to face the fact that our hates and injustices can even produce forces of evil that seemingly take on a terrifying life of their own.

THEN there is genuine human error. Human error can overlap with human sinfulness but I think we can mostly tell the difference. Accidents do happen, as we say. We get tired, we make mistakes of judgment or we don't quite understand how something works. So we drive our cars and fly our planes and people are killed in accidents. We are examined by doctors who mostly do their best, but they can't know everything and they sometimes make fatal mistakes. We make our decisions about how to act and we advise our children and friends about what to do in life, with every good intention, but we often don't know enough. We make mistakes and others suffer.

If you think about it, an enormous amount of human pain arises from ignorance, as opposed to mistakes. People form opinions about other groups of people without having any direct contact with them. We have a dreadful tendency to listen to people who speak with authority about others and to group others into categories of friends or enemies in response. 'All Asians are connected with drugs and crime,' we say. 'All Jews are after our money.' 'All homosexual people are promiscuous and lots of them are paedophile.' Or, more simply, 'That person votes Labor/Liberal. We don't like people like that.'

From this ignorant stereotyping of whole groups of diverse people we build punishing relationships, we form public policies and sometimes even go to war. Some of this is chosen ignorance, and some is not. Many of us don't have the opportunity to meet a wide range of people. We trust the views of others who may also be ignorant or who may be, unknown to us, of evil intent.

If you look at humankind down the centuries, so much happens to us because we do not know about something — our bodies, our psyches, our minds, science, nature, history, medical facts and so on. We have ideas, we experiment and by trial and error, we discover new information. We are always in a process towards greater truth and wisdom which seems to go on forever.

You would think that God could do something about ignorance to save us from much suffering. I suppose that if God did that, we would all be God and know everything. We would all have to be the same in intellect, in experience and style. Nothing would ever be new to us and we would have nothing to tell each other about. We would be born without anything to learn. We would never have the joy and wonder of discovery. Actually, when I come to think about it, this state of affairs would be awful.

BUT what about things that seem to have nothing to do with human activity, the random disasters and tragedies? Even before humanity began its more destructive relationship with the environment, when it appeared that earlier people lived far more gently and respectfully in relationship with it, there is little doubt that there were natural disasters. Ancient writings tell us of earthquakes, floods and droughts which were often interpreted as signs of the displeasure of the God/s. And, even though we may be able to discover some indications that ill-health is sometimes due to our own lifestyles, individual and corporate, few of us would claim that all illness and death comes in response to those things. It is as though, as fast as we find a cure for one thing, another terrible disease shows up among us.

What sort of God creates a universe which has within it the ability to produce these sorts of sufferings and death? There is no easy answer to this question. Sometimes it helps, again, to explore the alternative. What if the creation had within it no 'brokenness' and no potential to produce illness and death? What if it was a static utopia in which we lived out our free and messy journey? That has significant attractions, and yet, I suspect that it would produce a strange dissonance with human life. Maybe the whole universe is interconnected and alive with us in myriad ways. Maybe the whole of creation is always groaning, growing and changing, making its mistakes, evolving, interacting with all its life cells in a complex web of harmony and disharmony, just like us. Maybe everything lives in freedom with its Maker.

❦

How about a bit more reward and punishment to make it work better? I sometimes think that God could organise the universe in a clearer way so that we would have the satisfaction of seeing justice on a wider scale and would be encouraged to behave better. I especially think this when I would like to see others punished, less often when I face that I would be due for a measure of retribution! If we long for justice, however, maybe it is also because we can already see glimpses of that in life and these glimpses, plus the impulses of our hearts, encourage us to believe that this is the way things should be.

There is a rough sort of justice around us. Sometimes we nearly manage to set it up ourselves in our systems of government and judiciaries. Sometimes we can see people, including ourselves, getting what we deserve. Sometimes we even sense that who we are actually becoming as people is a sort of justice. We watch the tyrants and the sleazy people and we believe, deep down, that even though they win on one level of existence, they lose in some ultimate way.

We look at their faces and we know we don't want to become human beings like they are becoming, even as we envy their prosperity and power. We value some goodness in ourselves and in those around us, precisely because we see the unpleasant truth about those who are unjust. This is little comfort to those they damage and destroy (and, I believe, never should be suggested as such) but, as the human race, we sometimes know at our best that life is more than they are experiencing and enacting and that they are deathly people.

HAVING said all that, what would be wrong with a little more intervention by God? The first consideration would be a question of how the balance between the dignity of human freedom and this 'guided democracy' would exist.

Even guided democracies restrict freedom, the exercise of individual and corporate human responsibility. Would we ever grow up if God took more part in disciplining the peoples of the world? Children who never learn to live responsibly without the threat/promise of direct reward and punishment are not the best examples of mature humankind as a rule. They also have a quite different relationship with their parents than those who are set free to grow up. Maybe God wants a grown up relationship with us, a sort of sharing together in the developing of a good creation.

If there were a lot of direct rewarding and punishing, we would probably all behave better for the wrong reasons. In fact, we might become good in order to gain. Would this matter? I think that it would matter. There is a Christian theology called 'prosperity theology'. Those who preach it claim that people who are Christian are likely to be more prosperous in their lives and businesses. It inevitably leads to self-righteous judgments about the less prosperous and an unpleasant quality in those who are the 'good' and therefore 'prosperous'. It encourages us to sit comfortably with our wealth while others starve and struggle for survival. It invites us to punish those who suffer because of the sinfulness of others and because of the seemingly random events of life. Maybe God does not want a relationship with us which is distorted by very direct rewards and punishments.

Sometimes I feel that if there really were direct rewards and punishments, as apart from the natural consequences of our actions and attitudes which we can see, I might not be able to bear it. Have you ever really sat down and asked yourself what you would actually deserve in an absolutely just system of rewards and punishments? Now I don't think that I am too much worse than the next person but, if I was punished for every nasty thought and attitude, every wilful act that hurt or damaged another, every lie or half-truth, every individual and corporate injustice in which I participated and every time I lacked love — I could go on — I don't think I could survive it. Thank heavens, or thank God, or thank anything, that life is not delivering absolute justice to me! If you think about it, life is actually, necessarily, quite kindly and forgiving when it comes to rewards and punishments in relation to our activities. It thus invites us to be equally kind and forgiving of others.

Also, could it be that the ultimate aspiration God has for us is that we will do good for its own sake? The question of Satan to God in the book of Job is a valid one. How often do we really do good for its own sake, and yet is that not the highest form of human activity?

I remember an old woman of great dignity who used to receive Meals on Wheels. One day when I visited her, I learned that she had cancelled this service. Knowing that she was almost blind and quite incapacitated, I asked her why she had done this. She said, 'I couldn't stand any longer being brought meals by women who were obviously bringing them for some reason of their own. They would come in every day and tell me how they had given up all the things they wanted to be doing in order to bring me my meals. If they don't really want to bring me my meals, I don't want to have them.' People who do things because they want to please some God or because they 'ought', rather than because they honestly and freely want to do so, often end up oppressing others.

I recall another woman with whom I was discussing the traditional view of hell. I said I didn't believe in the fire and brimstone version, and she said spontaneously, 'But why would you be good if you didn't think there was a hell for those who aren't good?' I grieved for someone who was not really living a joyful and abundant life and who probably resented the thought that those naughty people, who she apparently saw as happier than herself, might not be heading for hell in another life. The good she was engaged in had, underlying it, a fear of a hell rather than the generosity of good.

Is justice possible anyway? In looking at human pain and tragedy, it can easily be seen that the choices which we are able to make are often very complex indeed. Even in interpersonal relationships, it is not always a simple matter of choosing what is good and right. Often there are real conflicts of interests between the several people for whom we care and the values which we want to uphold. All the different capacities of people to respond to situations come into play, as well as our varying personalities and understandings of what is best for us.

There is rarely one 'right' and just way forward for anybody. A mother with her family can easily think of examples of this sort of conflict on a micro scale. When it comes to our life together as a community and as a world, who would dare to claim that we can easily see where justice lies and how it could be offered to everyone. Imagine trying to supervise the world in a way which guarantees absolute justice for everyone! How, in the indescribable complexity of human life, with all its interweaving consequences of behaviour and events, could justice be delivered in rewards and punishments to us all? When I studied the Book of Job, our lecturer showed us a video of the film *Sophie's Choice*. This was a powerful portrayal of the dreadful complexity of life.

It is all very well to think that because God knows everything, it would not be impossible. I prefer to suggest that precisely because God knows everything, our motives, our histories, our varying opportunities, support systems and capabilities, that God is more likely to know that it would be impossible to deliver neat rewards and punishments. Perhaps God simply built in enough justice to symbolise what life could be like and in order to invite us to try to be just ourselves.

ODDLY enough, even though we may see that a clear justice is unlikely to be possible, we still hope that there won't be outright injustice — that is, really bad things happening to good people. We like to think that if we pray and are decent, we will be the one saved in the train smash. We can't help thinking that frequent tragedy in somebody's life must be linked with some meaning. Surely things can't be all that random? Are people being 'tested' or is there some hidden plan of God which would help us to understand if we could only know it?

I have met many people who struggle and strain to make tragedy and suffering meaningful. I recall a person who was trying to understand the death of a whole family in a frightful road accident. In the end, he decided that God had allowed the family to be killed because it made possible a Christian witness to the tow-truck driver who picked up their car. To most of us that would seem as almost obscene as a view of life and God, but if you decide that everything is specifically directed by God and has a hidden meaning, then you may end up with that sort of interpretation.

Still others believe that there is a 'learning' in all human suffering. Sometimes there is, but I confess to being very wary of this view.

It is often used to justify oppression and to require people to feel that they should be able to discern this learning in the midst of pointless and ongoing suffering. Sometimes I suspect we talk about looking for these learnings in order to save God from being blamed. I believe that we could at least respect ourselves, and others, enough to acknowledge that sometimes people learn nothing worthy from some suffering.

This is not to say that suffering cannot be transformed into a time of growing and learning, but it is to say that this is not always so. It is also to say that the possibility of learning something from it should not be a justification for the experience of suffering. Any learning is a by-product of, not an adequate reason for, suffering. If it were a reason, you would have to make a very convincing case which justified the obvious lack of suffering (and presumably need to learn) in some, compared to the obvious surfeit of suffering and learning in others.

ALWAYS the question must be 'What sort of God are we talking about if we hold the view we hold?' If there is a God who selects people to 'test' with injustices to see how strong they are or what they will do in response or even to learn, then we are dealing with a God who is less loving than most of us and who enjoys playing with the lives of people and watching them like butterflies stuck on a pin. Surely there is enough 'natural' suffering in life without a God who gives us little contrived tests!

If all our innocent suffering is connected with some hidden plan of God, then I suggest it makes life very perilous, especially since the 'plan' rarely seems to become at all clear. We would have a rather tricky God who is really only pretending to offer us dignity and freedom. Underneath our authentic and often tough journeys of life, with all their apparent choices and genuine aspirations, we would have this God who is overriding it all the time with the big plan. It would be like suddenly discovering that cats really rule the world instead of humans. (Occasionally I think they do!)

In fact, I believe that genuinely innocent suffering is quite random. It is not linked with any obscure punishment or plan, but rather is the consequence of being part of an unfinished and very free creation. The rain does indeed fall on the just and the unjust alike, and so does trouble. That is not to say that there is not also built into the universe a centre, a God, who cares about what happens to us. Why do I believe that? Because I experience a sense of that caring, a connection with me in my grieving, my weakness, my fear and my pain. I know others and read of others who have the same experience. I cannot prove the existence of this caring God. It is an act of faith to believe it. It also makes more sense to me than some other options.

WHEN trying to understand life, I sometimes find it useful to look at the broad alternatives for a world view. It helps to rule out some ideas as unacceptable to yourself, so that you can more fully explore what is left.

These are some of the options that I have considered:

- We can decide that at the centre of everything there is evil. Few of us can live from that option, because it carries so little hope and it somehow violates our view of ourselves and those we know. On the other hand, some people do try to live from evil.

- We can decide that there is nothing, or chaos at the centre of everything, or if there were something or somebody, that 'thing' or 'one' is now gone. Many people choose some version of this. They live their lives without trying to find meaning and pattern in it, other than that which they can see before them. Those people often have a very high sense of their own responsibility to live justly and creatively. However, they see themselves as being alone, among other human beings, in this endeavour. They live to please no God, but to satisfy their own understanding of integrity. All this I deeply respect. Of course there are still others in this category who live only for themselves because they see no larger picture and no purpose in doing anything else.

- We can decide to believe that in spite of the random justice and injustice of life, at the centre of everything lies love and good — we may call that energy, or being, different names. Those who choose this option then face life deciding how to connect with and interpret the activity of this one whom I will call God. There are, of course, many different views of this God, even within Christianity. All great religions have some sort of good and loving centre to the universe and different ways of working with that.

I BELIEVE that God is the ultimate source of good and love and that this flows towards us from God in an unconditional way. I believe that this good flows equally towards everyone and everything, regardless of their view of life or their behaviour. I think this loving energy can be accessed, if we choose, and that it helps to sustain us on the rigorous journey of life. It also engages with us in 'calling' us into a heightened awareness of new possibilities for the rebirthing of good, love and justice in the world, even though we may hear the 'calling' dimly and with ambiguity. Sometimes it is given as a gift, even though we have not asked for it. To decide that we will accept that eternal and unconditional good is present around us, within us and beyond us and that we will try to connect with that and be open to that, is a way we can choose to live. That is my choice.

And what about Jesus?

Lots of people ask me why I would take any account of Jesus at all — as a feminist, as a lesbian who has suffered at the hands of the Christian church, as a person who has a somewhat universal approach to God and who respects people of other faiths and none? I can only say that I find it immensely helpful to believe in a God who gives some indication of having experienced human life, and I think that is a central message embodied in the life of Jesus. The God who takes our flesh, lays down divine power and enters our journey has great credibility for me and the possibility of genuine grace through understanding.

I also find something compelling about the paradigm lived out in the life and death of Jesus which relates to the paradox of crucifixion and resurrection. Whether or not I believe in the precise historical truth of the events of the life and death of Jesus is less important to me than the significance of their meaning in understanding the nature of life. When I look at those events, I see layers of mystery and meaning which I believe that the church has not always offered very clearly to people. I will reflect on just some of them.

THE most common belief that the church offers people is what it calls the 'doctrine of the atonement'. The idea of the atonement has the capacity to be either the most saving or the most destructive understanding of the death of Jesus on the cross. Even though the atonement is the mysterious 'at-one-ment' of God with us, we use the word all the time as though it is about atoning for something. As soon as we do this, we create a terrible separation between the all-loving, self-sacrificing Jesus and a possible harsh God behind that Jesus who demands the sacrifice before we can be forgiven.

This God becomes the same God who in many cultures demanded

the sacrifice of pigeons, lambs, virgins and children. Even if this God said 'Just one more sacrifice and I will be satisfied if it is the ultimate sacrifice, that of my own son', it is still a harsh God. It is the God who Abraham thought he heard asking him to sacrifice Isaac in the Hebrew Scriptures. Many Christian people and many who think they know what Christians believe, live with this harsh God and a Jesus who they can never repay for saving them from this harsh God.

They live all their lives trying to repay the debt, and Good Friday becomes for them a powerful reminder of how much they still owe to the dying Jesus and the harsh God who demanded that he die. Many oppressed people have been further oppressed and brought into subjection by those who actually represent the powerful, cruel and perfect Father God who continually points to the suffering Jesus and reminds them of their wickedness in sending him to die.

So, what is the at-one-ment between God and ourselves? I believe we are helped in understanding it if we remember that Jesus said, 'I am the way, the truth and the life. Come, take up your cross and follow me.' This God says to us:

In becoming human, I have become one with you. There is no weakness, sinfulness, loss and deathliness I have not entered before you. On the day of my crucifixion, I will take upon myself all the things that stand between you and fullness of life. I will walk towards them, experience their violence, and take upon myself their humiliation, fear and pain. Watch, and you will see that I go through the same loneliness and agony of heart that you do. Watch and see which is more powerful — all the deathly things in human existence or the power of my loving, caring, faithful and truthful life.

As we watch this death, we see God demonstrate before us that this God has not turned away from anything that happens or could happen to us. He does not slide around them, or deny that they exist. He does not bargain with them, blame others or save himself from them with his godly power. He totally enters our life and stays within the things of our death for a symbolic three days. In all this there is nothing that we need to protect God from — all that we are and could be is carried within his body.

We had a Good Friday service at Pitt Street Church once where the people placed a large cross at the front of the church. They invited everyone to remember the hard things in their lives, the wounds delivered by others and by life, the weaknesses, the failures, the losses, all the things that were hard to bear and to take a stone from a basket and put it at the foot of the cross. Many people did.

Then the cross was lifted up, carried like a body or a casket and tenderly placed on a white cloth on the floor in the centre of the church. The edges of the cloth were wrapped around the cross like a shroud. The people were invited to believe that all their hard things were absorbed into the body of Christ for cherishing, comforting, healing and forgiving. They were invited to come and cover the cross with rose petals, to cherish the Body of Christ and their own wounds as did the women who tended the body of Jesus in the tomb. They were then invited to leave their hard things there and go forth to wait until Easter Day. On Easter Day, they returned and lifted up the cross to find an empty space outlined by fragrant rose petals. In this way, we enacted the moving and powerful possibilities in the paradigm of the crucifixion and resurrection of Jesus.

Last Easter I visited Pitt Street again. By chance, they repeated this service for the first time since I had left. I took a stone, experiencing my deathly life since 'coming out' as a lesbian, and placed it at the foot of the cross for healing. I am not sure I really believed in what I was doing at that moment. But it worked. I was healed.

Hard Questions for God

WHEN I was in Europe recently, I was given a profound and moving story which came from the massacre at Dunblane in Scotland and which offered me another possibility for meaning in the crucifixion. The story was told by one of the ministers from Dunblane who was trying to think about God and life in the light of the massacre as he went home one night:

> As I was reflecting on all this, I made my way to the school gates which had become a centre of devotion, transformed by the floral and other offerings placed there by residents and strangers alike. As I approached, the street outside the school was deserted apart from a handful of police officers, and a gang of youths aged, I suppose, about seventeen to twenty. As I watched, they took from their pockets sixteen night-lights — one for each dead child — and, kneeling on the damp pavement, arranged them in a circle and then lit them, using glowing cigarettes to do so.
>
> They stood around the candles for a moment, then one of them said, 'I suppose somebody should say something.' As they wondered how to do it, one of them spotted me, identified me as a minister and called me over with the words, 'You'll know what to say.' Of course, the reality was quite different. As I stood there, tears streaming down my face, I had no idea what to say, or how to say it. Words had not been especially useful to me, or anyone else, in this crisis.
>
> So we stood, holding on to each other for a moment, and then I said a brief prayer. That was the catalyst that enabled them too to start praying. A question came first: 'What kind of a world is this?' Another asked, 'Is there any hope?' Someone said, 'I wish I could trust God.' 'I'll need to change,' said a fourth one. As he did so, he looked first at me and then glanced over his shoulder to the police who were on duty. He reached in his pocket and I could see he had a knife. He knelt again by the ring of candles and quietly said, 'I'll not be needing this now', as he tucked it away under some of the flowers lying nearby. One of the others produced what looked like a

piece of chain and did the same. We stood silently for a moment and then went our separate ways.

In recent days I saw again on television the person who was once a naked child in Vietnam, running in terror from the violence of war. This image on our television screens, at the time of the war, was one of the turning points in the ending of that war. On that day, we saw the consequences of our violence — the slaughter of the innocent. In these two stories, I am not suggesting that the events had to happen in order for us to see the consequences of what we do, but that when they do happen, we sometimes have moments of truth like that.

Therefore, maybe, as we stand before the image of the cross of Jesus Christ it is another occasion when we see there the end result of our betrayals, our weakness, our sinfulness and our violence. We stand in total vulnerability before ourselves and our God. In Christian terms, we have tried to destroy our God.

We face our capacity to destroy the things of good and innocence and truth in our life and what it might mean to succeed in doing that. It is a moment when we are confronted and invited to lay down our knives, our violences and hates for the sake of the survival of our innocent and our innocence. It is also a moment when we realise, with relief, that we cannot kill God. There is a power for good which can defeat our evil.

FOR me, Jesus on the cross is the revealer of the way as well as the creator of the way. This Jesus challenges that fullness of life is about our being rewarded if we are good and punished when we are bad, and that being good will inevitably make us happy and prosperous. This Jesus heads towards all the powers of oppression, exposing them as he goes. He demonstrates that in an incomplete universe, God walks with us and gives himself to fight for justice to the death.

He walks bravely past the traitors who think that only they know what is right and who believe that they are called to destroy people who don't agree with them. He travels along with weak and puzzled friends whose courage fail, who sleep through his agony, who can only watch his suffering and weep and still claims them as friends. He stands in the midst of those who see the truth and wash their hands of the responsibility of knowing. He hangs there among those who cast lots for anything of his they can carry away, who shout in support one day and become the meanest of crucifiers the next, according to whom they see as most convincing at the time. He dies between two thieves, honestly crying out in his aloneness and pain.

And, in all this, the victorious life of God can be seen in Jesus as, although he is saved from nothing, he is not determined by anything. With dignity, courage, with receiving from his friends as far as they are able to give, with faith and truth, he moves into all our realities and even as he dies, becomes the victim of no-one.

There in his death, deep down some of us can see something which is never defeated. In the old stories of many cultures we can see the same crucifixion/resurrection paradigm in the mythical or real heroes and saints. If you go to Bali and watch a dance about the battle between good and evil that is put on for tourists, you will see a similar paradigm emerging from ancient Indian Hindu culture. The people are in trouble because of evil forces. The king comes to visit them and is concerned for them. He sends his son to save them and the son is captured by the evil forces, the dragons. They hang him up on a tree to kill him, but, at the moment of his death, he leaps off the tree and becomes a God. He then returns to sprinkle healing water over the people. I hope I have understood what was being portrayed accurately enough, but it was something near to that story.

Even in our own Anzac story the same paradigm is dimly there. We celebrate people who were sent on a seemingly hopeless mission, mainly by people who were not prepared to face the cost of that mission themselves. Most of them died and whether or not they achieved their mission is, at least, ambiguous. And yet some of us see in that event, if we can separate it from its violence, something which is about losing but nevertheless winning.

In the landscape of this country, I believe we can see the paradigm and it forms our culture and life. From the peril of the fire, we see greener leaves spring forth from the blackened stumps of the gum trees. In the desert, the life stirs in secret ways. In the cities, the grass grows, whether we nurture it or not.

This truth stands in contradiction to all our theories about what is ultimately dangerous to us or life-giving for us. Even as we do not understand it well, nor are able to describe in detail what we see, we know something which informs our world view and enhances our life.

Some General Thoughts about Surviving Well Enough

WHEN someone shares with you an account of a traumatic journey through life, you can either sit there trying to think of the answers you will offer to them for the next part of the journey, or you can say, 'How on earth have you survived all this?' Even if they are barely surviving, or have only survived for part of the story, they probably do have their own ways of surviving. Most of us don't stop to ask ourselves how we are surviving, however, we just act and react to things as they happen.

I have found that it is useful, in preparing to survive a rather tough journey of life, to try to discover your own type of spirituality. I would describe spirituality as the way in which you connect with and/or express your connection with the 'other' in life. That can be experienced as the presence of God, wonder, awe, or something greater which is beyond yourself or to be found within yourself. You don't have to be religious to be a person of spirituality. For many people, the development of their spirituality may have nothing to do with a belief system. It may be a very delicate, inarticulate part of yourself, something you don't discuss or can't really explain.

To deliberately explore the way in which your life is supported, healed and restored is to live more intentionally connected with the things which empower you. Although we can make suggestions to others about these connections, our own way of being empowered may not work for them. There is a certain degree of uniqueness about each person's spirituality.

I remember when I first became a parish minister I had just learned the helpfulness of meditation. I decided that meditation was a great idea for everyone. I found some resistance among the members of the parish and thought to myself that one day they would see the light — it was probably a matter of their spiritual maturity. In the end, some people really challenged me and pointed out that they were just different.

A group of us then did the little exercise which follows and, to my surprise, I found that some people restore themselves and connect with their inner life by intense physical activity. That was hard to believe for someone like myself, who cannot imagine physical activity as other than necessary exercise and likely to be tiring.

The variety we discovered in our group was quite significant. It made us realise that we needed to be respectful of the way each one of us works with the developing of our spirituality and helped us to understand some of the tensions that were present when we tried to arrange corporate activities for restoration and relaxation.

THE following is a simple set of questions for reflecting on this:

In your life journey

1 Remember your most vivid experience of being carried beyond yourself — an experience of being in the presence of God, or some loving power beyond yourself, a moment of awe or mystery, of greater clarity and strength:

Where were you?
Who was there?
Were you in a large or small place? Mountain or sea? City or country?
Was it among people or with one other? Or were you alone?
Were you still or moving? Were you speaking or silent?

2 If you had to find something which reminds you of God, or a higher power than yourself, what would it be?

You may find that you choose a different image at different points in your life. As this happens, it may give you a sense of your changing needs and where you are on your spiritual journey.

3 If you had to find something which reminds you of yourself, what would it be?

As you do this, it enables you to pause and become more aware of what is happening to you and who you are at the moment. This respects your response to life — for example, as lonely, peaceful, energised, together, flying apart, stuck or something else.

4 Where do you go to heal or restore yourself? Are you alone, or with others? What do you do there?

Your answer may be similar to that for Question One but it is another way of asking it which may be more helpful to you.

5 What is your favourite poem, text, song, book, cartoon, saying?

This gives you a clue to a theme which is important to you.

6 What is your favourite music?

You probably play it a lot anyway, but it is good to recognise it as part of your survival resources, and one which you can sometimes carry with you. Are there other art forms from which you draw comfort and energy?

As people answer questions like these, they are likely to discover their own general spiritual themes. Is healing and renewal found in the grand or the womb-like space? Are we refreshed and energised by being alone or with others?

If you can remember an environment in which you were renewed and connected with a peace or energy outside yourself, it is sometimes possible to find a place like that again, or bring it to your memory again when under pressure. You can even place around you things which remind you of 'saving' or inspiring moments or of special people in your journey and to draw energy from them. Every time I set up my workplace, I find myself carefully arranging all my 'icons' around me — lots of things which have been given to me in particular situations or that remind me strongly of the giver who is special for my support in life. I have particular books, a kaleidoscope, a paperweight, some photos, a vase, a candle or two, some small boxes and pictures. As I work, I look at them and play special music. Oddly enough, Mozart's *Requiem* is my best 'writing music'. (I don't know what that means!)

The simple exercise above can be used for people to reflect on the answers, and find the symbols that are important to them and which describe their state of being in a silent period alone. It can also be used by people in a group, who spend a time alone and then share anything they choose with others in the group. The sharing sometimes explains genuine differences between people who are otherwise in close relationship. It can also be a non-threatening way to share who you are at that moment. It is surprising how hard it is to tell other people how you are at any moment, compared with sharing that if you are holding something which you have found as representing an image of yourself.

MANY of us live carrying the guilts and pains of the past with us, rather than the creative and life-giving things. We are also often predominantly focused on what we want in the future so that we hardly experience the possibilities and gifts in our present. Those who are spiritually growing live with a heightened degree of awareness about the present — who they are in the present, who others are in the present and what gifts and resources are around them for enhancing life. When we are able to do this, life is more real and our energy becomes directed into our present situation rather than what happened in the past or what may happen in the future — a much more creative and healthy way to live.

I remember a spiritual director I had in the past telling me about what she called the 'sacrament of the moment'. She said, 'When you are stressed or grieved, look around you. See the beauty of the shadows and the light, the colours in things, the movement of a leaf, the signs of life on another's face, the grass in the concrete. All around you are special gifts of the moment for you to live from.' At first I thought that sounded a bit romantic, but I decided to try doing it. I was astonished at how unaware I had become of the things around me — how I had hardly noticed so many lovely and sometimes small gifts waiting for me there. I am still surprised at how separated we can become from the things that are close to us and which wait to heal, comfort and energise us. We can also be just as distanced from the people who are offering us supportive care and resources for living. I am sure that we can all hear someone we know saying 'Nobody cares about me' when there is support all around them. Sometimes that person is myself.

※

SOME people imagine that spirituality it is an exclusively personal thing. I believe that it is a false view to imagine that, even if we spend most of our time on an introspective journey, we are not spiritually formed by our community environment. If our meditation life is strongly used as an escape from the world outside us, then that in itself forms our spirit. Those who claim to be interested in the spiritual development of people and see themselves as separating out from society and encouraging the turning away from social and political realities, are, I believe, offering a diminished view of the spiritual possibilities. It is also an abrogation of human spiritual responsibility not to participate in the creation of a world where all people may live in wholeness and in an environment where each spirit may fly free in joy.

If you live in a society where your class, race, gender, age, culture, ability or sexual orientation is regarded as inferior, then already your spirit, the essence of your being, is travelling on a tough journey. If it survives in determination, in courage and self-affirmation, then it will be all the stronger for the struggle, but it may well be wounded. Alongside those who survive there may be many more who live forever with less life. If you live in relationship with a formally religious institution by choice or by culture, that too is both formed by you and forming of you as it gives models for the spiritual life and ways of interpreting the journey. For some, the presence of religion is alienating and therefore also formative of their spirituality.

The culture of a society, in itself, impacts on our sense of being. If I stand within the culture of the United States, I immediately feel as though I am struggling for my existence in its loud, closed-in, confident, over-the-top style. If I go to Japan, I feel clumsy, large and intrusive and feel the need to try to make myself smaller and more elegant so that I am not so obvious. If I go to England, I wonder why everyone is so distant and sure of themselves, without sharing enough words to connect us. Each of these experiences tells me something about my understated, somewhat inarticulate, homely and faintly cheeky Australian spirit. When I return to my place, my spirit stretches itself out again in relief.

If this corporate journey is circular it is because, as we together form our life, it affects us all in the process of its formation, according to the role we play. The life we achieve together is then forming for us and others as it impacts on our capacity to live with fullness — body, mind, heart and spirit. At this very moment, Australia is, I believe, making choices about how mean it will become on all fronts and we should recognise that whatever corporate spirit emerges will profoundly affect who each one of us becomes in our spirituality. We do not ever live alone.

I have written in an earlier chapter of this book about the way the landscape interacts with our spirit. In all this, we are on a spiritual journey of infinite variety.

Rituals to mark and honour the journey

Not everyone finds it helpful to have rituals or rites of passage in their life journey, but many do. Of course you need someone with the confidence to initiate a ritual, and that is not common in a society which has a self-conscious, Anglo-Celtic base. We are all familiar with rituals like baptism (or other rites of entry into a group), weddings and funerals.

Quite apart from the more obvious rites of passage, I have found there are other helpful ways of marking the journey. They don't need to be elaborate. A moment can be made significant by just saying, 'Wow! This is a moment to celebrate. Let's drink to it!' Many people think that their life journey is insignificant, not worthy of being marked and honoured. In fact, no life journey is insignificant. Almost all of us make tough or special decisions, survive difficult times and could well celebrate or recognise many more moments of importance.

To recognise what is happening to us, and pause to do so, is to make the moment significant. Religious communities try to do that in their regular gatherings for worship and sacramental life. They are really hoping to enact a ritual which invites people to believe that their lives are important to God and can be brought before God for honest accountability, grieving and celebrating and for renewal. There is a mixture of thanksgiving and praise for the company of God on the journey and an openness to new possibilities in the power of God and each other's support for the next stage. The church sometimes does that very well and sometimes not so well.

For many people, however, the rituals of the institutional church are not helpful. Perhaps they do not reflect the authentic spirituality of many people. Perhaps many of us do not fit into the church culture, or that of any religious institution. Nevertheless, there are still times when some people would find it helpful to be supported by others in either marking and celebrating a time in their lives or enacting a ritual which affirms their liberation, forgiveness or healing. Sometimes amazing things happen in direct response to this. Sometimes the ritual becomes a signpost to a new hope about things, an indication of the love of God, or of a connection with universal love, and/or with our friends, which carries us forward.

I remember being asked by a group of women to come and lead a ritual in their small town where a large number of women had been raped and where community life was beginning to break down in fear and mistrust. The women did not really know what they wanted, except that they needed to gather women together and find new courage and community. A few of us worked on what would happen. In a way, we used the understandings which we had underpinning the best of our church liturgy and adapted them. I have found that, in a sense, all encouraging and healing rituals are basically the same in essence.

The women were invited to gather in a local church, which was made available for the occasion and they came in large numbers. We firstly did some things which reminded us that we were not alone and that we were people of dignity and courage. In the front, we hung a large quilt which had been made by hundreds of other women at a conference as a patchwork expressing their lives in both joy and pain. This symbolised the fact that we were not alone. We lit purple, green and white candles and affirmed that we were women of dignity, women who weep for the suffering of the world and women who had hope.

We told the story of the horrors of the rape and the fear and loneliness which followed. Then an old women told the story of a mine disaster that had happened years ago in the same place and how the women had survived and supported each other. We formed a large circle, sang some songs together and passed around flowers that had been made by women in another city as a sign of their caring. We ended by singing a blessing song for us all.

As we had supper together afterwards, we found women spontaneously arranging networks of support for the coming days — the reforming of community in the face of its threat. The rapist was eventually caught, but in the meantime, women rediscovered their power to be strong and to care for each other and their community. The ritual was really very simple, as most good rituals are. It just reminded those women that they were part of a wider community of caring, it acknowledged and respected the reality of their traumatic situation, it reminded them of the strength of women who had gone before them and claimed their own good energy and caring for the coming time.

In essence, I think that is the form of most rituals. The fact that these things are ritualised focuses all the realities and possibilities. In symbols, stories, acts and imaging they rehearse new life and community. The fact that a ritual is structured and has boundaries makes it manageable for many people to enter and participate. It also becomes a sort of survival memory when things become tough. I often think we have hardly begun to recognise what courage, strength and new life would be enabled if we worked on this area of life with confidence and creativity.

In the End, the Passion

As I have written this book, I have been having a conversation with myself as well as with others. In the evolving of the writing in response to that conversation, some things have become even sharper than they were for me previously.

I have realised that virtually every survival and every living of the fuller life has to do with being open to moving ourselves into a wider perspective, seeing ourselves in a bigger frame. It is as we see ourselves as part of something bigger, that the vision for both our living and surviving is enhanced. New resources are perceived for survival, not just in added personal support from others but in the recognition that we are part of a great human story, even as we struggle in our own moment and place.

The energy to go on, the courage to face things and the hope for the next day may come from history or from the brave struggle of others in another part of the world. It may come from the sight of a group of tiny ants labouring up the wall, carrying a breadcrumb ten times their own size. This encouragement is not about seeing others as worse off than we are, and thereby reminding us that we should be grateful for our lot. On the contrary, it comes from seeing others as having strength, courage, faith, love and hope in the face of equally difficult life journeys. It is about seeing them hold together in community and in feeling their invitation to join this community of human and cosmic struggle.

Part of that widening of the perspective has always included for me the concept of a God who is my encourager and who can enlarge my life beyond what I thought were the boundaries of my own love, energy, courage and hope. I suppose you could say that I include God in my conversation of life. Nevertheless, I watch with genuine interest and respect the credibility of those who walk their spacious journey in another way, in other company, or who define the travelling differently.

I believe that it is within the very 'conversation' which our lives have with each other that our lives are best sustained. As we make any sort of non-destructive and honest connection, we are not only informed about the experience of others in an intellectual way, but our very gut — our bodies, hearts and souls — take energy and healing from each other in a myriad of ways. Those ways are not simply about talking with each other — they sometimes, in their medium, take us by surprise.

At one point during the writing of this book, I went to see the movie *Wilde*, which is about the life of Oscar Wilde. Obviously I identified with some of his struggle for the respect for the love which cannot always be named, even if his lifestyle did not always appeal to me. As I was watching the movie I kept hearing the music, which had been written by Debbie Wiseman for the film, and I found it quite special. On the way home, I bought the CD of the soundtrack.

Weeks later, I was feeling rather discouraged by some of the responses to my own life and I played the music from *Wilde*. I don't think I was inspired by Oscar Wilde but by Debbie Wiseman's heart and musicianship as she contemplated his life. I was not thinking to myself about the life of Oscar Wide as I heard the music. I was being encouraged and comforted by the sound and feeling which lay within the music. I don't even know what Debbie Wiseman's feelings were when she wrote it, or who she is, for that matter. I was co-opting a gift from her and receiving from it something for the ongoing of my own life. It felt as though we were all interacting in a conversation between people who are never likely to meet each other. It reminded me that we are all, if we are open to it, in some cosmic connection of concern and the endless renewing of life and hope. That is what I believe.

I think that the good life has about it a creative passion for the supremacy of love. This love is not sentimental. In my woman's body, as many other women do, I carry a paradigm about the bringing forth of new life, and that cannot be sentimental. It is about the amazing conceiving of new possibilities, and about the nurturing of that conception in a myriad of ways. The nurturing involves a generous sharing of all that you are with the evolving new life — a cherishing of it, as you rock it in a womb-space under your heart. It does not pay for its place there, nor for its sharing of your resources. It is cared for there because of your love of life itself and your cherishing for this vulnerable newness. Then, one day, you enter the labour and pain of bringing something to birth and both you and the new life grow in this magnificent undertaking.

I believe that deep within most women is this knowledge, whether they have literally given birth or not. We know that little that is worth anything emerges in life without some cost and generosity. It does not come from 'efficiencies' which ruthlessly take from people their hopes and talents and kindnesses. It does not come from 'the markets' which are like a terrible competition to rip as much as possible from everyone else, regardless of what happens to people on the way. It is not a matter of the 'user paying'. It is far more gracious than any of that. It is more reasonable that the 'rational' because it cares and gives in ways which create other caring and giving. Creative and good life for each of us and all of us is not a business plan but a harmony of collaboration and liberation.

The full life has a passion for searching for truth and for paying the price of its upholding. It claims love for itself as well as for others. It laughs at its own pomposities and messianic tendencies and goes and sits on the grass for a picnic to cool itself down, or raises its glass to the wry and astute comments of its critical children. It acknowledges that its passion is only sustained here and there as a sort of sign of what might be.

The passion for life carries us well beyond passivity and powerlessness into a state where we matter, others matter and everything (well, nearly everything) matters. It makes life the supreme adventure of big mistakes, big cheers for surviving and sometimes living a new order of things, coasting along in peacefulness where possible and a lot of very ordinary things in between.

In the end, the passion for life is, thankfully, held safely in the history of the human struggle that has gone before us, in that which stands beside ourselves now and on into the generations that will come after us. When we put the best of all that together, the passion for love and life gathered together, then we are able to image us all walking firmly towards our deaths. We can see ourselves honestly grieving and fearful as we go and yet still moving on with determination. We can see that, paradoxically, this walking towards death has led us one step further towards love and life.

Writing this book has felt, some of the time, like walking towards a death. To try to put into print what you have experienced and what you believe is to replay deaths and moments of life. It is also to risk discovering in the conversation which then, hopefully, ensues, that much of what you have risked putting into print for others to see must die because it cannot live in the face of their truths. This death is the lesser one, however. The greater death is not to attempt the connection with each other that leads us into the mystery of cosmic life, life beyond any of our imaginings.

And the wonder of it is that among all the grandeur, the bigger dreams, all we are required to do is to be honestly human together, ordinary, everyday people, nutting along our rackety path of life, with all its detours, its fallings down and its marvellous little miracles. This, in itself, is the passion.

At some profound level, it is about being 'real' and being real is costly and marvellous. When I think of this I remember the old, old children's story called *The Velveteen Rabbit*. The toy rabbit longed to be real, as he sensed the old toy Skin Horse was real. He asks the Skin Horse how you become real and the Skin Horse says, 'It doesn't happen all at once ... You become. It takes a long time. That's why it doesn't happen to people who break easily, or have sharp edges, or who have to be carefully kept. Generally, by the time you are Real, most of your hair has been loved off, and your eyes drop out and you get loose in the joints and very shabby. But these things don't matter at all, because once you are Real you can't be ugly, except to people who don't understand.' (Margery Williams, *The Velveteen Rabbit, or How Toys Become Real*, Heinemann, 1922)

Marge Piercy's poem 'For Strong Women' images this real and passionate journey in another way. I invite strong men to adapt it for themselves, imagining a strength which arises in strong loving and the adventure of vulnerability. Part of her poem reads:

*A strong woman is a woman who craves love
like oxygen or she turns blue choking.
A strong woman is a woman who loves
strongly and weeps strongly and is strongly
terrified and has strong needs. A strong woman is strong
in words, in action, in connection, in feeling;
she is not strong as a stone but as a wolf
suckling her young. Strength is not in her, but she
enacts it as the wind fills her sails.*

*What comforts her is others loving
her equally for the strength and for the weakness*

> *from which it issues, lightning from a cloud.*
> *Lightning stuns. In rain the clouds disperse.*
> *Only water of connection remains,*
> *flowing through us. Strong is what we make*
> *each other. Until we are strong together,*
> *a strong woman is strongly afraid.**

That is how I understand the journey. She speaks for me. Living is, indeed, an everyday passion and 'strong is what we make each other'.

---

* 'For Strong Women' by Marge Piercy, copyright © 1977, 1980 by Marge Piercy and Middlemarsh, Inc. From *The Moon is Always Female* published by Alfred A. Knopf, Inc. Used by permission of the Wallace Literary Agency, Inc.

Rituals and Liturgies for the Journey

For those who feel wounded or betrayed
and who find a religious ritual helpful

OPENING SENTENCES

LEADER:
>Our God is a God who longs to be with us

PEOPLE:
>Who reaches into our deepest places
>who weeps within our tears.

L: Our God is a God who holds us in the womb-space
of compassion

P: Labouring to bring us to birth in the new life of freedom,
tasting the blood of our pain.

L: Our God is like a rock

P: Unmoved from love,
unshaken by the anger in our righteous protest
firm beneath our feet
in the eternal creating of our holy ground.

The grieving journey

L: *Let us recall the journey of grieving,*
the place of safety and joy which has been left
and the loss along the way:

(The grievings, losses and disappointments are named)

L: *Let us taste the tears in this journey we have had together.*

(The bowl of saltwater 'tears' is shared and the pain honoured in silence)

READINGS AND REFLECTION

The affirmation

All: *There is no death*
from which you cannot rise in us, O God.
The power to fail
can never kill the gift of life,
unless we choose not to receive it from you.

Your Spirit is never defeated
by the woundings of life
however unjust, however painful.

Your grace in Christ
goes well beyond our understanding
and your love for us is never measured
by our love for ourselves.
Even as we walk a hard journey
we will claim together
this great hope.

We still need help for the future

L: *Let us place in the hands of God,*
all that disturbs us,
all our longings for those who we hold in loving concern.

(The people share their hopes and longings)

THE LIGHTING OF THE CANDLE

(The candle is lit and the people stand around it)

L: *Place your hands towards this flame.*
As its warmth spreads towards you,
receive the healing love of God and our love for each other.
In the name of the Christ,
who has walked every journey before you
and sees deeply into your hearts in understanding,
we announce a new day.
In the name of Christ,
All: *Amen.*

BLESSING

L: *Go in peace*
and may the God of grace encircle your soul
the God in Christ reach out to touch you
and the Spirit shine light on your path.
All: *Amen.*

A ritual of support

Using non-religious language and with less interaction in words and a focus on one person in its beginnings

Supporting a friend

(The friends gather)

OPENING

LEADER:
>At this moment in our friend's life
>we pause and gather around her/him.
>We are stronger and more caring when we are together.
>In between us, around us and within us
>is an energy for healing, comfort, courage and love.
>In the silence, let us remember that power.

(A silence is kept)

The grieving

(A pathway of red cloth is placed in the centre and a bunch of flowers to the side)

L: Let us recall the journey of grieving,
>the place of safety and joy which has been left
>and the losses along the way.
>As we speak, let us place a flower on this red cloth,
>as the pathway of pain of this life.

(Either the friends or the person name some of these things. As each person speaks, they take a flower and place it on the cloth)

L: (Name) we give you these flowers to carry with you
>in the next part of your journey.
>They are the sign of our company with you.

(The flowers are given)

READING

An encouraging poem or story

Strength for the journey

L: *We all need each other and many gifts for our next days.*
In the silence,
let us consider the most important resource that we need.

(A silence is kept)

L: *Let us go around the circle and share our needs.*

(The people say one word each to indicate their needs)

L: *In vulnerability, we have shared these things.*

People:
All of us need each other
and all the good that lies between us
for our human journey.

L: *Our lives are significant.*
Our travelling is new every day.
Let us celebrate a common hope.

(Glasses of wine or coffee are poured and passed around)

Let us drink to our friend! (Named)
Let us drink to each other!
Let us share a meal together. (if appropriate)
Go in peace.

(Music begins and people mingle)

Grieving the child

For those whose child is born with a disability or has become disabled

OPENING SENTENCES

LEADER:
> Carried with love under our heart:

PEOPLE:
> We waited for you.

L: Held close in the depths of our beings:

P: We waited for you.

L: Born from the life of God:

P: We imaged this child —
sound of body, mind, heart and soul
small gift of beauty and life.

This was not to be

L: But this, our child, faces life with a disability.
In its very beginnings there is placed a struggle for fullness of life.

It's not really that we weep for ourselves, O God,
although we do weep for ourselves too.
We wanted the best start to life for this child for its own sake.
We longed for it to have all the options for growing and being.
Life is usually hard anyway and we wanted it to have every chance.
When we saw the new reality,
we prayed and we prayed
and you didn't seem to hear us God.

We also really wanted a God
who would protect all children in their vulnerability
and now we don't know how to see you God.
We don't know how to understand what has happened to us
and our precious child.

> *Sometimes we cannot help but wonder if there is something*
> *that we have done which has caused this?*
> *But what sort of God would you be that would*
> *punish our child because of something in us?*
> *We know that is not the God we have known.*

P: All this is loss, O God.
All this is too much for us, O Jesus Christ.

L: In the silence
let us honour our pain.

(Period of silence)

Signs of the honouring

(A purple cloth is placed on the table, or on the floor in the centre)

L: This purple is the royal covering of pain that lies over our life.
This pain is beyond the commonplace,
it has dignity and significance.
It is to be respected and marked.

P: We will light a tiny candle
the flickering of the hope, the life, the remnant of our faith.

(A tea-candle is lit and placed on the cloth)

READINGS
The cry: Psalm 13
The assurance: Romans 8:22–27 & 31–39

The affirmation

L: Let us affirm our faith:
All: We believe that,
in the face of loss and grief we are free to cry out,
to protest in righteous anger,
to respect our own pain.

We believe that this cry never goes unheard,
that it is not lost in the silences and pits of our sadness.

We believe it is taken into the heart of our God
who weeps with us and walks with us
through every moment that has been,
and is to come.

We believe that,
as we bow our heads,
the Spirit covers us with her bright wings,
sorrowing in our sorrow and lifting our faces
to the warmth and love which waits for us,
cherishing us and giving us strength
for this unknown journey.

We believe in this God who says
'I will be with you, and that will be enough',
even as we find it hard to believe it will be enough.
In faith, we will move in to the next part of our life,
carrying close to our heart this new child,
this child in need of special care.

We will need help

L: Those were hard-won statements of faith, O God,
and often we cannot hold to them.
It looks like a long journey ahead
and we will need all the help that we can get.

P: Please gather the right companions around us
for this journey,
the ones who will carry us when our feet and souls are tired,
the ones who will have faith for us if our faith falters.

(The friends pray their own prayers for the family)

L: In Christ you said to us that if we knock, search and ask,
you will send to us the Holy Spirit, O God.

We are knocking, searching and asking now.
Send your Spirit in power upon us
for healing, faith, courage, endurance, and all that
we need for these next days.

P: *In the name of the Christ, Amen.*

The new child

L: *The child we expected is not the child we have.*
In this moment let us farewell the old child.

(Period of silence)

L: *Here is the child we have,*
the new child,
the precious one that belongs to its parents and to all of us
for sacred safe-keeping all the days of his/her life.

(If it is appropriate, the child is brought into the centre and surrounded by the people who lay their hands upon her/him)

P: *We welcome this child with love.*
We will watch over this child
and hold it surely within our community of hope.
The life of this child is a slender thread of gold among us.

(A gold thread is placed around the candle)

BLESSING

L: *Go in faith.*
And may God the Creator be nearer than breath,
Christ our friend hold your hand
and the Spirit surround you with grace.

All: *Amen.*

(This liturgy is for our son, Christopher. From *The Glory of Blood, Sweat and Tears*, Dorothy McRae-McMahon, JBCE, 1996.)

Ritual for those who are betrayed by the church

GREETING

LEADER:

Christ be with you

PEOPLE:

And also with you

LIGHTING OF CANDLES

L: *Let us remember who we are:*
We are the people of dignity.
Down the ages, we have been the people of God,
the people who know themselves to be called
to freedom, courage and truth.

P: *We light a white candle for that dignity*
and the power of God in us.

L: *We are the people who were for those who suffer.*
We are the people who walk with the Christ
towards all who grieve,
who are oppressed and exploited.

P: *We light a purple candle for those who suffer*
and the power of Christ is in us.

L: *We are the people of faith and hope.*
In the Spirit we celebrate our energy and strength,
our power to heal,
and our calling to walk with God
in the re-creating of the world.

P: *We light a green candle for our hope in the Spirit.*
We are not alone.

NAMING OUR REALITY

(Either the leader, or the betrayed person tells the story)

PRAYER OF CONFESSION

L: *We are the Body of Christ, the church.*
We are called to heal, to free,
to live with justice and love.
But we betray that calling.
O God, the power of that betrayal is immense,
because we carry the authority of your holy name
and the terrible power to destroy the innocence of trust.

P: *Call your church to repentance, O God.*

L: *We name before you our conviction*
that these, your loved children,
have been abused by your church
and that the church has become a barrier
to your love and justice.

P: *Call your church to repentance, O God.*

L: *O God, we believe that your church*
has made choices to stand with the oppressor
rather than the oppressed
and we grieve its weakness
and lack of honesty.

P: *Call your church to repentance, O God.*

L: *As we gather around those who have been wounded,*
we call into our circle
all those who have suffered
from the unfaithfulness of the church.

(Silent reflection and possibly naming of those people)

L: *Our God weeps with us,*
is angry together with us
and dies in our dying.
But the word to us, in Jesus Christ,
is that nothing in heaven and on earth
can separate us from the love of God.

All: *Amen.*

READINGS

Psalm 121
Luke 2:46–55

Affirmation

All: We believe in one God,
The Mother and Father of us all,
giver of birth and rebirth
out of our nothingness.

We believe that
as we embrace our victim child
our tears become a healing balm,
our anger restores to strength and worth
and that to pray is other than an easy way through.

We believe that
life can be claimed in the face of the sins against us,
that repentance is the journey towards forgiveness
and that your renewal comes as gift
in the most surprising ways.

We will live together in faith
as if all this is possible.

Laying on of hands and anointing

(The people asking for healing kneel and the friends lay their hands on those kneeling)

L: Christ has died.
Christ is risen.
Christ will come again.

Life is stronger than death.
The victory has already been won for you.
Receive the gentle healing,

The cherishing which is yours in Jesus Christ.
Receive the gift of freedom
From the powers of evil which have surrounded you.
Your faith, and our faith, has made you whole.
In the name of the God, the Loving Parent,
the Child Christ, and the Spirit of Comfort.

All: *Amen.*

(The people are then anointed with fragrant oil)

L: *You are the loved children of God.*
All: *Amen.*

Litany of love

L: *Love reaches past the words we cannot say*
and the words that are not heard.
Love can bear to hear the pain
and stays with the tears.

(A bright ribbon is linked with a central cross and the people)

L: *Love empowers helplessness,*
even before the answers are clear.
Love finds a pathway
between us and God,
beyond the barriers of injustice.

(Another ribbon is linked with the cross)

L: *Love longs for us.*
Love seeks us out.
Love is shared.
Love is of God.
P: *We long for your healing*
We are searching for you in your pain.
We share our love for you at this moment
And we pray that God will be with us in that sharing.

(Ribbons link all the people)

EUCHARIST (if appropriate)

BLESSING

L: *Go in freedom and courage.*
Go as those who walk in the company of Christ.
Go to discover the Spirit dancing before you
and the grace of God between you.

All: *Amen.*

Hold your heads high, our liberation is at hand

For those engaged in struggle

GREETING

LEADER:

> Lift up your hearts!

PEOPLE:

> We are warmed by our hope in Christ.

L: Lift up your voices!

P: For even the stones cry out.

L: Lift up your heads!

P: Our freedom is near at hand.
Thanks be to God.

HYMN

This is who we are

L: As we know your nearness, O God,
we know more clearly who we are.
We are your people who struggle with many things.
We see your reign at hand,
but it still seems beyond our reach.
In these things it seems far away:

(The people share the struggles in their life and work)

At intervals the leader will say:

L: O Christ, hear our prayer

P: Be with us we struggle, O God.

or an appropriate sung response.

ASSURANCE

L: There is no time or place
which is far from the love of God.
Hold your heads high,
our liberation is at hand!

All: Amen.

READING:

Luke 21:25-33

The signs of the reign of god

L: In thankfulness,
we celebrate the signs of the sovereignty of God
which we have found in our life and work together here.

(The people light a candle and name the sign)

L: In faith, we join these our signs
with those of our sisters and brothers around the world.

(Silent reflection)

L: With an awareness of our unique place
in the eternal plan of God,
we remember some of those who have gone before us:

(The people name those who have been their inspiration)

L: And all who will come after us.

(Silent reflection)

L: We are not alone.
P: We stand in a great company,
with the whole communion of saints.
L: They have prepared the way:
P: And so will we, by the grace of God.
Amen.

L: *In us will the flowering of the Spirit be seen.*
In each one,
Christ will call forth a blossoming of new things.
The peace of Christ be with you.
P: *And also with you.*

(The people give a flower to each other and pass the peace)

HYMN

Commissioning and blessing

L: *Take up the task with hope and faith!*
P: *We believe that we are the children of God.*
L: *The world is always waiting for us to emerge:*
so, go with courage into the costly path of Christ,
go with imagination into the creative life of God
and go with freedom into the life of the Spirit.
All: *Amen.*

For my friend Brian Wren, hymn writer, and for those who want to begin with vulnerability and end with hope and faith together.
(First published in *The Glory of Blood, Sweat and Tears*, Dorothy McRae-McMahon, JBCE, 1996.)

In the end, the passion

OPENING SENTENCES

LEADER:
>In the end, there is a passion:

PEOPLE:
>Deep in the heart of God.

L: It will not let us go:

P: Even if it travels with us
past the moments of death.

L: It rises again and again
in the eternity of love:

P: A mystery, a wonder, God undefeated.

It's often hard to believe

L: It's hard to live with passion, God.
You lived that way,
always honest with yourself and other people, even your friends,
always determined to take the risk of living really free,
challenging powerful people,
actually caring about things most of the time
and they killed you.

(Silent reflection)

L: We never come close to living as passionately as that, God,
but still it feels dangerous much of the time.
What if we make choices about our life
which seem to be the best we can do
and then we see them for what they are, and were,
and can't live with ourselves?
They were passionate decisions God,
borne of our blood, sweat and tears,

and we mostly thought you were in them
at least a little.

(Silent reflection)

L: Mostly we are just longing to be loved
and so we make our choices towards that.
It's hard for us to do otherwise.
You know that, God.
Some of it's about
wanting to keep what we have,
in power and things
and maybe add a little more.

(Silent reflection)

L: You understand all that God.
You have felt all that we feel,
longed for all that we long for.
That's why, some of the time,
we believe that you will forgive us.
Let us ask for the forgiveness of this God.

P: Forgive us and love us,
make sense of our struggles, O God of grace.

THE ASSURANCE

L: The assurance in the Christ
is that this God loves us with such a passion
that God travels with us into death
and defeats that death forever.
Amen.

P: Thanks be to God!

READINGS AND REFLECTION

The affirmation of faith

L: Let us respond to the Word:

All: *Even as we seem to be dying*
in weakness,
in fear,
overwhelmed by all the forces against us,
there are moments when we know
that we will never be determined
by any of that.

There is a God
who says to us weep strongly,
be strongly afraid,
care strongly,
choose life strongly in faith
and I will live strongly
in all of that.

There is a God
who moves from hill to mountain top,
who stands high in the depths of the pit,
who gasps free of the waters of drowning
and plants the cross-shaped tree
on the very shaking ground on which we stand
as though our trembling earth is like a rock.

There is a God
who steps free
of the binding chains around our souls
and calls us in a voice
which always knows our name,
and always knows our pain,
who lifts our feet
as though our life
stands cupped in a saving hand
and cherished forever in a life-filled place.

Call us on

L: Call us on to the adventure
of your passionate life, O God.

P: Carry us past the boundaries,
the near horizons of our small dreams.

L: Paint our world in vivid colours
so that we see
a whole new vision of your possibilities.

P: Hold the cup of living water to our lips
and breathe into our souls
the life of your Spirit.

L: Pour over us the oil of your anointing
that we may stand tall
as the royal children of your birthing.

P: Fill us with a fire which burns from a flame of truth,
refining our beings
so that we dare to take in our hands
your cross of courage, justice, hope and love
and raise it abroad in all the earth.
We ask this in the name of the one
who walks this way before us
to the end of time.
Amen.

BLESSING

L: Go forth in the miracle of the grace of God.
And may you be touched
by the fire of the Spirit,
the gentleness of the Christ
and the wisdom of your Maker.

P: Amen.

(An adaptation of a liturgy first published in *The Glory of Blood, Sweat and Tears*, Dorothy McRae-McMahon, JBCE, 1996.)